Advance Praise for
Funny, You Don't Look Like a Rabbi

"Many people fantasize about changing careers but never take the leap. Lynnda Targan jumped headfirst, and the story she recounts will embolden and inspire others. It was no easy path to choose the rabbinate, considering the hurdles for women—particularly moms, let alone one starting the process at age 50—but Rabbi Targan felt the pull of our text and teachings, and crossed the threshold with moxie and prayer. This memoir reminds us all of what's possible."

— Abigail Pogrebin, author of *My Jewish Year* and *Stars of David*

"Lynnda Targan's journey to the rabbinate is anything but typical. She writes of overcoming her challenges and obstacles with determination and grit, as well as with the help of her family, her deep Yiddishkeit, and a few 'angels' along the way... An inspiring story of personal transformation and ultimate faith."

— Angela Buchdahl, Senior Rabbi, Central Synagogue, New York City

"A riveting journey of achieving the improbable. . . [Targan's] resilience, perseverance, tenacity and unwavering commitment to family and faith absorb the pages of this poignant memoir on loss and redemption. . . . A gutsy, liberating, page-turner of a memoir."

— Regina Calcaterra, *New York Times* bestselling author of *Etched in Sand*

"With levity, warmth, and personal truth, Lynnda Targan describes a feminine version of a traditionally masculine journey. It is not so much a tale of battling and overcoming (although there's a fair amount of that, too) as much as a tale of listening, offering, receiving, trying, listening again, and then trying a new way. Reading this book is like hearing a good friend's life story, wanting the best for her, and knowing that the only reason she's telling it to you is because she wants the best for you, too."

— Rebecca Barry, bestselling author of *Recipes for a Beautiful Life*

Funny, You Don't Look Like a Rabbi

Funny, You Don't Look Like a Rabbi

A Memoir of Unorthodox Transformation

RABBI LYNNDA TARGAN

White River Press
Amherst, Massachusetts

First published 2020 by White River Press, Amherst, Massachusetts
www.whiteriverpress.com

Book and cover design by Douglas Lufkin
Lufkin Graphic Designs, Norwich, Vermont
www.lufkingraphics.com

ISBN: 978-1-887043-72-4 paperback
          978-1-887043-60-1 ebook

Library of Congress Cataloging-in-Publication Data on file with the publisher.
LCCN: 2020007584

To Larry, Beth, Eric, Charlie, Nasreen, Sage, and Darren:

Your love and nourishment support me in all
of my transitions and transformations.

— CONTENTS —

— ACKNOWLEDGEMENTS —

To my patient and loving family, I say thank you and thank you: Beth Seltzer, Larry Targan, Sheri Daniels, Todd Lewis, and Vicki Lewis. Many, many, thanks to my esteemed Mussar group: Dr. Marlyn Vogel, Dr. Betsy Richman, Sharon Greis, Karen Model, Dr. Penni Blaskey, and Joy Gordon; with much gratitude I thank Hersh Richman, Dr. Bob Vogel, Bonnie-Kay Marks, Shirley Brown, Susan Cole, Dr. Steve Barrer, George Seltzer, Dani Shapiro, Cyd Weissman, Madlyn Rovinsky, Charla Sussman, Karen Silverberg, and Rabbi Fredi Cooper. You have all offered your encouragement and thoughtful comments, for which I am beyond thankful. Blessings and thanks go to my esteemed early editors, Ghena Glijansky Korn and Rebecca Barry; and finally, to the marvelous Ann Campbell who pushed this book through to fruition. . . without you it would be lost in the ether. Many, many thanks to Linda Roghaar, Jean Stone, Doug Lufkin, Kitty Florey, and the entire team at White River Press for believing in my work and bringing it to light.

Shehechianu: Praised Are You Lord our God, Presider over the Universe, for granting us life, for sustaining us, and for helping us to reach this day. Amen.

Were the sky above us of parchment made,
And every twig and reed a quill;
Were every drop of sea water ink
And each of us a book could fill:

Still we could not tell the wondrous story,
Of the Creator's work in all of its glory.

From the *Akdamut,* a medieval anonymous
hymn used for the holiday of *Shavuot* prior to
the recitation of The Ten Commandments.

— AUTHOR'S NOTE —

This is a memoir, a work of nonfiction that I've written based on journals and diaries and from memory. Every painstaking attempt to convey details accurately has been made from the inception of this project. Wherever possible and permissible, I have used people's real names. To protect the identity of others, names have been changed or expressly eliminated.

— FOREWORD —

*B*ACK IN THE FIFTIES when I was growing up, there was a popular prime time TV show called *What's My Line?* A guest would be asked to "enter and sign in please," and a panel of four celebrities attempted to guess the visitor's profession by asking a series of leading questions.

The panelists were plenty smart, but if the show were on the air today, and I were a guest, I would likely stump the panel and win the game. I've been told that I don't look the part or fit the stereotype. Compared to men, women are still a distinct minority in this occupation.

So, whenever someone introduces me, it's usually followed-up with a question:

"Guess what Lynnda does?"

Not one person has ever been correct.

"I'm an ordained rabbi," I respond with a touch of pride and humility.

"Really? A rabbi?" people exclaim with wide-eyed curiosity. "Well, you sure don't look like a rabbi. Certainly not my father's rabbi! No black hat, no long stringy beard and curly *payos* (side hair locks). Maybe if we'd had rabbis like you back in the day,

I would have liked Hebrew school," they tell me, even though they likely wouldn't have said the same thing to a man.

But there weren't rabbis like me then. I would never have been a guest rabbi on *What's My Line*, because female rabbis didn't exist at that time. Women rabbis weren't ordained until two or three decades later, in the seventies, and even then, there were only a few. Thousands and thousands of men have been ordained, but there are only approximately 800–1,000 or so female rabbis that exist even today—worldwide!

That fact alone might explain the curious response of many people when they realize what I do. With a quizzical look on their faces, they continue questioning.

"A rabbi? What made you decide to become a rabbi? Are you a practicing rabbi? Are you affiliated with a movement? Do you serve a pulpit?"

This book answers those questions by revealing how I heard the calling and transformed myself in midlife to become a working community rabbi. It tells a story of seeking and finding personal, professional, and spiritual fulfillment, despite many challenges and lots of adversity. It is meant to inspire others to follow their passion, no matter what age, and no matter how unreachable the goal seems. And mostly it cautions against cookie-cutter expectations of others in order to be real and happy in one's own skin.

It wasn't as though I was spending my days on the couch eating chocolate truffles and watching soap operas when I first felt the inklings of a spiritual awakening. I was living a busy, engaged, happy, and privileged life infused with meaning and purpose. My husband and I loved each other. He was an excellent partner, dad, and a solid provider. I worked as a teacher and a journalist, wrote a newsletter as a volunteer for the LaLeche League of nursing mothers, sat on boards, took care of my house and children, had lots of friends, and traveled the world for business and pleasure.

But though my cup did runneth over, I felt that there was something missing in the fountain of my soul. I experienced an almost daily emotional and spiritual barrenness, a sense that I was not realizing my potential, not giving back to the world with the moral obligation of *noblesse oblige*—that I was living a life according to outsiders' expectations. I was searching for something larger than myself and I knew that I had to change direction to find satisfaction. I needed a life makeover to discover my essence. But what to do?

Swiss psychologist Carl Jung called this longing the "statement stage," when we look for ways to make a difference in the world and live a life more focused on service. By becoming a rabbi at fifty-five years of age, when most of my friends were retiring or slowing down, I was gearing up for an entirely new journey, a complete turnaround. I had to take control and become a kind of personal entrepreneur of my own life, dedicated to the business of self-actualization through transformation.

The path was tough stuff. I faced many hurdles and tests along the way: rejection, serious illness, work overload, feelings of inauthenticity, shifts in my marriage, a bombing in Jerusalem, and 9/11 in New York City. But I learned how to set my intentionality (*kavanah* in Hebrew), create realistic goals, break tasks down to manageable pieces, embrace uncertainty, take a leap, live in the moment, and focus. Along the way I developed confidence, fortified by grit and resilience. In the end I was ordained as a rabbi. As poet Robert Frost noted, *"I took the road less traveled by, and that has made all of the difference."*

There's a Jewish teaching from *The Ethics of Our Fathers*, which states, *"From all of my teachers I have learned."* Though this book is organically presented in a Jewish cultural framework, it poses universal life questions that all of us must confront in order to find our true calling or passion at whatever stage and passage we find ourselves. Using the model of my own spiritual path, the book will hopefully motivate readers to look inward, outward, and upward, to recognize when your life needs to be transitioned into something else or transformed entirely, and how to shift thinking. I hope that it will lead you to find a unique and meaningful place in the world and be happy in it. Meanwhile, thanks for accompanying me on this journey.

— CHAPTER 1 —

Love, Loss, and Abandonment

"Forsake me not, Adonai, my God;
be not far from me."

(Psalm 38:22)

MY LIFE CHANGED FOREVER on an otherwise unremarkable day. And although more than six decades have passed, the breakup that cut through the purity of my early childhood with such laser-like impact has left wounds that are still raw and tender to the touch. Even today, my parents' parting is as fresh and wrenching as last night's nightmare.

I can recall sitting at the dining room table, an innocent nine-year-old painting a wheat-colored Collie with oils from a paint-by-numbers set. The image bore a striking resemblance to our dog Spot, whom I adored, and it was bathed in a light that came streaming through the prisms of a crystal chandelier hanging above the dining table. I heard my mother's purse snap shut as she headed towards the nearby front door.

"Hold down the fort," she called out. "I'll be right back."

"Okay," I answered, barely looking up and not missing a brushstroke, oblivious to the ominous pulse of the day. I was in high spirits, being creative—doing what any unsuspecting child might enjoy in a quiet, contented moment.

My mother, father, sister, and I—and our dog Spot—had recently moved from our crowded two-bedroom apartment into a beautiful, furnished model, three-bedroom, split-level house in an attractive development in suburban Reading, Pennsylvania. For the first time since my sister had been born four years earlier, I had my own room, my dedicated space, complete with a little corner of privacy to read and write and be alone when it mattered.

I loved our new house with its sumptuous, hilly backyard that flowed gracefully onto a knoll that was perfect for running races and sledding in the snow with our new friends and neighbors. I had never experienced so much secluded outdoor land and freedom before, and it was exhilarating.

The front yard was carpeted in emerald-colored grass bordered with sculpted shrubs and adorned with a country-like flower garden that had been meticulously planted by my mother, with my sister and me as her assistants. Home ownership was a big step up for our little family, and I reveled in our apparent success.

To my child's sense of timing, it hardly seemed like ten minutes had passed since my mother had hurried out the door, when my father's gold-and-white 1957 Dodge, with the futuristic-looking fins, pulled up along the curb in front of our house. Both of my parents emerged from their sides of the car simultaneously. It was an odd and unexpected sighting. I hadn't imagined that they had been out together, and it seemed too early for my father to be home from work.

My mother wobbled stiffly into the house first, her red eyes apparently swollen from crying. Her demeanor portended trouble. Big-time-never-before-seen-trouble. My stern-faced father rushed past her, bumping against her tiny shoulders at the foyer entrance, and he ran upstairs to their bedroom, taking the steps that divided the living and dining areas two at a time.

Confused, I looked back and forth at the two of them as though they were opponents on a tennis court.

I followed my father up the stairs. "Daddy!" I called.

He didn't answer.

I continued down the hall, stopping short at the threshold of my parents' bedroom. I watched incredulously as my father flung an open suitcase onto the salmon-colored, silk-tufted bedspread, its corners tucked in neatly, and began dumping piles of clothes pulled from his drawers and closet into it.

"Where are you going?" I asked perplexed, the stirrings of panic rising in my intestines. He didn't acknowledge me as he continued to deposit garments into the open suitcase by the armful.

"You just came back from Philadelphia," I noted as I continued my questioning.

My father traveled weekly on Wednesdays from Reading to Philadelphia, staying over in the company apartment that Reading Corrugated maintained for its salesmen. I was used to his one-night-a-week absence, though, indeed, the house lacked a certain cheeriness when he was away.

Bewildered, I pressed on. "Where are you going now?"

Hints of fear and dread began to deepen.

No answer.

"Why are you going away again?"

Continuing to ignore me, my father swiped a dozen ties off the rack, then tossed them into the pile of clothes lying willy-nilly in the middle of the suitcase. In silence, he grabbed shoes from the bottom of his closet and held them in the crooks of his elbows. I looked up. My mother was standing in the doorway like a marble statue. Her eyes, now overflowing with tears, were angry.

"Go on, tell her," she hissed at my father.

"Tell me what?" I implored.

"Your father's leaving us," my mother said, her voice quivering in the back of her throat. "This time he's going for good. He's not coming back to live with us ever again. He doesn't love us anymore. He's in love with someone else, and he's moving to Philadelphia."

Wide-eyed and dazed, I looked at my parents. It was unthinkable what my mother was saying. My father was going away? Leaving us? For another family? That he loved more than us? How could this be?

But their pained expressions confirmed the truth. We were breaking apart. And I was devastated even beyond my understanding of the calamity that had befallen our family.

It turned out that my parents had met furtively at the corner convenience store to talk, or more precisely, to agree to dissolve their ten-year marriage in less time than it took to hard-boil an egg. My life had entered the eye of the storm, and I knew in my belly that I was about to be windswept by the gusts.

With deep, wailing sobs, I darted down the two flights of steps to our den and hurled myself facedown on the sofa, where I pounded my fists on the raw, nubby fabric. My feet kicked the couch with rapid-fire movements, causing it to bob up and down and hit the wall with each thrust.

"Damn you," I heard my father roar to my mother upstairs. "Why'd you have to tell her that way?"

"Why did you have to do this to us?" she lobbed back.

My father slammed his packed suitcase down at the foot of the landing in the dining room area, walked to the kitchen, and descended the few stairs from the kitchen to the den. He squeezed next to me on the couch as I lay on my stomach, continuing to pulse my legs as though I was paddling underwater. But I was going nowhere. I was stuck in a setting that appeared to be my new reality.

"No, no, no!" I screamed over and over again without looking up.

My father sat motionless and speechless.

"How could you do this to us?" I wailed.

In the 1950s, broken families were uncommon among my parents' coterie of friends, and certainly nowhere to be found in my extended immigrant family. Divorce was a curse. Isolating. Disenfranchising. A failure. An embarrassment. A disaster. At my young age, I visualized everyone else's parents to be a cohesive family unit with a mom and dad kissing at the door when the dad came home from work like the TV moms and dads of that era. I could never have imagined the drama of the scene unfolding before my eyes.

"I'll come see you all the time," my father offered as he put his hand on my back.

I wiggled away from his touch.

Sadness and doom lingered in the air between us like radioactive material. How could our father abandon our family, throw us away like a bowl of moldy fruit in the refrigerator?

A family couldn't exist without a dad, I thought. Especially our dad. Daddy was our good-time Charlie, the man with the fairy dust who broke the rules and made us laugh, and he was leaving, moving to Philadelphia, an hour and a half away, because he loved someone else.

In shock, trying to absorb a child's vision of Armageddon, I turned over to look into the depths of my father's eyes. Sniveling I asked, "When are you leaving?"

"Now," he said softly.

"Now? As in this very minute?"

It was clear that my father, already wan and emotionally spent, wasn't primed to hang around any longer than necessary for more histrionics. He shifted his body to leave.

"Will you take me to the pool to swim?" I asked hoping to prolong his departure, bargaining to hold on to our family unit as I knew it for just a little while longer.

"Not now," he responded. "I have to go."

"Please," I begged.

Perhaps, I thought, he might change his mind about leaving us after a swim, the cool water enabling the situation to calm down. Or maybe, before he retreated too far away and rode down the path of no return, he might reconsider his decision, double back to the house, put on his chef's apron, and whip up our typical family barbeque. Dad always had an impish grin on his face while he flipped boneless chicken breasts and big beefy burgers on the grill. My mother's emblematic hearty salad would be served as a companion to the meal after she had joyfully set the table with pretty patterned napkins and turquoise Melmac dishes. I desperately wanted to rewind our lives back an hour, to our own imperfect normalcy, the way we turned our clocks back in autumn to move forward.

"Not today," my father answered. "I have to go."

He brushed the sweaty, uneven bangs off my forehead and lightly kissed me goodbye as I turned around. He didn't offer a hug, and I didn't ask for one, both of us probably fearing that I might collapse under his hold.

I started sobbing again.

He walked up the stairs fast, abandoning me as I howled in the den, without looking back or saying a word. He jockeyed past my mother and my little sister, Sheri, who was holding onto my mother's skirt, whimpering, "Please don't go, Daddy. Please don't go!"

I heard my father shut the door behind him, and I listened to the motor in the Dodge turn over as I sat alone on the edge of the couch, trying to catch my breath between sobs and process the implosion of my life. In a single, spectacular instant, my faith in a universe of goodness had been shattered. Poof went my idealized perception of a secure home with two present loving parents, the sheltering of my nuclear family.

I wondered what would become of us. My mother didn't work outside of the home. She was a "housewife," like the majority of women of that era. She was good at it, artfully maintaining our home as beautifully as an innkeeper with fresh, lilac-tinged sheets and vases filled with colorful flowers, which she cut and arranged like a florist. Her cooking skills could rival any professional chef, and she could whip up a luscious meal for twenty or so guests in an instant's notice. But she'd never worked outside of the home after she was married.

Who would support us? Would we starve? Would they send my sister and me to an orphanage to live like Little Orphan Annie, scrubbing floors under the wicked eye of a mean Miss Hannigan?

If I hadn't read Nancy Drew mysteries or Archie comic books under the covers with my flashlight after lights-out, or if I had balked less at cleaning my room, would my parents have decided to go their separate ways? Might they have loved me more than they disliked each other? What was divorce going to look like for us? I had no answers, only the questions of a naïve youngster, and they were blanketed in misery.

◆◆◆

From that day on, the trajectory of my life assumed a radical course, as my fragmented nuclear family plunged into an ineffable darkness. My parents' separation was the end of my childhood innocence, of my feelings of trust and security in the world, and it became the first day of my passage into the streets of the forlorns and the have-nots. Everything that was familiar disappeared like smoke into ashes. I would never again paint by numbers or stay within the blue lines of conventional life-definition. I would be challenged to forever exist in gray landscapes.

Inevitably, I had to learn that transcendence after tragedy, trauma, and loss—if it is to occur—must be launched like a rocket from the wound. And it demands improbable elasticity. Over time, post-divorce, in my quest to heal and manage my disappointment and loneliness, I developed an empathic heart for the suffering of others and a deep-seated desire to fix brokenness. Unwittingly, I had started the process of becoming what psychologist Carl Jung called the "wounded healer." And the diminutive seedlings of my spiritual calling began to germinate in a vacuum of existential loss before my age had reached double digits.

— CHAPTER 2 —

In the Beginning

"Childhood is a garland of roses."

(Talmud Shabbat 152a)

AFTER MY PARENTS went their separate ways, Bella and Hymie Yaskolka, my mother's Polish parents, who were used to managing crises, came to the rescue. In their worldview, children were sanctified, cherished beings entrusted to humans by God. I was in a unique position, the first grandchild and great-grandchild on my mother's side, and a second-generation American child born into a family of immigrants who had fled pre-Holocaust Eastern Europe. The moment I arrived in 1948, I became an instant celebrity in our family, hailed like the Messiah and anointed in love into the House of Yaskolka. In the ethnocentric eyes of my grandparents, great-grandparents, and their relatives—who mostly all spoke with heavy Yiddish accents—Jewish children would build Jewish families. They would determine and seal the identity of the Jewish community and solidify a Jewish longing in America, where they were free to live Jewish lives devoid of fear of the religious reprisal they had experienced in Poland.

Survivors of the Holocaust in the State of Israel, which had been proclaimed only two months before my birth by the United Nations General Assembly, was at war with a coalition of hostile Arab states and Palestinian-Arab forces. The struggle for the soul of Jewish identity in Israel and the Diaspora was an ongoing battle. Particularly after the annihilation of 6 million Jews, including 1.5 million Jewish children in Europe—what was tantamount to a third of the Jewish population worldwide—less than a decade before I was born, it was the sacred, if unspoken, mission of the Jewish community to grow and recover what had been lost at the hands of the murdering Nazis.

I was considered "interest on the family interest," according to my family's vision. Each child was a phlegm-filled spit in Hitler's dead eye. The more children the better. As a Jewish-American child I represented continuity—hope for the future. In English, I was even named Linda Hope. And the national anthem of Israel would later become *HaTikvah*, "The Hope." My parent's chose the Hebrew name of Leah for me, after one of our enduring biblical matriarchs, the mother of six of the heads of the twelve tribes of Israel, and the only daughter, Dina, sired by the patriarch Jacob.

We know through DNA that my maternal side of the family was descended from the biblical priestly clan. But unlike the ancient Jewish priests, they were devoid of any of the outward trappings of scarlet robes, diamond diadems, or inherited wealth. Similar to Tevye's family in the fictional *shtetl* (a small Jewish town in Eastern Europe), Anatevka, in the play *Fiddler on the Roof,* my mother's immigrant relatives were impoverished dairy farmers from Lodz, Poland, an important textile town landlocked in the center of the country about eighty-four miles southwest of Warsaw. My great-grandfather, Abraham, a pious bearded man with twinkling blue eyes, who always wore a *kippah* (religious head covering) over his thick gray hair, immigrated to the United States in 1914 at the height of the largest Jewish migration from the Pale of Settlement in the mostly western region of Imperial Russia, a piece of land where Jews had been permitted to live. Between 1870 and 1920, they were fleeing rampant anti-Semitism, pogroms, and menacing poverty that threatened to destroy their communities. *Zaida* (Yiddish for grandfather) Abe was one of more than 2 million Jews during that period who came to the *Goldena Medina*, the Golden Land of America, where the streets were purportedly paved with gold, looking for opportunity.

When they arrived, they wore frayed clothes on their backs and carried a little *peckle* (bag) full of underwear and family photos, and held very little in their holey pockets. For the most part they also arrived with few marketable job skills, no English, and limited connections other than family members who were already residing in the United States, and who had struggled to send them the necessary money to make passage. What they did possesss were many concretizing Jewish rituals and faith in a presiding God who would guide and protect them in a free and democratic land.

In 1920, six long, lonely years after my great-grandfather Zaida Abe had left the "Old Country," he sent for my great-grandmother Rose and their boys, one of whom would become my grandfather. Days and days later, after having been packed into steerage on stormy seas, they ultimately disembarked from the boat, named the *New Rochelle*, on Ellis Island in New York. When my great-grandparents reunited in America, they conceived my great-aunt Ann, thus completing their Polish/American family consisting of five children. Everyone always described them as humble people with basic needs, beautiful, loving, genuine, and sweet as the Fox's U-Bet chocolate syrup that they drank in their daily seltzers.

Their middle son, my head-turning dapper grandfather Chaim, assumed a Yiddish nickname, Hymie, in America. He married my plain little grandmother Bella, also an immigrant from Poland, whom he met while they both were working at a schoolbag factory in New York City.

After their marriage, my grandfather adjusted to the New World's vicissitudes through work, laboring at three jobs at once, which helped solidify his English. Zaida earned a living primarily as a furrier, skinning the hides off of animals for the retail fur trade. He augmented his income by managing funds at the local credit union and by driving a yellow cab through the streets of New York during the late-night shift. Also, because he was an excellent driver, he became the family's guardian angel— the self-appointed chauffeur who seemed to be on call any time of the day or night to deliver or retrieve people or handle the myriad household errands.

My grandmother Bella was a typical housewife who didn't venture out enough to learn much English. A marvelous traditional Jewish cook, she was considered the quintessential *balabusta* (homemaker) with her long, busy days spent cleaning the apartment, shopping for food, and cooking full, brimming platters of chicken *fricassee* (a stew) and carrot *tzimmes* (a sweet stew typically made from carrots and dried fruits) from recipes etched into her heart. Most nights, extended family members on both sides who were trying to get on their feet after World War II, clamored for a place at her table to partake of the hearty nourishment and to share stories in a mixture of lively Polish, Yiddish, and a drizzle of English.

My grandparents' lives had been informed by the Jewish ethics and teachings they had garnered in Poland and now continued in America as best they could, observing the *mitzvot,* the commandments in the Bible, despite backlash from both assimilating modern and hard-core, ultra-Orthodox Jews, as well as grumblings from the secular community. Like many other Jewish immigrants of their day, they fought valiantly to continue to maintain traditional Orthodox Jewish customs, like observing the Sabbath and keeping kosher, and hanging on to familiar values in their own little American/Jewish enclave. At the same time, they subtly assimilated to the new and strange Americanisms, with the secular clothes they wore and the language they spoke in the streets. It was a delicate dance between traditionalism and modernity, universalism and particularity.

◆◆◆

In the early days of their marriage, my grandparents gave birth to and raised two daughters, my mother, Bernice, *Brina* in Yiddish, and nine years later, my aunt Shirley. They were adoring parents who doted on their daughters, and later on their grandchildren, who today would no doubt be perceived as hovering helicopter parents and grandparents. Their overprotective natures made my mother crazy.

As loving as her parents were, there was a part of my mother that rebelled against their ubiquitous presence and their "limited" Jewish way of life. Even with her fluent, perfectly nuanced Yiddish, she longed to be recognized as a full-fledged American, like her American friends with American parents, who spoke English without an identifying accent. She yearned to be independent and to wear the chic, trendy clothes that appeared on fashion models on the cover of *Harper's Bazaar*, as well as other *au courant* celebrities in the pages of *Look* and *Life* magazines.

Every day when she left her apartment, she would roll her skirt up at the waist so that it skimmed the flesh above her knees, apply lipstick to her colorless lips, dab Chanel N°5 perfume behind her ears and on her wrists, and pray that she wouldn't get caught by tattling neighbors or relatives—*yentas*, as she called them—who congregated together like busy bees in a swarm.

Our tightly knit extended family was chock-full of colorful personalities, archetypes for quirky "fictional" movie and television characters with their old-school European peccadilloes. But they were kind, generous, genuinely moral individuals who espoused their Jewish values and cared deeply about transmitting them to subsequent generations. For most of them, the ethical lessons communicated through parables, stories, and modeled behavior were judged just as important, if not more so than the multiplication tables and other academic facts as building blocks for a successful future taught in elementary school.

My grandparents and their extended family also took care of their neighbors and the community. Even as a small child, I witnessed their generosity—how they visited sick people with trays of meat and bowls of thick, healing, homemade soup; how they showed up in good and bad times for holidays; how they organized joyous rituals and life cycle events; and how they lent money to the needy when pantries and pocketbooks were sparse on the home front. As early as I can remember, I was impressed by their hospitality to strangers, how they invited them to eat at their buffet with the rest of the family.

Dirt-poor by most American standards, they seemed rich in spirit, never faltering in an ability to be caring, righteous, nourishing, and stable. I always felt lucky to be a child born into their loving circle. Their grounding would become the stabilizing force I would cling to after the divorce saga, and I would return to it in my later years of spiritual seeking.

◆◆◆

In her late teens, my mother-to-be rejoiced at the opportunity to visit extended family in other cities where she noted that it would "expand her horizons." She was on her way home from visiting cousins in Baltimore when she met my father-to-be in 1947. The Baltimore cousins were somehow distantly related to my father, and they had all been invited to my father's sister's wedding in Philadelphia. My mother, who wasn't related closely enough to receive an invitation, planned to catch a bus back to New York while her weekend hosts went to the wedding reception. As they were saying goodbye outside the wedding venue hall, my dad caught a glimpse of my mother. She was eighteen and petite with deep sunken turquoise-blue eyes, a stunning Elizabeth Taylor-look-alike whose eyes were so blue they appeared violet. My father, a twenty-two-year-old wannabe *bon vivant* with a confidant swagger, approached her and flirted unabashedly. Emboldened by her Chanel Nº5, she flirted back.

There was an irresistible alchemy between them, like a scene from the Broadway play *Kismet*. He said to her in no uncertain terms, "You're not getting on any bus to go home." Putting his arm around her waist, teasing and tempting, he upped the ante: "I'll drive you home later, doll, after the wedding is over. You can attend the wedding as MY guest." Not appropriately dressed for a formal wedding, my mother tried to protest, but my father proved to be too irresistible. She stayed and danced all night with the suave, dashingly handsome stranger who had swept her off her feet. Music rang in her ears as she swooned. . . . *"Take my hand. I'm a stranger in Paradise. All lost in a wonderland. A stranger in Paradise. . . . "*

Years later, my mother told me that the chemistry between her and my father was "hotter than an oven on broil." But there was also a plethora of clues that made a long-term marriage for my parents a poor risk from the outset. My paternal grandfather, Louis Lewis, my father's Russian/English father, had been abandoned by *his* wife, a *shonda* (disgrace), a particularly dishonorable scandal given his generation and the era of the late

1930s. Soon after her departure, he found solace in the arms of a woman he'd met who was living on the West Coast, while he and his two kids lived in the East. This hifalutin woman embraced his daughter but not his son, who would later become my father. Nevertheless, my grandfather ran off with her, dumping my father in an orphanage after his mother had moved out, thereby abandoning him a second time.

My Dad spent his early school years moving around from orphanages to foster homes, or bunking down and relying on the largess of various friends. Unable to depend on handouts forever, he lied about his age and joined the Navy when he was sixteen. During World War II he manned a submarine in the South Pacific off the coast of Australia. He always lamented his lack of formal education, having left school in the eighth grade, but he was a fighter, a hard worker, and gifted in street smarts.

Returning from combat after the War, my father lived on his own in Reading, Pennsylvania, working as a salesman in the corrugated box manufacturing business. Lean and a well-toned jock, he played baseball in the minor leagues and was a championship diver. He was also a coveted bridge player with masterpoints and a 12-handicap golfer who hit the greens a few times a week at Galen Hall, a tony country club in nearby Wernersville, PA. On paper he was a very desirable, hunky bachelor.

Following a brief, feverish courtship, my mother and father were married in a fancy, formal New York Jewish ceremony. My dashing father was dressed in top hat and tails; my veiled mother, covered from neck to elbow in white satin modesty, had a long lace bridal train trailing behind her back. After the wedding, my mother waved goodbye to her loving family in Brooklyn to join my father in Reading for what she hoped would be an exciting marriage adventure and kosher passage outside of the Jewish-American *shtetl* where she'd been raised. My maternal grandparents were sad to see her moving so far away from home, but delighted that she had seemingly found someone strong and capable to "take care of her" and "protect" her as they did. My grandparents' dreams were fulfilled well beyond their myopic expectations. Their gorgeous daughter and handsome son-in-law would have "beautiful" children who would extend the family legacy and perpetuate their Jewish values. *Siman Tov U'Mazel Tov!*

Although as a teenager my mother's recurrent dream had been to escape from under the sheltering wings of her "greenhorn" parents, when she followed my father to a new life in blue-collar Reading—where my grandfather Lou had retreated after leaving his West Coast lover to marry a different woman named Floretta, a prissy Quaker, whom he called "Reet"—it was a complete culture shock. Her detached in-laws provided no sense of Jewish community or family unity like the Yaskolka clan. In fact, Reet had never laid eyes on a Jew before she met my grandfather.

My mother found that she missed the presence of her parents, aunts, uncles, cousins, and childhood friends in New York. She was off-kilter from the outset in the rural hinterlands of Reading among the Quakers and Amish, and almost as soon as their honeymoon was over, my parent's relationship began to deteriorate.

As a first-generation secular Jewish-American, raised as a neglected orphan, my father enjoyed showing off what he earned. It was a badge of honor for him to be a popular American red-white-and-blue, belong-to-a-hoo-ha-country-club guy. Before my mother's arrival in Reading, golf and cards had filled my father's leisure calendar, but neither of those pastimes held any interest for her. There was no ritual on Friday night *Shabbat* (the Sabbath, the prescribed biblical day of coveted rest), as there had been in the Yaskolka household. Even though she identified herself as mostly non-observant, my mother felt disengaged, sad, and lonely. The adjustment was painful—and she was already pregnant with me.

I emerged eight months after my parents' wedding, delivered at St. Joseph Hospital, aided by nuns, when my mother was just nineteen years old. My sister was born there as well four years later, without extended family or close connections nearby to help or *kvell* (be happy and proud).

Like her own mother before her, my young mother spent most of her time cooking, cleaning, and taking care of her two little girls and a husband, crowded into a small development apartment in a neighborhood pretty much devoid of Jews. My mother, also like her mother, was a talented *balabusta,* an organized homemaker, and an imaginative cook. Her priority was home and hearth, as was expected of most women of the day. Out of respect for my grandparents and a nod to familiarity, she tried to maintain a "kosher style" kitchen, but eventually ceded to my father's desire for *traif,* nonkosher food, in the house. When my grandparents visited, they scurried around screaming, "Hide the bacon!" Caught between both old and modern traditions, my mother was unable to fit compactly into either mold, and she was out of sorts.

My father was a wheeler-dealer, a guy who liked to work long hours to make lots of money, which he believed held the prestige card that had eluded him in his early, deprived life. When he wasn't working, the "king of the household," as he branded himself, felt entitled to go out and pursue his favorite activities—golf and cards.

My mother did her daily chores, volunteered at the school, and collected money for charities like the American Cancer Society and The Jewish National Fund that supported Israel. I enjoyed accompanying her door to door in our neighborhood with little tin cans, *pushkas* in Yiddish, and handed out paper receipts when someone made a donation. "Say thank you," my mother prompted as the coins dropped into the charity cans.

Her garden was also a source of pleasure and pride. Tending it filled lonely hours. My sister and I helped her weed and dig holes for the beautiful white alyssum which edged the multi-colored annual flower garden that she planted and whose genus and species she could recount as easily as the days of the week.

She also grew piquant herbs, and together we cut mint and rosemary that grew uninhibited in clay pots. When she was cooking, she showed us how to enhance the flavor of food by tossing the fragrant greenery into hearty soups and stews. As her *sous chefs*, we mixed, whisked, and ground the colorful herbs like human mortars and pestles while she whipped up delicacies for supper whether my father showed up or not.

My mother grumbled about being starved for companionship and devoid of ample adult stimulation. She was pretty much low energy by the end of the day. When my father bolted through the door, charged up and high-voltage, he was dismayed to find my mother in bed quietly reading, or hanging out with us on her starched pillows, watching TV. Their nearly nightly petty confrontations and continual exchange of snarky remarks in front of my sister and me promulgated perpetual stomachaches and created exhausting domestic anxiety.

◆◆◆

After we moved into the new house a few miles away, we had high hopes for improved family *karma*. Sadly, not much changed except the venue and the school district. My father was gone more often, proffering that he had to work harder to afford the new house.

As it turned out, my father wasn't bringing home the money he'd professed to be earning during their brief courtship, and their finances were straitjacket-tight. My mother honed her parents' Great Depression mentality by becoming a parsimonious spender, careful and discerning as she budgeted for grocery specials and bargain-basement stylish clothing for my sister and me. But my mother's frugality did not stop our life-of-the-party father from picking up the bar tab at the country club for his notably wealthier golf and card cronies. Afraid of going broke, my mother would kick him under the table when he scooped up the check for the entire crowd. He despised her attempts to handle him, and he resented her arbitrary boundaries. Their marriage, turned charade, was always on the brink of falling into a morass of deep debt, and she worried endlessly about managing their fragile finances. Her anxiety made her harangue my father more, and the more he felt controlled, the more the power struggle between them became intractable.

The space their relationship inhabited turned into a hard hat area, the combustible debris of a failing marriage falling quickly, conflagrations starting at every turn. It was evident to my sister and me that my practical, responsible mother tried to contain the loose embers, but there was a lot of squabbling, and we could sense that our mother was growing increasingly miserable. Valium, the doctor-prescribed drug-of-the-day for "depressed" women, became her friend. The side of her that once had been joyous and funny vanished with ever-increasing frequency.

◆◆◆

Despite the ubiquitous household tension, my father was enormously charming and a lot of fun. When he was available, he took us to the swim club and taught us how to do the breaststroke and to execute perfect cutaway dives off the high diving board at the deep end of the pool. He bought us putters to use on the putting green at the golf club, and he took us to the driving range to help him hit a bucket of balls. Afterwards he rewarded us with hot fudge sundaes from Penn Supreme ice cream, and drove us up to see the famous Reading Pagoda, radiant in red atop Mount Penn for an unforgettable view. He also taught us how to dance the Cha-Cha and the Merengue, holding each of us tightly as we swayed to the recording of trumpets playing "Cherry Pink and Apple Blossom White."

On nights when he came home late, no matter what time, he tiptoed into our bedrooms, woke us gently and told us to follow him to the kitchen, where he whipped up a plate of sunny-side-up "dippy eggs" that oozed with yellow-yolk gooiness that we sopped up with a toasted sesame bagel. My mother wasn't happy when he disturbed our sleep and our routine and messed up the spotless kitchen, but my sister and I loved the serendipity of the late-night feasts that he always presented with comic flair.

However, on the flip side, our father could be volatile and explosive. His abandonment as a child left him with an angry, unresolved core, and he wrestled with a conflicting *yetzer ha ra* (bad inclination), and *yetzer ha tov* (good inclination), the Jewish version of the Chinese *yin* and *yang* of innate opposing psychological forces. As a child it was hard to predict which of daddy's *yetzers* might dominate the day, and what might be the catalyst to flip the switch.

One Sunday, after weeks of planning, my mother and sister and I got all dressed-up to attend a showing of *The Ten Commandments,* the Cecil B. DeMille movie about the liberation of the Jews from Egypt and Moses receiving the Ten Commandments from God on Mount Sinai. It was a four-hour film with an intermission, and we needed to be on time. As usual my father sauntered home late from his golf game. By the time he arrived the movie was well into the second hour, and it was too late to attend. You could see my mother seething as she snarled at him the second he walked in the door, unshowered, still wearing his sweaty golf attire.

"Goddamn it! Just once, you might have been reliable and made it home on time to have our family outing," my mother screamed at him. "Now look how you've disappointed us again. You crushed your daughters' hearts, you thoughtless bastard!"

In response he hurled an 8-ounce glass of milk at her at close range, drenching her beautiful, gray cashmere sweater. The round white angora collar matted to her neck and the matching gray wool knee-length skirt was soaked with enough milk to stick to her skin and reveal her underwear beneath it. My sister, mother and I stood there horrified with sad, wide eyes like people in a Keane painting. Cecil B. DeMille had nothing over my parents in the drama department. And it was exhausting and relentless.

— CHAPTER 3 —

Brooklyn Shabbat

"Remember the Sabbath day to sanctify it."

(Exodus 20:8)

HE BAD TIMES IN READING were punctuated by pleasant visits with our dear grandparents who provided an interlude from the chaos in our house. When we visited them in Brooklyn, it was a welcome change of scenery, a respite, an oasis of recovery. Their loving Jewish-infused home was a complete contrast to ours, and the festive vibe that always accompanied our arrival fueled us like fertilizer in soil. Those visits provided a continual beacon of light for my future spiritual endeavors.

In stark contrast to the company of our warring parents, each day with *Bubby* (Yiddish for grandmother) and Zaida was like a holiday. Their Jewish daily rituals were infused with a sparkling spirituality that conveyed a mindful slowing down, a paean to Godliness. My grandfather and his brothers and their father *davenned* (prayed) every morning, walking over to the neighborhood *shul* (synagogue) with their *tallisim* (prayer shawls) and *tefillin* (phylacteries) to join the *minyan* (prayer quorum of at least ten observant men) before 7:00 a.m. Bubby always had breakfast waiting for them when they returned.

In the afternoon, the men in the family leapt to their feet for the second set of three prayer sessions mandated for each day. The women and girls watched silently as the men turned eastward towards Jerusalem, bowing and *shuckling* (swaying) back and forth in tune with the Hebrew holy words of the liturgy, barely audible beneath their breaths. I witnessed *Yiddishkeit*, the Jewish way of life, customs, and practices, in its full expression at 1077 Blake Avenue, my grandparents' tiny apartment, and it was better than therapy, super vitamins, Valium, or antioxidants as an antidote to the spiritual and intrapersonal system failure that was overwhelming my nuclear family.

In Brooklyn, the weekly encore presentation was Shabbat. Just as God had finished the work of Creation in six days and rested on the seventh, the Jewish people were biblically commanded to *"remember"* and *"observe"* the Shabbat with the cessation of labor. For my grandparents and the extended family who took these commandments seriously, Shabbat was an inviolable commitment.

In place of the labor of the workweek, Shabbat appeared with its own rhythm and exclusive customs, a designated time of "delight," according to the prophet Isaiah. Shabbat's imagery is that of a bride, pure and dressed in white, and is ushered in when the sun's rays begin gathering and setting on Friday night. It ends on Saturday night, *motzei Shabbat*, twenty-five hours later, or when three stars are visible in the sky. What happened in between the sunsets—this soulful, weekly, cyclical event that honored the comingling of sacred time and space—was what most captivated my early Jewish consciousness.

Preparation for Shabbat in my grandparents' house began as soon as the last one ended, and we counted the days until her dramatic arrival. As the secular week drew to a close, the flurry of household activity intensified in anticipation of the setting sun. During the final countdown on Friday mornings, we awoke to the smell of freshly baked *challah*—at least four traditional, braided loaves (two for the Friday night meal and two for the Saturday lunch meal). The seductive odor drifted out of the oven into the bedroom where I was sleeping with my sister and Aunt Shirley under pink chenille blankets that covered two twin beds pushed together. Piping hot and fresh out of the oven, Bubby's challah was as sweet and scrumptious as cake—better even than the wonderful homemade Amish baked goods that we were used to finding in local Reading stores.

Following my olfactory senses into the kitchen, I would find my grandmother, who had arisen in darkness, standing in front of the waist-high butcher block station, with pasty flour clumps in her hair. She was rolling out *luchshen* (fresh noodles) with a wooden rolling pin for the chicken and vegetable soups that would be served later that evening as part of the Sabbath meal. When the *challot* (plural of challah) were finished baking, fresh apple pies with domed pastry toppings for dessert were pushed into the one and only oven that worked overtime to spew out the abundant Shabbat food. The seductive scents from the challot and the apple pies wafted throughout the rooms and spilled out into the narrow hallways outside the apartment.

Shabbos, which was how the Ashkenazim pronounced the Sabbath, begins with lighting candles and reciting blessings. As a child observer, I didn't understand the blessings chanted in Hebrew, but it felt good hearing the mystical words that had the power to change the mood in the room from a buzz to a hum. Something palpable shifted. My grandmother lit the five white candles in her candelabra, which were inserted into aluminum candleholders known as *bobeches,* precisely twenty minutes before the sun set, so as not to violate the rules of kindling on the Sabbath. She tied a kerchief under her neck, a *tichle,* as a sign of respect to God, and covered her eyes with the palms of her hands as she said the blessing for lighting the candles: *"Praised are you Adonai our God, ruler of the universe, who has commanded us to light the candles of the Sabbath. Amen."*

Immediately following the candle lighting came the *Kiddush,* the sanctification of the Sabbath with wine, chanted by my grandfather, and the *Motzi,* the prayer over the two braided breads that had been prepared by my grandmother in the wee sunrise hours.

The parade of food followed immediately. Dinner was singularly spectacular—a pleasing, satisfying gift, a glorious interval from the frenzy of the week for the laborers in the family, and a time for marvelous food, family chatter, blessings, singing, and *kibbitzing* with the children. Savoring a little shot of *schnapps* thrown down the men's throats for good measure was *de rigueur,* as well. *L'Chayim!* To life!

◆◆◆

Though Shabbat is a weekly holiday, Bubby and Zaida taught us that there are many other beautiful holidays throughout the Jewish year that offer specific rituals and practices. One autumn *Rosh Hashanah* morning when I was about six or seven years old (Rosh Hashanah marks the commencement of the Jewish New Year), Bubby introduced me to the world of organized Jewish formal prayer in their East New York, Brooklyn, shul.

While I was still in bed shortly after the sun came up, she asked me if I wanted to hear the blowing of the *shofar.* "Sure," I said, not knowing what a shofar was. Later I learned that it was a ram's horn traditionally sounded on Rosh Hashanah to shepherd in the New Year. My mother dressed me in a frilly pink dress and black patent leather Mary Janes, and then my grandmother walked me to the large neighborhood Orthodox synagogue where my grandfather and his brothers had been praying since the first glimmer of sunrise.

Bubby and I mounted three flights of heavy marble steps until we reached "the women's section," the place beside the *mechitzah,* the separation where men and women were ritually divided by strict Orthodox Jewish law. I called this area the "balcony," since what transpired around me was truly theatrical. The mood was solemn, the music, majestic. Both far away and a story below us, men with heads covered by long black-and-white striped, flowing silk garments, or *tallesim* (traditional prayer shawls), were swaying, trance-like, in rhythmic movement. Their mumbling, a constant humming like bees buzzing around honey was audible throughout the sanctuary. Beyond the food, family, and holiday rituals that I'd already experienced, this community scene was entrancing.

In the middle of the service, the blowing of the shofar—which sounded like a bleating sheep—began blasting. I was told that its mesmerizing musicality is meant as a spiritual clarion call to the congregation to wake up and reconnect with Judaism's highest ethical principles and to renew a strong relationship with the God of Abraham, Isaac and Jacob at the time of the New Year. It was out of the blasts of the shofar—which is commanded to be heard by both men and women—that renewed inklings of an unconscious calling to my Jewish future reverberated.

Even though I was young, I was aware that women at this time and in this setting had only supporting roles. Few questioned the system. The biblical matriarchs were as yet unmentioned in the traditional liturgy next to the patriarchs, and there was relatively no discourse about them or their stories. Nevertheless, I watched and listened in amazement. I couldn't comprehend the magnitude of what I was witnessing, or recognize the spiritual meaning of the services, but I remember feeling surrounded by an awesome power. And at the same time, as a girl, I perceived that I stood apart from the core of the service.

Seated up high, distanced from the liturgy, which was being chanted in a "holy" foreign language, Hebrew—not the conversational Yiddish of my grandparents' discourses—I became a curious bystander, eons before I could entertain the notion of ritual participation. Most of the hat-wearing women I was sitting with were busy chatting and greeting each other with the traditional New Year's greeting, *Shanah Tovah*, which means, "a good New Year, a sweet one to you and yours." A few followed the service silently with prayer books open on their laps, but otherwise they were soundless spectators in a male-dominated tableau.

I was hypnotized by the choreography of the service, and I wanted to understand more of the mystery of the moment. I asked Bubby a lot of questions, but she kept shushing me with her index finger over her lips. I never did get satisfying answers from her or anyone else in the family about what I had experienced that morning until decades later when I consciously launched my own spiritual journey in earnest, and started peeling away the layers of the "service of the heart," as it is named. During that time, when I began to develop the vocabulary to ask informed questions of teachers who had already learned from the rabbis whose wise Oral Tradition filled the sacred books, I would start to understand. When I was able to immerse myself in those sacred books that I would penetrate one page at a time, the course of my life changed.

◆◆◆

Back in Reading, the Jewish rhythm of my grandparents' Brooklyn culture had continued to be nonexistent. After we had moved to the new house, I was only one of three Jewish children at the large public school I attended. Despite my mother's class visits to fry *latkes* (potato pancakes) at *Chanukah*, which was celebrated around the same time as Christmas, Christmas was the larger, glitzier-seeming force that surrounded me. Even though some of the teachers invited the Jewish children to share holiday stories and traditions, we mostly felt like outsiders, marginalized by the tinsel, especially in public prayer sessions. As a result, I learned the *Lord's Prayer,* all the stanzas of "Onward Christian Soldiers," and every Christmas carol before I knew one line of a prayer from my own tradition. Sometimes I was forced to pray to Jesus, though my parents told me that Jews didn't believe in Jesus as our "Savior." With no clear model, or formal Jewish education, elementary school was a confusing time, religiously and spiritually.

Though Jewish children were clearly a minority in our school system, the Jewish community in Reading was organized, close-knit, and self-sustaining, albeit diffused by suburban sprawl. Outside of the synagogue, the "Y" was the center of Jewish social and cultural life. It was there in Madame DuValle's ballet class, at age seven, that I met Sheila Roth, who years later would unexpectedly play pivotal secular and religious roles in my adult life in another city. But as a youngster I yearned for the sense of community and religious purpose I enjoyed whenever we visited my grandparents in New York.

At ages eight and nine, it was enjoyable to attend Brownies at the Y, and an affiliated summer day camp, Camp Asodi. My parents, with limited finances and disparate religious connections, didn't feel it was necessary to send me—a girl— to Hebrew school. Finally, because I craved for the social connections that accompanied Jewish religious literacy, I begged my parents to hire a tutor, the cantor of Kesher Zion Synagogue, Cantor Klonsky, to work with me privately until I could catch up with my peers who were already enrolled in the synagogue's formal Hebrew school program. We studied together for a few sessions, but the fantasy of joining my friends at the synagogue would never be realized. My study routine fell apart soon after my parents' separation.

◆◆◆

The illicit relationship that had doomed my parents' marriage had purportedly started innocently enough. My father's younger sister, Aunt Norma, at whose wedding my parents had met, lived in Philly and my father visited her when he was in town on Wednesday nights for business. It was his pleasure to enjoy a home-cooked meal with her and her husband and two daughters in their northeast Philadelphia row house. My aunt, a jolly soul, belonged to a Wednesday night bowling league. She was a good bowler, but she looked forward even more to getting out of the house and away from her contrarian husband. She invited my father, also a good bowler, to join her.

The first time my father accompanied my aunt Norma to the bowling alley, he met and immediately became smitten with one of my aunt's teammates, a married woman with two small children who lived in a row house in the same neighborhood as my aunt. Soon afterward my father and the woman began having an affair.

My mother found out about their clandestine meetings only after they had been cavorting secretly for years. As soon as she confronted my father at the corner convenience store with evidence of the affair, she told my father to "get the hell out." That was the day our mother announced with heart-wrenching conviction that our father was leaving us because "he loved someone else." Allegedly, Daddy tearfully admitted his infidelity and begged my mother to let him stay to keep the family together. He promised to give up the affair, but my mother, raw from discovering proof of the ongoing betrayal, was resolute, convinced that there had been other women besides my aunt's friend and that my father was a "serial cheater." My father moved into his mistress's house in Philadelphia and the rest of us were left to teeter along on our own. For my mother, sister, and me daily uncertainty was a miserable place to reside, and we were all deluged with a consummate spate of worry and fear.

◆◆◆

A few months into the separation, my father declared bankruptcy, a result of his spendthrift lifestyle going awry. With no money put aside for emergencies or living beyond the next bill cycle, our little family descended even farther down a dark rabbit hole under the weight of simultaneous financial and psychic loss. Hebrew tutoring and any extracurricular activities were cut off. Worst of all, the bank repossesssed our new house and all the furniture in it. One day I had to watch the moving men carry out most of our belongings, my beloved player piano among them, into a waiting truck, never to be seen again. We were left with our beds, some books, our clothes, and a few odds and ends. It was a trauma no child should ever have to bear, the kind of event that soils a childhood with a stain that is impossible to scour out.

My husbandless mother was now without money, a job, financial security, or extended family nearby, and she was responsible for feeding, sheltering, and clothing two young girls. She didn't even drive, which wouldn't have mattered anyway, because we couldn't afford to own a car. Without private transportation, however, it was impossible to get around in suburban Reading. With staggering rapidity she became a poverty-stricken, displaced housewife at a time when support groups like Parents Without Partners and Single Mothers by Choice didn't exist. It was only after I became a mother myself many years later that I understood the depths of her distress and fear.

Alone and vulnerable, my mother talked about moving back to her hometown of Brooklyn to be nourished and supported by my grandparents and our many kind, adoring relatives whom, she supposed, would always be ready to step in whenever needed. But for me more change seemed daunting. Initially I didn't want to move anywhere, including New York. Though being with my grandparents was always a delicious experience, I was aware that East New York had a shady, crime-ridden reputation. I petitioned my mother in writing to reconsider: "Dear Mommy," I wrote, "Please, please, please, don't take us to that crowded, awful Brooklyn where so many bad things happen on the streets. . . ."

But the impending move was already a *fait accompli*. With no other options available, my mother had finalized plans to start anew in New York. So off we went. And thank God we did. Without my grandparents, we would have languished in an even blacker hole than we were already in.

— CHAPTER 4 —

New York, New York

"New York, New York, a Helluva Town . . . "

(Music by Leonard Bernstein,
Lyrics by Betty Comden and Adolph Green)

*M*Y GRANDFATHER DROVE from Brooklyn to Reading to retrieve us, and back again, all in the midst of a blinding snowstorm that seemed to continue without mercy. My sister had the mumps and moaned most of the way behind swollen cheeks, lying on my mother's lap, sucking her thumb in the backseat. My mother was quiet and sullen. To make matters worse, the moving truck that was carrying what was left of our scant belongings got stuck in a ditch in the snow two blocks from our new apartment. We arrived at our destination with nothing but the clothes and gear we had traveled with. Needless to say, the move to New York was a brutal transition.

My mother, still harboring a fear of driving, would have been happier living in the heart of New York City, with access to public transportation and proximity to Manhattan's culture of theatre and museums, but she chose to nest in the suburbs with a grassy backyard in a quiet neighborhood where we could ride our bikes in relative safety, and where my sister and I would have the ability to attend the best public schools.

Unfortunately, our new apartment was a prototype for downsizing before the concept became popular. Less was not more. From our attractive three-bedroom, two-and-a-half bathroom house in Reading, where I'd enjoyed my own "space," we moved into a miniscule one-bedroom apartment in the back of a small duplex that was owned by Italian Jews in the suburban Brooklyn section of Mill Basin, which was comprised mostly of intact upper-middle-class families.

The solo bedroom had room for two twin beds, which my mother and sister claimed because I liked to stay up late and required less sleep than either of them. I was relegated to slumber in an undersized, twin pullout chair-bed next to the small dining room table that was squeezed into a cramped alcove. The bathroom was so tiny that two people could only be in it at one time if one person was bathing in the bathtub. I hated the lack of space and privacy, but this was the new reality. It was an early lesson in how to deal with the hard things in life. To move ahead a day at a time. To settle for less and strive for more.

Our doctor and family friend, Dr. Josephs, had a daughter my age, and my mother arranged for us to walk to school together. She and her friends were kind, but I had a difficult time being the new girl in town—from a divorced family—and attempting to break into established cliques where everyone else appeared to be well coiffed and high styled, exuding the appearance of wealth. I also felt socially isolated when the crowd went to synagogue for afterschool Hebrew classes that would lead to a *Bat Mitzvah* at age thirteen. Lack of funds for me, with no one stepping up to the plate to subsidize my studies, left me home alone in our dark, little apartment while my friends went to learn the history of our Jewish people and how to recite Hebrew prayers.

Having divorced parents also set me apart as a target for bullying. In response, I tried to embrace my identity and seek individuality. In the sixth grade, with five other Lindas in my class, I changed the spelling of my name to LYNNDA. My teacher, Mr. Moriando, would call on me mockingly, "Lynnda, with a Y and two Ns . . ." and the class would explode in uproarious laughter, leaving me humiliated. With my pride and attempts at distinctiveness squashed in the classroom, I struggled on all fronts.

◆◆◆

As the years progressed, my father's visits to New York were less frequent than they had been in Reading, and when he came around he brought the "other woman" with him, which meant we had to share our daddy-time with her. She was nice enough to us at the beginning, even fun, but her presence exacerbated my mother's gloominess. She constantly lambasted my father, pointing out his shortcomings, telling us that he was not forthcoming with legally required child support. Even though my mother was the more responsible parent in the trenches with us for the long haul, I was irritated at her for criticizing my father, and I blamed her exclusively for our have-nots. We were often at odds with one another.

It took a little time, but to my mother's credit, she got herself together, studied for her real estate license, and passed it. She began selling apartments in high-rise buildings, making new friends, and earning some money, which somewhat lightened the spirit in the house. But lonely and anxious about our accumulated debt, and constantly worried about having to apply for food stamps or some other form of subsistence, my mother couldn't shake her lingering depression. I watched her continue to take a lot of Valium, which made her seem even more listless and despondent than ever.

My grandparents, an enduring source of happiness and support, were by then living close to the boardwalk in Brighton Beach. They supplemented our income and continually filled our freezer with meat and chicken, and our refrigerator with Bubby's hearty home-cooked soups. Whatever we required, they brought. When I was with my grandparents, at least for a little while I felt safe, loved, and nourished. We were never hungry for food, but I was starving to find a peaceful place for myself, a place free from worry about the basics, a comfortable place among my peers.

Eventually, my father married his girlfriend, roughly five years after the day he'd packed his suitcase and left our house. When the newly married couple came to see us for the first time after their quickie-wedding my sister and I noticed the new wife's baby bump.

"Are you having a baby?" I asked her, shocked, and praying that it wasn't so.

"Yes, I am," she answered blithely. "Your father is going to be a father again. Isn't that great news?"

No, it wasn't great at all! It was devastating information. God help us! Fantasies of parental reconciliation are common among children of divorce—even if there isn't a nail's head of a chance that the parents could or should be together. Any small illusions I'd harbored of ever having a "normal" family were now terminally defunct—dashed by the implantation of an embryo. While I stewed in the car, my father and his new wife smiled playfully at one another. Their clear lack of compassion for our feelings irritated me like alcohol on a brush burn. I felt betrayed, wounded, and abandoned all over again. Their insensitivity was too much for an insecure teenage girl to handle with any kind of aplomb, and my sister seemed clearly wigged out as well.

When my mother found out about the impending baby, she was filled with rage, which aggravated her depression. Lonely and bitter, she seemed to be moving in slow motion. Panicked on all fronts, I tried to digest the changes coming down the pike, but there was no respite anywhere. Days and nights in our little apartment were painfully glum, even more so than usual. Something had to shift.

— CHAPTER 5 —

Philadelphia

"I believe the children are our future.
Teach them well and let them lead the way . . ."

(Songwriter Linda Creed)

IT WASN'T LONG after the birth of my baby half-brother, Todd, that my father began bringing other women besides his new wife to join us on our New York visitations. He was in love with someone else other than his wife, he told us when the new baby was just a few weeks old, but he was committed to staying in his marriage—sort of. "I can never do to another child what I did to you and your sister," he told me. So he played around in full-frontal view and continued to profess his guilt about how he had betrayed his first family and how he missed us desperately.

He began nudging me to leave my mother and settle in with him and his wife in Philadelphia, tempting me with promises of material security and a chance at higher education. He declared, "If you want to get a college degree, come live with me and establish residency in Philadelphia for your last few years of high school. Afterwards, I'll send you to a state college."

Whoah! The prevailing message given young women of my generation was to learn to type, be a nurse, or earn a teaching degree to "fall back on," before marrying a nice Jewish guy who would take care of us—forever. My mother had crapped out by following that erroneous propaganda, and I wasn't betting the dice on it for my own life. Unlike my mother, I wanted to have the ability to provide for myself financially with a stockpile of cash stashed and ready for emergencies. I knew that a good education was the ticket.

Unable to envision any other option for a college degree, I agreed warily to reside with my father and his wife. On Flag Day, June 14, 1964, at age fifteen, five weeks before my sixteenth birthday, I moved to Philadelphia, leaving my mother and sister behind in Brooklyn. My mother, exhausted from years of struggling, barely uttered a whimper about my departure. She sat propped up on a pillow in bed with a wet washcloth on her forehead while I packed my bags.

Many years later she told me she was "sick to the core of her bones" that I'd had chosen to leave. She rationalized that maybe something good could come from a change of scenery for me, or perhaps I might find opportunities that she couldn't offer. But she prayed with all of her heart and soul that I would return to her in Brooklyn after the summer. That didn't happen. The chaos that was to follow put the *kibosh* on both of our immediate hopes and dreams.

◆◆◆

The day I arrived at my father's house, the row home that his wife had once shared with her first husband and kids, I knew that my decision to move to Philadelphia was a colossal mistake. As I stood in the doorway, suitcase in hand, I recalled the living conditions that my sister and I had endured in that house during intermittent visitations. I wasn't used to my home, big or small, being anything other than immaculate and organized. Even on her most compromised days, my mother had been an impeccable housekeeper, neat and orderly. "Cleanliness is next to godliness," she'd chirrup as she dusted and vacuumed with broad sweeping gestures. But my father's house was godforsaken, I thought. Shockingly neglected, despite daily domestic help. How could he live like this?

The appearance of the house was an outward manifestation of the covert psychological mildew that had been festering there for years. For starters, my father's wife's kids from her previous marriage had suffered their own traumas from their parents' divorce. They were constantly acting out, especially her eleven-year-old daughter, with whom I was supposed to share a room. In their eyes, not only did they have to cope with a new baby from a strange, new father figure and abandonment by their birth father, but now they were facing a teenager intruding into their already chaotic lives.

For all of her feigned friendliness towards me when I had been living at home in my mother's house, my father's wife shed her amiable skin the moment I crossed the threshold on Kerper Street. She became a stranger, and worse than that an enemy. "Listen young lady," she barked at me almost as soon as I put my suitcase down on the stained carpet. "We have rules here, and you'd better get used to them right away." There was a venal tone in her voice that I hadn't heard before, and I was scared.

"Your father always wanted to have a boy," she continued. "Ha! Now he does. The king is born. Long live the king! You are not to touch that baby. Ever! Understand?

"You can't step foot into our bedroom," she droned on. "You can't eat anything after dinner. The kitchen is closed! And you will have a lot of chores to do. Is that clear?"

My descent into a new kind of hell was meteoric. I turned to my father, looking for help. He had a feeble expression on his face, like a sad clown. The corners of his mouth sloped downward while he remained silent. It was obvious that I was an unwelcome intruder in this house, and his wife wanted to swat me out the door like an annoying fly.

From that day on I never touched my darling little brother as a baby except when my stepmother left the house and my father or the housekeeper brought him to me. And I never stepped foot into their bedroom as I'd been told, although her own children marched around there insouciantly at whim.

If I were home, which I tried not to be, my father's wife kept me busy doing household tasks. With her constantly barking orders like a drill sergeant, I had little time or space to study and to do my high school homework, and since my stepmother's daughter went to bed early—clearly an escape mechanism—I couldn't use our bedroom to read or write. I don't know where I harnessed the strength or fortitude, but I became resourceful and resolute in taking care of my study needs. I set up a desk with wobbly legs for myself downstairs in the wet, unfinished basement, where I studied by the light of a bent, green apothecary desk lamp that my father bought for me at a flea market. Besides being wet, the room was dark, dank, and cold. The occasional mouse or roach scampered over my toes. But I stayed focused. I was determined not to fail even though my stepmother remained a relentless adversary.

In general, my father tended to look the other way, or run off to play golf, have a drink or two or consort with other women to avoid dealing with his wife's poor treatment of me. I was too petrified to complain to him, because she kept me in line by making up stories. "Your father has a bad heart," she told me repeatedly, her face in mine. "If you run to him, you'll put him in a pine box before his time. Do you want to kill your father?

Send him off to an early death? You will if you aggravate him," she warned vituperatively.

Once in a while my father would walk in on one of these terrifying scenes and catch her in the midst of spewing her abusive diatribes directed at me, which then generated a massive blowup between them. "What the hell are you doing to my kid?" he would shout at her, his bloodshot hazel eyes bulging from their sockets.

"Isn't that just like you to stick up for her?" she would snort back at him.

"She's a kid, God damn it! A kid! Jesus Christ, there's never any peace around here," my father bellowed. "What's the matter with you? Can't you see what you're doing to her?"

"Lynnda, let's go," he would say as he held the outside door open, ushering me swiftly out of the house.

Most of the time after leaving the war zone, we drove to the Dairy Queen for soft-serve chocolate ice cream with hot fudge topping and wet walnuts. For an hour or so I was able to exhale, and be content to receive some protected time alone with my father. But the next day I would pay for it with a new spate of malice, or the silent treatment.

His wife did her best to keep me isolated and under her control. When my mother or grandfather called the house, my stepmother would say to them, "Nobody by that name lives here," and hang up on them abruptly. After the call she would send a new wave of jibes my way.

"You know your *grrrrreat* family back in New York? Well, they don't give a shit about you. They never call you or send you anything, so you better straighten up and act nice here, because other than us you have nobody. You hear? Nobody cares about you at all."

Still, my maternal family called often and tried to open the communication channels. My father's wife hid stacks of letters, birthday cards, and greetings sent to me by friends and family. Years later, I found them bundled with a rubber band behind the TV in the curio when a technician came to service the set.

Living with so much stress and anxiety I began to develop breathing problems. On one occasion, against my protestations, my stepmother was called to school to address my frequent asthma-like symptoms. She told the school nurse that it was an attention-getting device, and when I came home she warned me to stop my acting routine.

"Your phony-baloney illness will not get you sympathy from me, or anyone else, so you better shape up," she snarled.

◆◆◆

"Pain is indispensible to growth . . . ," wrote Rabbi David Wolpe in his important book *Faith Matters,* which touched a nerve when I read it decades later. Looking back at the time I spent in my father's house, it is clear that somewhere along the way, almost gallantly, I rallied my inner resolve to prevail over my abusive circumstances. I figured out that the best antidote to adversity is accomplishment, and I had faith in myself that I could overcome the victim storyline. I discovered that I was a survivor and that with tenacity I would find a course to success.

I tried out for the cheerleading team and was one of only three girls in the sophomore class to make it. Besides cheering for the football and basketball teams, I was cheering for myself, for my spirit to triumph, pom-poms in hand.

Cheerleading opened a door for me, and I became popular with boys and girls. I made lots of friends and spent most of my time at my neighbor Shelly's uber immaculate house and at my best friend Jayne's, where we had many sleepovers. The time spent there revived me. The bathrooms and sheets were crisp, the house sparkled, and loving parents welcomed me. Jayne and I studied together, and she often let me borrow her beautiful Villager clothes or one of her pretty gold circle pins to wear to school the next day,

Some of my teachers, especially one of my early English teachers, recognized my affinity towards language and literature and mentored me. I received excellent grades for my efforts, and my advisers encouraged me to take on more and more advanced assignments, which I did with pleasure.

And soon I would meet the person who would change my life forever.

— CHAPTER 6 —

All You Need Is Love

*"Open your heart to me,
my sister, my love, my dove."*

(*Song of Songs 5:2*)

DESPITE ITS LOVELINESS, after fourteen months, a relationship that I was having with the captain of the football team ended. I started dating a few boys here and there, but the Divine sparks weren't flying, and the bells weren't ringing. Suddenly, although I wasn't really looking for a new guy, a cute one serendipitously showed up on the radar screen.

I met Larry at Northeast High School in Philadelphia when I was a sophomore and he was a junior. We both had a teacher named Mr. Whitehall for English. Larry's class took place during the fourth period; mine was during the fifth. I was an English major, and Mr. Whitehall was a painfully boring teacher and cranky to boot. The students taunted him mercilessly and, ordinarily, it was drudgery to show up for class.

Then one day Larry, an adorable, audacious young man with flashing, laughing eyes and a mischievous grin was sitting at Mr. Whitehall's desk in front of the room, greeting our class with a wave as students filed passed him on the way to their seats. Larry was being punished for "disruptive behavior" and was spending his lunch period in detention in our room. Whenever the teacher turned his back, Larry carried on with infantile antics, and the class devolved into uproarious laughter.

It seemed as though every day after that Larry was sitting in detention throughout our class, and, much to Mr. Whitehall's consternation, whenever Larry was around, the classroom decorum disintegrated. He made silly faces behind the teacher's back, and we hailed him as our savior from the humdrum of the tiresome class.

From what I could discern, Larry had a captivating, impish nature—different than my serious, goody-goody demeanor—and I found him charming. After seeing him a couple of times during class, I looked forward to his unruly presence, which was oh so much better than listening to Mr. Whitehall's lackluster lessons. Day after day of looking over at Larry sitting irreverently in detention, I developed a Pavlovian response whenever I glanced in his direction. Even if he did nothing, I would burst out into giggles.

We became friendly that year, talking in the school's corridor between periods, but for a long time our paths crossed only peripherally. Larry had a bit of a playboy reputation—he was the proverbial, irresistible "bad boy," fun to be with, but no commitments. I avoided dating those types, or even trifling with the idea. Who needed a broken heart? But getting together with Larry was apparently meant to be, *bashert* in Yiddish.

◆◆◆

Two years after we first met, when Larry was a college freshman and I was a senior in high school, we reconnected on a hot summer night in June at a mixer sponsored by a country club that my friend dragged me to attend under protest. I was dating a couple of young "suitors," as they were labeled back then, and the one I liked the most had abruptly stopped calling after warning that he needed me to be more of a "woman." In other words, I wasn't putting out enough. After breaking up with him, I was pretty blasé about getting involved with another man so soon.

When we arrived at the mixer, I walked over to greet a friend and gave him a peck on the cheek. Then I heard someone say: "Hey, don't I get a kiss too?"

It was Larry. After we bantered back and forth like a B movie, he asked, "Are you still dating Gary?"

I told him the Gary fling was over, and he was surprised.

"Wow," he said. "I thought you really liked him."

"I did," I told him. "It wasn't very pleasant in the end, and I hate to admit it but I do miss him in a strange way. It's like losing a baby tooth—there's a hole there for awhile but you know something bigger is coming to fill in the gap."

"Hey, maybe I could fill in the gap," he suggested winningly.

"Maybe?"

"How about next Saturday night?"

"How about it?"

Starting the next evening, we talked on the phone whenever I could manage to steal some time while I sat in the basement doing my schoolwork. It was fun getting to know each other better, and I found that Larry possesssed a depth I hadn't expected. He also had good manners and was surprisingly reliable. When he said he was going to call, the phone rang precisely at that moment. I called him Big Ben. And he always made me laugh.

On our first official date, he picked me up in a dilapidated, 1958 green-and-white Chevy Impala and took me to see the movie *Can-Can*, followed by a bite at the local hangout, Lee and Mel's. We were already excited about what was developing between us, and when he opened the door to the car for me, I felt like royalty. As he sat down in the driver's seat, he took my hand. My heart cooed like a dove.

◆◆◆

That summer, Larry and I were inseparable. He was attending summer school to make up one of his courses, which meant he couldn't spend his usual summer frolicking at the Jersey shore, which he loved. I had no summer plans besides a part-time job in a lingerie store, so we courted over Phillies' baseball and college basketball games.

Larry came from a lovely, modest, hardworking Jewish family with good values. From the time he was a young teenager, he'd always had a job, which meant that he always had discretionary spending money in his pocket. After allocating currency for expenses, he was more than willing to devote a portion of his income to our entertainment, like movies and eating hamburgers at local joints.

Living in my house of horrors, I couldn't have been happier to enjoy his time and attention. His cut-up sense of humor buoyed my spirits and kept me in stitches. And wonder of wonders, he remained every bit the gentleman, great fun to be with and as reliable as Yellowstone's Old Faithful, a complete contrast to his "bad-boy" moniker.

We fell in love, madly, deeply, passionately in love. When I wasn't with him, I ached for his presence, and the warmth of his lovely family who welcomed me with open arms.

◆◆◆

I'd earned a reputation as a hardworking student, and my high school guidance counselor advocated for me to gain admittance to a local college. At age nineteen, two years after I'd started attending the Community College of Philadelphia, Larry and I became engaged. He presented me with a brilliant one-and-a-half carat marquis diamond set in platinum, with two baguettes on either side of the center stone. He bought the ring with money he'd earned in his spare time, supplemented by some funding from his parents, who wanted me to have a nice ring, even though my generous future mother-in-law had, up to that point, never received a diamond of her own.

Sadly, it was 1967, at the height of the Vietnam War, and Larry was given a low draft number. His father, Jack, having served in Saipan during WWII, leaving Larry's mother and sister and the rest of the family for four years, was like other veterans. He had hoped he had fought in "the war to end all wars" so that no one would ever have to participate in another one. Larry's parents were understandably petrified about sending their only son overseas, especially to an unpopular foreign war that none of us believed was necessary. I lived in daily fear of him being drafted.

Fortunately, Larry was able to join the army reserves, which was a bit of a hedge against his low draft number, and might even delay his induction into active duty—we hoped. The reserves weren't a complete fail-safe, but they were the best option at that time.

On the day that Larry took the bus to Fort Dix, New Jersey, en route to his basic training, I left my father and his wife's house of misery forever. With only one small, half-empty suitcase in hand, I understood that, while I had accumulated nothing material in Philadelphia, I had triumphed in resilience and accomplishment. The love I shared with Larry had served as the healing balm for my tumultuous early years, and my new community of Larry's family and friends felt to me like a wealth of riches. By then I had also earned an Associate's Degree from

Community College of Philadelphia, which gave me a heaping dose of self-respect.

It was June 1968 when I said a wrenching goodbye to my beloved Larry at the bus station and moved back to Brooklyn to live with my mother and sister for the six months or so that he would serve in basic training and active duty before our marriage. I was almost twenty years old, and I planned to work in New York before enrolling in Temple University to complete a bachelor's degree in English/Education.

◆◆◆

Back in my mother's apartment, I found that my mother was in a healthy state with a good job and lots of friends. Much of the depression had lifted, and her winning sense of humor bubbled back to the surface. My sister had also grown up in the four years that I had been living in Philadelphia, and now we were like-minded contemporaries. After what we'd been through together in the dimmest days, it was a sterling reconnection. Despite our years of living apart, and many subplots, we coalesced like the finale of a noble play. We shopped and went to movies together, and I spent a lot of time hanging out with her and her boyfriend, who would later become her husband. And we laughed a lot.

Having my sweet grandparents and the rest of our lively extended family nearby again was also a source of great joy. Personal contentment was something that I had longed to experience during my teenage years in Philadelphia, and back in Brooklyn it permeated my being.

During that summer, I worked on Wall Street in a small investment-banking firm where my great-aunt Ann was employed, and I earned more money than I ever had at any of my earlier part-time jobs. I loved being back in New York and was dazzled by the fast pace of the city and the sophisticated culture of restaurants, museums, and theatre.

Our wedding was scheduled for early December, but I began to wonder about going back to live in Philadelphia where I had been ground up and spat out like chewing tobacco before I met Larry. Would our marriage be strong enough to make up for all I had suffered in the City of Brotherly Love? Maybe it would be better for us to stay in New York or to start fresh elsewhere? I worried a lot, but my fears were always allayed by a phone call from my reassuring fiancé.

◆◆◆

Wedding plans accelerated toward the big day, and on December 1, 1968, Larry, now finished with basic training, and I were married in Floral Park, New York, in a ceremony presided over by an Orthodox rabbi and cantor that neither of us had ever met. Both of my parents walked me down the aisle, and fifteen family members stood with us under an enormous *chuppah* (wedding canopy) made of white stephanotis. Following the ceremony we sipped champagne in fancy flutes, danced the *hora* and the bunny hop, and ate a not-so-memorable glatt-kosher chicken dinner. Right before we left the catering hall near the end of the event, I changed into my "going-away" outfit, a blue mini dress and matching coat ensemble. Larry threw out my garter to the single men, and I tossed my bouquet to the single women, aiming directly at my sister, who caught it. And off we went, leaving our guests waving at us at the door.

After our honeymoon in Florida, which was a relaxing aftermath to wedding planning and army life, Larry and I began building our lives together in Philadelphia. I started attending classes at Temple University, which had accepted my community college credits, and we moved into a small, rental two-bedroom apartment in a dark walk-up in the far northeast part of the city that we outfitted with second-hand furniture—the best we could afford.

With no handy washer and dryer, we did our laundry at my in-laws' house on the weekends when we visited for Sunday night deli dinners, and each week I borrowed my mother-in law's vacuum cleaner to sweep the scrungy carpeting which contributed to the dinginess of our apartment.

My father stopped by periodically, the same old aging good-time-Charlie of my youth, bringing the luxury of bagels and lox on Sunday mornings, a meal which we could ill afford on our meager budget.

As a full-time student at Temple University I was very busy, but I enjoyed my classes and the camaraderie with my fellow-students. Larry was working for a knitting mill and finishing up his three remaining courses of college work at night. His mother had donated her eleven-year-old Chevy to us, the car we'd used on our first date, but we were so poor that we had to either save pennies to buy gas or take public transportation at the end of the week before Larry got his pay check. We struggled financially, but we had many cherished friends and lots of happy, normal times. It was a good life lesson in delayed gratification and the benefit of working hard to improve one's state of being.

Fairly soon after Larry went to work for the knitting mill, the company declared bankruptcy. He quickly visited his college placement office, and answered an ad for Integrity Textiles, a successful fabric company that had been launched in 1929. He interviewed for the job and was offered a position with the prospect of an exciting and lucrative career with a solid future. The only caveat was that we would have to leave our family and friends and move to Chicago.

— CHAPTER 7 —

The Cushy Life

*"Go forth yourself from your land, from your relatives, and from
your father's house to the land that I will show you."*

(Genesis 12:1)

LARRY ACCEPTED THE POSITION in Chicago with
the proviso that the company allow us to stay in
Philadelphia for six months, long enough for me to complete
my much-coveted college degree. On the last day of my classes,
in January 1971, we packed up a new Rambler, that Larry's
father had cosigned for, with our sparse belongings, including
the new vacuum cleaner we'd recently acquired, and drove like
the Beverly Hillbillies to another walk-up apartment that we had
rented 1,200 miles away. Skokie, Illinois, a lovely, safe suburban
enclave—later made famous by the neo-Nazis who fought to
march in the town largely populated by Holocaust survivors—
became our new home.

Much to our surprise, the transition was seamless. Though
we missed our family, the Chicagoans we met readily offered up
their finely honed midwestern hospitality, warm and welcoming

like hot apple cider before a glowing fire on a chilly "Windy City" day.

We also met many transplanted "East Coasters" who became our family surrogates. And much to our delight, through one of my father's cronies, we discovered that my friend Sheila from Madame DuValle's ballet class at the Y in Reading, had also moved to Chicago with her husband. We reconnected at a neighborhood ethnic restaurant and relaunched our early friendship, happy to find that the four of us had a lot in common. It was at Sheila's initiation that we began celebrating some of the Jewish rituals, life cycle events, and holidays that had gone by the wayside in our first two years of marriage.

◆◆◆

I taught high school English at a suburban school near our apartment and worked as a stringer for a community newspaper, with many of my stories appearing as front-page features. Larry quickly built up the midwestern territory of his company's business, cracking it open for expansion beyond anyone's expectations. For the first time ever, we accumulated a little money. We bought a couch and a couple of paintings for the walls. We put a few dollars in the bank and started to pay off my student loan, which my father was supposed to repay, but didn't. On occasion, we could even afford to eat at fancy restaurants and enjoy Chicago's excellent theatre offerings.

Two years later, in 1973, Larry and I had our first child, a son, Eric, who was ten weeks premature. Born breech at three pounds, one-and-one-half-ounces, and fourteen inches long, his scrawny arms and legs flailed as though he were still in utero. The distance from his tiny waist to his neck was the size of my pinky, and his little ears flimsily attached to either side of his face were devoid of cartilage and could be moved around like silly putty. Larry fainted when he touched his thin skin through vents in the incubator, earning the nickname "Fainting Sam" from the neonatology nurses who lovingly cared for our little baby. We were scared by how small and vulnerable he seemed, and unprepared for the kind of parenting a premature infant would require.

We were lucky. Eric was alert and breathing on his own, even in the first hours after his arrival, and other than his size, he was healthy. Because of his low birth weight, which at one point dipped to two pounds, fifteen-and-a-half ounces, we had to leave him in a city hospital for a month until his weight rose to four pounds, four ounces. Alas, our blood family was too far away to help with the daily routine of feeding, rocking, and cuddling our new son, but our amazing Chicago friends hopped to it. Every day for a month, our friends Jill and Ron, Genie and Allen, and others drove me to the hospital, keeping me company while I rocked and fed our tiny preemie. They also brought meals to our house when we arrived home exhausted from administering the last nighttime feeding.

My mother flew to Chicago when Eric first came home from the hospital. She was over the moon crazy in love with him and arrived loaded down with presents for her first grandchild. My proud, sweet, grandparents flew in for a two-week visit a month later to help out at his *bris,* the ritual circumcision, which had been delayed because of low birth weight. They were ecstatic that they had lived to welcome a great-grandson—emphasis on boy—into the family and the *Covenant* of God. It was marvelous watching them interact with him, a *tireleh boyalah* (dear little boy), absolutely smitten, cooing, and cajoling.

◆◆◆

Adjusting to motherhood and mothering a demanding preemie, in particular, was challenging, but I adored our baby and I was having fun. I enjoyed my part-time job at the local newspaper, and I loved my circle of supportive mother-friends, like Jill and Sheila. But the joy was short-lived. When Eric was just ten months old, we received grim news from New York. My beautiful, petite mother was diagnosed with advanced breast cancer at the young age of forty-five.

The prognosis was dismal from the get-go. The tumor was large and aggressive, and even with the advantage of the big treatment guns in an excellent, prestigious, New York City hospital, we were told that she had less than a 20 percent chance of surviving her disease for five years. Most likely the metastatic breast cancer would invade her brain or her bones, or both. I was twenty-six, and my sister was twenty-two. We were destroyed by the news.

I shuttled back and forth from Chicago to New York to be with my mother as often as possible, leaving Eric with Larry, and my heart with whomever I left behind. Despite my mother's poor prospects for long-term recovery, she clung to life like a koala bear hanging on to a Eucalyptus tree.

In the midst of the meta-crisis, Larry and I bought our first house in Highland Park, a northwestern suburb close to the shores of Lake Michigan. The three-bedroom, two-and-a-half bathroom charmer was a wood-sided, split-level structure, and was much like my family's house in Reading that had been repossesssed by the bank.

Situated in an established neighborhood that was turning over to young couples with small children, we made a new circle of friends, spending many hours together at the park or the nearby beaches. Sometimes we went to antique markets and shopped for bric-a-brac for the new house. We bought a station wagon for future nursery school carpools and acquired an adorable fuzzy ball of a golden retriever puppy that Eric named Sally, after the dog who appeared in his early reading books.

I wanted to have another baby, but because my pregnancy would be considered high risk, I was reticent to conceive, fearing that if my mother ever needed me, I would be unable to fly to New York to be with her. We kept delaying the expansion of our family, worried that the dreaded Angel of Death, lingering nearby, was waiting for any excuse to swoop in and scoop up my mother like the Wicked Witch of the West in the *Wizard of Oz*. For four years we lived with the ups and downs of my mother's illness—dramas, surgeries, brutal cancer treatments, and a roller coaster of emotions that left me feeling an incalculable, overwhelming amount of responsibility and stress for someone in her late twenties. Treatment decisions fell to me and my generally quiet, guarded twenty-two-year-old sister. We coped as best as twenty-somethings could who didn't know a lick about managing breast cancer.

◆◆◆

One morning when my mother was groggily recovering from surgery, a radical mastectomy, she instructed my sister and me to lie to her if the disease ever recurred. "I'm going to recover from this," she told us defiantly. "Too many people care about my welfare for me to die now. But if it comes back, I don't want to know. Okay?"

Okay?

Sixteen months later, just as the doctors had predicted, an aggressive tumor presented itself in my mother's spine, making walking tentative and excruciating. We lied about the new tumor because we promised her that we would, and we told her that she had osteoporosis, a debilitating but not necessarily fatal disease. Amazingly, we never used the "C" word again in her presence.

Day after day we stealthily sidestepped the subject, forcing the reluctant healthcare team to corroborate our fraudulent story, perpetuating a secret that kept us all feeling drained. The insidious lies floated like a poisonous mist over our entire family, including our grandparents, who hovered daily near our mother's hospital bed without understanding the reality of their daughter's sickness and true fate.

The consequences of this charade were immeasurable, and to this day I think about what we might have gained as a family had we all been able to discuss the truth, cry openly, lament the unfairness of the situation, tell each other what we meant to one another, and ultimately, say a heartfelt goodbye to my mother. But we had bought the deception ticket at the outset, not knowing where we were going, and, alas, the train of dishonesty chugged on toward a bad destination without ever changing its course.

And then after four years of waiting and watching my mother bravely fight her disease, I became pregnant. The promise of new life in the face of certain death offered a welcome repose, a chance to concentrate on joy instead of dwelling on the murkiness of doom. But even as I cherished the thought of adding another baby to our family, elation over my pregnancy didn't last long.

— CHAPTER 8 —

Saying Goodbye

*"Teach us to number our days so that
we might acquire a heart of wisdom."*

(Psalm 90:12)

I WAS APPROACHING my thirteenth week of pregnancy and in New York for a visit when my mother's lab work showed that she had too much calcium in her bloodstream, a side effect of bones breaking down due to the cancer and its treatments. She needed to be taken to the hospital and, once there, the news beyond the blood hypercalcemia was horrific.

Her lead doctor told me, "Your mother has lumps and bumps everywhere. Despite all that we are offering, which frankly isn't much at this point, the tumors are pervasive throughout her entire system. There's nothing else we can do for her except try to keep her comfortable. Her days are numbered."

After treatment for hypercalcemia, my mother left the hospital with somewhat renewed energy. For a brief interlude she felt pretty good—surprisingly well and seemingly unaware of the gravity of her condition. What followed were intermittent respites that allowed us to share good times in the white spaces between cancer management and palliative care, laughing and feeling hopeful again that perhaps the doctors were wrong and she would live to become a grandmother a second time.

But as the weeks ambled on, new illness-related cruelties continued to develop—mouth sores that sprouted like weeds in a garden, loss of motion in a hip because a tumor was growing there—a reminder that she was and would remain separated from the land of the well. My sister and I felt like little unarmed tin soldiers standing around her hospital bed with no ammunition, trying to do battle with the cancer and witnessing her systemic demise. She hated watching us watch her, and we hated watching her watching us. Yet, the three of us there together were joined metaphorically at the hip.

◆◆◆

The end came like a stealthy cat, ready to strike when no one was prepared for the surprise attack. I was well into the fourth month of my pregnancy, waiting to fly east for Rosh Hashanah, which I imagined with great sadness and trepidation to be the last holiday I would likely have with my mother. I was home alone, trying to temper the symptoms of a cold, and Eric was at nursery school when my brother-in-law called from outside my mother's hospital room.

"Your mother took a turn for the worse, Lynnda. She's filling up with fluid and she may not make it through the night. You better come today and not tomorrow."

Immediately, I called Larry at work and we changed our flight reservations. A few hours later, we landed in New York and proceeded straight to the hospital. When I entered my mother's room, I was shocked by the sight before me. She was awake and alert, but I froze at her dull appearance. Her condition had deteriorated considerably since I had last seen her two weeks earlier, and she had become a *goses*—a person known in the Jewish tradition as suspended between the states of life and death.

My mother's chances at a good outcome had been horrible from the onset. Now, standing next to her fragile, cancer-ravaged body, watching my beloved grandparents hanging over the railing of her hospital bed, witnessing their precious firstborn daughter wasting away—and not even knowing definitively that she had cancer—we were all gripped by fear and dread. I realized that I had been deluding myself, thinking I could let her go when it was her time to pass on. My mother was forty-nine years old; I was thirty. I still needed her guidance and friendship. We had reached yet another new place in our relationship when I'd made her a grandmother. Now, a second grandchild was on the way. My son and unborn child needed a doting grandmother who would give them the same unconditional love that I had been given from my terrific grandparents. I stood beside her and prayed that whatever happened she would be at peace.

Though my mother recognized me and acknowledged my presence as I leaned over her bed, she was too weak and debilitated to hold a conversation beyond a few words. Straining to hold back tears, I anxiously started to blather on, talking faster and faster, hoping she could hear me. The doctor had told us that the sense of hearing is often among the last of the senses to lapse before final expiration.

I talked to her about my pregnancy; I lifted my wide maternity top to show off my abdomen, stretched to the size of a large melon as new life was taking shape beneath it. I relayed the most recent mischievous antics of Eric, the first boy in his generation to be born into our extended family. I shared the latest information on Larry's success in the textile business. My mother loved Larry, and she was delighted that he was able to care for me financially in a way she had never known herself. I filled her in on my work for the newspaper. I made her aware of current events—what was happening in the world she was leaving. I talked and talked. About friends and relatives. About flowers. About holiday food. About anything to maintain a living connection between us.

My mother drifted in and out of consciousness as I chattered incessantly, a soliloquy of desperation. She smiled and looked around each time she opened her eyes, telling me to leave and rest my pregnant body. When she seemed to be mostly out of it, we went to a cousin's apartment a few blocks away. But the moment we arrived we were called back to the hospital and informed that our mother had begun actively dying as soon as we left her bedside. A short time later she died quietly, the day before Erev Rosh Hashanah, as we stood around her disbelieving and helpless against death, which had finally swooped down and snatched her away.

Like my parents' separation twenty years earlier, my mother's death inculcated to me once again that life is precious and precarious, that our greatest gifts and assets can be whisked away from us in a single, chilling instant. That we have to savor each day as though it were our last, because it might be.

◆◆◆

My mother, the snappy dresser who looked like a model in life, replete with perfect makeup, false eyelashes, and kickin' shoes, was buried the next day according to Orthodox tradition, dressed in muslin shrouds, deferring to my grandparents' wishes, lying in death in a plain pine box without dowels. Her love of fashion in life was juxtaposed against the simplicity of her burial dress, *tachrichim*, in death. My grandparents beat their chests as they clung to her casket, weeping so hard I thought the earth would rupture. Family and friends buried the casket while the sky clouded over, making way for steady torrential rains that flooded the cemetery, splashing mud everywhere. It was like a scene out of a Fellini movie.

I read the words of the *23rd Psalm* at the funeral without conviction: *"Yea, though I walk through the valley of the shadow of death I will fear no evil, for God is with me. . . . "* I was fearful of living a life without my mother, and doubtful that God's presence was near or could be sustaining in the midst of such miasmic grief. Where are you, God? I kept asking. My mother was being lowered beneath the surface of the earth. I felt utterly deserted by God in that moment, and abandoned again by my parents.

◆◆◆

We all left the cemetery and went to my sister's house, my mother's last residence, for the requisite "meal of consolation." Because of the imminence of Rosh Hashanah, Jewish law dictates that mourners only sit *shivah* for two hours instead of for the normal seven-day, intense mourning period, a blueprint for the bereaved that early Jews had brilliantly created to facilitate the grieving and healing process while allowing the community to step in and be a consoling force. The impending holiday trumped the customary mourning rituals and meant that we would have little time to share stories about my mother's life, to catch our breath, to transition into being motherless daughters.

The day after my mother's death, the holiday dinner at my grandparents' apartment in Brooklyn, usually so lively and filled with good cheer, was ghastly. My grandmother, not knowing how critically ill her daughter had been, had prepared the usual holiday banquet with enough food to feed "starving children in Europe." But when we looked at the food, as gorgeous and comforting as it should have been, none of us felt like eating. The silence in the house was impenetrable, broken only by the sound of a small child, our son, who knew he had lost his grandmother but didn't understand the concept of gone forever. An opaque sadness took hold of all of us and was relentless in its grasp.

In the days that followed, my sister and I cleaned out what was left of my mother's meager belongings. Knowing her to have been such a meticulous fashionista when she was well, it was upsetting to find that most of her clothes had spots and stains, the hems falling down carelessly on her beautiful skirts and dresses, signs of an uncharacteristic inattention that had settled in as she had become weakened by cancer and had no occasion to wear most of her beautiful wardrobe or check it out.

We divided up some of the dishes, serving pieces, and decorative arts that my mother had avidly collected at flea markets and antique stores, and a few pieces of inconsequential jewelry. Remembrances, nothing more.

Crestfallen and bereft, Larry, Eric, and I returned to Chicago.

◆◆◆

Pregnant and grieving, I wanted to pull the covers over my head and stay in bed as the autumn winds kicked in over Lake Michigan, causing the air enveloping us to become a typical freezing Chicago winter. But with a young child who needed me in the house and my pregnant body to nurse for the sake of our unborn baby, I had to rouse myself. My friends were very helpful and a huge source of consolation, but the mourning process, without my extended family nearby, was soul shattering. I walked around zombie-like, performing my duties perfunctorily. My chest felt heavy, like a hard slab of granite was pressed against it as I contemplated life without my mother. I knew I had lost the unmatched continuity of a mother's unconditional love, the guiding voice that cheered when I accomplished something good and offered solace in tough times. In its place was silence at the end of the telephone line, an empty space at the table, an extinguished light that had once illumined my female history and future.

Our relationship had not always been ideal or even good at times, but we had achieved a sweet renewed closeness right before I got married. After I became a mother, I could empathize with her struggle to raise two children as a single parent with insufficient financial, emotional, or social resources to ease the burden. In recent years, we'd even talked about how much I appreciated her courage. Now the loss of her left me unmoored.

At the time of her death, Larry and I weren't affiliated with a synagogue in Chicago or an organized Jewish community that might have been uplifting in service to my grief. I clung to a well-known poem in our tradition, *We Remember*, written by Rabbi Jack Reimer and Sylvia Kamens, which is often read at funerals or memorial services. Though I had heard it recited often, in my time of bereavement it resonated deeply:

When we are weary and in need of strength, we will remember her.

When we have news we crave to share, we will remember her.

When we have decisions that are difficult to make, we will remember her.

As long as we live, she too will live, for she is part of us, as we remember her.

❖❖❖

As the onset of an early Chicago winter grew more brutal, white precipitation started dropping and dropping. It became the winter of a record snowfall—105 inches before we would see a blade of grass again. The branches of the old trees in our backyard were bowed by packed snow and clear, hard icicles. The snow was so heavy on the roof that we had to pay a company to come out four times over the course of two months to shovel it off, fearing that the weight of the snow might cause the roof to collapse as it had in other homes, factories, stores, and warehouses around the area. Leaks sprouted up all over our house, forcing us to put buckets and bowls in the corners of rooms on the carpeting and hardwood floors to catch the steady drips of water.

Our Golden Retriever thought the bowls and buckets of water were meant for her, and splattered the water clumsily with her paws as she tried to drink from vessels that were too tall for her reach. It felt as though our house was a perpetual sopping mess, a state that mirrored my inner spirits. I was drowning in melancholy. In the midst of it all, my cervix began to dilate too early to deliver safely. Not wanting me to give birth to another premature baby, my doctor ordered complete bed rest. I was to get up only to go to the bathroom or when absolutely necessary—like if there was a fire.

What a challenging trick it was to mother an active, energetic five-year-old boy who needed lots of activity and stimulation while the weather outside was miserable and I was bedridden. Much to his disappointment, after he came home from school, Eric sat with me on the couch in the den, or on the floor reading, putting puzzles together, or watching television. Unless he was invited for a much-welcomed playdate or Larry came home early from work, it was just the two of us all afternoon, engaged in "quiet" activities while the cacophony of dripping water into aluminum pots rattled my brain like Chinese torture. We were both antsy and stressed, but I pushed myself to maintain a pleasant exterior for our little boy.

As a diversionary tactic, Larry bought me a Cuisinart food processor, which back then was a newly minted, state-of-the-art kitchen item. Eric and I diced, chopped, and sliced everything in the refrigerator, while I sat at the kitchen table, with my legs elevated on the mustard-colored vinyl chairs. Afterwards, I ate everything we prepared. The pounds were piling on, and I began to look and feel like a super-sized muffin.

I was a despairing and nervous specimen-in-waiting, worried about everything. At least once a week Larry sent a bouquet of beautiful orange and green parrot tulips with gift cards proclaiming, "Spring is coming and so is our new baby. Keep the faith!" But even stunning tulips couldn't lift my malaise or make me feel optimistic. The snow continued to plummet. Huge drifts piled up in front of our windows and doors, and the roof kept leaking—drip, drip, drip into the aluminum pots— testing my patience. Spring and the new baby were nowhere on the horizon, at least not that I could see beyond the foggy windows glazed with ice. And more challenges, far worse, were coalescing closer than I might have imagined.

◆◆◆

An hour after a routine doctor's checkup revealed that I was about to deliver four weeks early, I was rushed to the hospital with a police escort guiding our way down the snow-laden highway.

At first, the birthing team seemed unconcerned. The baby appeared to be over seven pounds, heart rate perfect, and in a good position for delivery. Labor was short and I delivered a gorgeous, chunky baby girl weighing in at seven pounds, twelve ounces. But from the moment she emerged, her breathing was labored. After a few tense hours of observation, my pediatrician thought it prudent to medevac her to a high-risk neonatal unit (NICU) for closer monitoring. Watching her being rolled away was excruciating.

Later that night the neonatologist from Evanston Hospital where our baby was being treated paid a visit to my room and told me—without emotion—that our baby had hyaline membrane disease, an acute lung disorder now known as respiratory distress syndrome. It was obviously not great news, but he said they could "handle it handily." I was petrified. I remembered that President and Mrs. Kennedy's baby Patrick had died of hyaline membrane disease, and if they couldn't save that baby with all their resources what would become of ours?

My grandparents were anxiously awaiting the birth of this baby, who was to be named after my mother, their late daughter, a symbolic gesture fleshy with meaning and importance. Their daughter's memory would live on through our new daughter. It was healing for them in their deep grief to contemplate the naming, and I couldn't bear the idea of having to explain this new drama. When they called after the delivery, with glee in their voices, I was as evasive as possible about the situation. Worrying about how they would take the news added angst to an already tense situation.

I checked myself out of the hospital the next day to be with our new baby at Evanston's Neonatal Intensive Care Unit, a facility with a fine reputation for taking care of "sick" babies. I was warned that our daughter was breathing on a respirator. Indeed, tubes were cascading out of every possible bodily opening. Soft white cotton mittens had been placed snugly on her hands to prevent her from pulling out the lifesaving tubes.

I cried when I saw her, even though she was the largest baby in the room amongst the scrawniest preemies. Under lights to combat jaundice, she was blindfolded and dressed in only a diaper. A pink bow was clipped to a mound of jet-black straight hair, humanizing her against the backdrop of pulsing machinery that was keeping her alive. She was so pretty, so perfectly formed on the outside. How could she be so ill? Watching her labored breathing was reminiscent of witnessing the last breaths my mother had taken before she died. Oh God, no!

To stay connected to her I pumped my breasts with an electric suction machine that honked and snorted and pulled at my mammaries like I was Elsie the Cow. The white stuff came flowing out of me like nectar from the gods, and was quickly poured either into a feeding tube attached directly into her stomach, or frozen in plastic bags for a later feeding. It was an exhausting process, but I clung to the opportunity to do something life-sustaining for our baby while she struggled with what the doctors were now calling, "persistent fetal circulation," a fancy term for infant pulmonary shutdown, which meant that instead of her breathing system opening up at the moment of birth, her lungs had not inflated.

Suddenly, the situation went from bad to worse. At midnight on the second night after she was born, Larry and I were lying in bed when a call came in from the chief neonatologist of the unit, the quiet, unassuming doctor who had visited me in the hospital the day before with an optimistic prognosis. "Mrs. Targan," he said in a measured monotone. "I'm afraid I have some disturbing news for you."

"Did our baby die?" I asked gripping the sheet in utter terror.

Larry looked on in horror, knowing that something really bad was happening.

"No, ma'am," the doctor responded.

I shook my head to let Larry know she was alive.

"She's in critical condition. However, we have a few tricks up our sleeves. We're going to put her on an adult respirator. Of course, we run the risk of causing her blindness by doing that. The eye nerves of a preemie may be too weak to sustain the pressure of high-volume oxygen. But she's a big baby so it's not likely to be a problem. And we're going to try a drug that we used before. It wasn't successful earlier, but we think it may be worth the effort attempting it again. If these things don't work,

I'm afraid your baby will expire. Would you like to come to the hospital to be with her?"

Blindness? Expire? I heard nothing else.

With Eric asleep in the next room, we couldn't run to the hospital. And, anyway, did we really want to see our precious baby "expire?" What to do? We went into crisis mode, a state of being that had been all too familiar for too long.

Instinctively, I picked up the phone to call a rabbi I had interviewed for my newspaper, a well-known counselor who ran a support group for parents who had lost children. Despite the late hour, the rabbi sounded as though he was waiting for my call.

"We may be about to lose our baby," I reported, my voice quivering. "My mother just died four months ago. This baby was to be named for her. My grandparents, in New York are planning to name her in a synagogue. They don't know what critical condition she's in. What should I do?"

"You know, Lynnda," he answered calmly. "First you must be assured that your baby's illness is not your fault. You did everything possible to insure her healthy passage. The situation reminds me of a farmer who plants rows of crops, and for some inexplicable reason, one plant in the plot does not thrive. It's sad, but sometimes there's loss in the natural order of things in a random universe."

Losing my mother, as awful as it was given her young age, seemed to have been within the natural order of things. Losing a child did not. I couldn't bear the thought of it. I started to shake.

"What am I supposed to tell my son? He was expecting to welcome a new baby brother or sister into our home. He's been anticipating her arrival for months. He knows she was born and that he hasn't seen her yet. Now she might die. I don't know how to handle this."

"Tell him what I told you for starters and fill in the pieces as it becomes necessary, tidbits of information that he can comprehend at his level. Meanwhile, I'll pray for your baby. Perhaps it won't be necessary to offer any words of condolences to your son. Let's hope . . ."

◆◆◆

All night Larry and I held onto each other, numb, crying, and silently praying from the depths of our souls, bargaining with God to be lenient with us and our little daughter. At seven o'clock in the morning the phone rang. We both thought it was the doomsday call. I stared at the phone not wanting to answer it, petrified to hear the worst news imaginable, but insane from the ringing. I lifted the phone from its cradle.

"Mrs. Targan," the neonatologist began, speaking in his earthy monotoned voice.

I held my breath.

"I think we might have finally turned the corner," he said. "The baby seems to be responding, and her blood gasses are returning with better numbers."

I exhaled.

"We're not out of the woods yet," the good doctor reported, "but I am feeling hopeful. The next twenty-four to forty-eight hours will be telling. We have reason to think that she will recover, but we are saying this with guarded optimism."

Hey, baby girl, way to go! You're a fighter. Hang in there, I thought, while the doctor continued to recount the details of the night's events in the neonatal unit where our cherished little baby continued to fight for her life.

"We'll come to the hospital soon," I said. "Thanks so much. Thanks so much," I answered choking back tears that kept running down my cheeks like water in an infinity pool.

"Guarded optimism, Mrs. Targan. Guarded optimism."

◆◆◆

Our daughter, Beth, stayed in the hospital for almost a month. I continued with the breast-pumping routine, and she continued to be fed my milk, her health improving steadily every day. When she could finally be disconnected from the respirator, we rocked her and held her close. Friends volunteered to bring us food in between feedings, to take care of Eric, to keep us company, to offer prayers and support. I fought to be brave, more so as I sometimes watched other parents in the unit, loving parents like us, say an excruciating goodbye to their little babies who didn't make it.

On the day we took Beth home from the hospital, accompanied by Larry's parents who were visiting from Philadelphia, I called the rabbi I had spoken to on the night we thought we might lose her. I reported to him that by the grace of God our baby was doing well. I was told there were no apparent residual effects that the medical team could discern, and so far, no problems with her eyes. For the first time in a month, my heart began beating at a normal pace. The doctors would keep a close watch, but they weren't anticipating any problems.

"This is a true miracle," the rabbi responded almost giddily. "Astounding news! Thank God. I'm so happy for you and your family. Why don't you bring the baby to the synagogue, and we'll name her here officially after your mother, *aleaha shalom* (May she rest in peace)."

"My grandfather already named her in their Orthodox synagogue in New York," I told the rabbi.

"It's okay. We'll do another one here if you want. Bring your friends. This is truly a cause for celebration."

A few weeks later when we had settled into the sleeplessness of infancy again—the result of the baby nursing every two hours around the clock—we hosted a Chicago *Simchat Bat* (celebration of the daughter) for our precious gift from God, in Solel, the rabbi's synagogue in Highland Park. Our new baby, named Beth in English, acquired the name *Brina* (after my mother, Bernice), *Froidal* (after Larry's paternal grandmother), the daughter of *Yeduda Leib* (Larry) and *Tzvia Leah* (me). It was an extraordinary celebration—warm, loving, personal. We were filled with gratitude. Our friends brought wine, desserts, good cheer, and blessings. We considered ourselves the luckiest parents alive with our lovely little family, a boy and a girl, what the old-timers called "the rich man's family." We soaked up the *nachas*, the delight of our baby's survival, like bread dipped in olive oil. But we had barely savored the joy of new life when yet another family tragedy began to unfold.

◆◆◆

While basking in the glory of our precious, healthy little girl, we received a horrible phone call from Philadelphia. Larry's handsome, sweet, adoring father, Jack, had died unexpectedly of a massive heart attack after a short hospitalization. He was fifty-nine.

We flew back east again with our two children, a six-week-old baby barely out of the NICU, and a five-year-old boy who had lost another grandparent a few months earlier. Shaky and disbelieving, we found ourselves in the back of another funeral limousine too soon after the loss of my mother, this time following a hearse carrying the body of Larry's dear father to the cemetery for burial. My fifty-eight-year-old mother-in-law was in shock, scared, and vulnerable. Even before Dad was placed in the burial soil, we wondered how we could possibly board a plane and fly more than 700 miles away, back to Chicago, leaving her behind without her beloved spouse of thirty-six years.

During the shivah period that followed and once we were back in Chicago, we began to realize that, sooner rather than later, we needed to be closer to our families. We were feeling like coconuts that had been shaken on palm trees during a hurricane. The distance between Chicago and Philadelphia simply had begun to feel overwhelming. Though we loved Chicago and had thrived there with good work and loving friendships, a nice home, and the pleasures of the city, we started to long for our East Coast family connections, to be able to huddle together in triumphs and tragedies. Wistfulness for family in close proximity crept in regularly, especially after painful phone calls to my mother-in-law or my sister, who regularly expressed how much they missed us. We continually asked ourselves and each other what we should do. It was a hard and confusing time in need of reckoning. In our hearts, we knew that we were compelled to return to the place where we had begun our lives together. But change also seemed daunting.

— CHAPTER 9 —

Pursuing Transformation

"The self is made, not given. It is a creative and active process of attending a life that must be heard, shaped, seen, said aloud into the world, finally enacted and woven into the lives of others."

(Barbara Myerhoff)

OR A BRIEF PERIOD OF TIME we moved on with our lives, a little family of four, as normally as possible. Our frazzled nerves began to calm after the loss of two parents and the near-death of our daughter. Beth was a gorgeous and delicious baby, with big round teal-blue eyes similar to my mother's, and dark, wispy hair that stood straight up as though she had put her fingers in an electric light socket. She had a sunny disposition, an endearing smile, and a contagious giggle. She was so adorable and engaging that everyone on the street and in the supermarkets stopped me and told me that she should be a baby model. Meanwhile, Eric was adjusting to the intrusion of his new little sister, waffling between kissing her over and over again on her forehead and holding his hands over his ears when he heard her cry, or just dismissing her completely when he was tired of her being nearby. All was very homespun and welcome.

As for me, I was a proud and glowing mother. Having my own sweet nuclear family helped me recover what had been lost in the fragmented family life of my youth and the more recent tragedies. I counted my blessings instead of sheep every night.

Continuing to work as a part-time stringer for the newspaper, I also accepted substitute-teaching positions at the local high school, which paid well. I counseled women who were breastfeeding preemies, as I was, which was not really encouraged or fashionable at the time. My work schedule allowed me to drive car pools and exercise regularly at a trendy new workout studio with excellent day care, and I played tennis twice a week. In between, I met other mothers for play dates, children's music classes, and hurried lunches in homey cafés and small restaurants. And I did a lot of cooking. My friends and I even formed a "gourmet club" to try new recipes and bond with other couples around the ritual of creating and sharing food.

Larry was doing very well in his business, loving his work, and whistling when he set out for his office every morning. His career afforded us a financially privileged lifestyle, and we relished eating out at restaurants, attending theatre and other cultural events, buying furniture and some beautiful decorative arts for our house, traveling to exotic destinations and taking the kids on family vacations.

Sheila and my new best friend, Leslie, and the rest of our gang were always around, and we continued to gather for Shabbat and holiday dinners, Sunday picnics, birthday parties, and beach days on the shores of Lake Michigan—all of which helped us loosely maintain and keep our Jewish rituals somewhat relevant. We were a loving community of friends, all compensating for our distant extended families, dedicated and present to each other in good and bad times.

Yet with all this privilege and joy in the aftermath of devastating losses and near-losses, I continued to feel that I was missing something—something that was unclear to me. I couldn't define the feeling as anything more than a restlessness. Some days I barely noticed it. At other times it was painfully annoying like a large mosquito bite on fresh skin. It was a sensation that as yet had no words, no reason for being, no explanation. It was just there. And troubling. So I began searching for the unknown.

It was the first inkling I had of an awakening of a desire to find an inner life, one that couldn't be identified or named. In the few empty spaces between busyness, I couldn't shake the sense that I wasn't self-actualizing or realizing my potential— that I was awakening to a call to do something else—something deep that I yearned to access. And I wondered how I could be pining for something unidentifiable when I was so blessed with good fortune. I felt ashamed that I wasn't grateful enough for my blessings. And worried that I might have been hyper-focused on life's high drama for so long that I couldn't coexist with a peaceful status quo.

Gestalt therapist Ilana Rubenfeld identifies this feeling, apparently a woman's midlife phenomenon, as the "fertile void." If so, I was ovulating the need for a journey within. Was there a calling calling?

◆◆◆

Ralph Waldo Emerson once said, "When you make a decision to do something, the world conspires in your success." After ten years of living in Chicago, one of the senior partners in Larry's firm announced his retirement in Philadelphia, and Larry was summoned to move back to the City of Brotherly Love. The opening presented itself as an enormous opportunity for him to advance his career, to buy into the company as a partner, and to solidify our finances. Plus, we would be going home. Wasn't that the package we'd been waiting for?

Given the opportunities for future success, you'd think I'd have been dancing the Watusi in the streets after we got the word, but when reality set in that we were going back to Philadelphia, we both suddenly felt wary and ambivalent. We had lived in Chicago for ten years. The Windy City with its inclusive midwestern hospitality had been good to us. I felt like a New Yorker at heart, but Chicago was a vibrant substitute. We no longer kept in touch with our old friends in Philadelphia; family members were long embedded in their own routines without us. I would need to find work, schools for the kids, new doctors and dentists . . . I was suddenly nervous about being uprooted from another home and making sweeping changes again. Even with all of the enticements, moving seemed terrifying.

In truth, if Larry was to stay with the company, we had no choice but to relocate to Philadelphia. Therefore, we sold our house, bought a lot in suburban Philadelphia, and started building a new house in a new development of ten homes all inhabited by young families. On moving day, I flew to Philadelphia with the two kids, while Larry drove fifteen hours in the car, accompanied by the houseplants and our golden retriever, Sally. I had to hold back tears, hiding my anxiety from the kids who were primed for an adventure as we sat on the tarmac, awaiting takeoff. I felt numb.

Our family reunited a day later at a furnished two-bedroom rental in my mother-in-law's apartment complex, where we lived for three months until our new house was finished. Larry began work as a partner at his new office, Eric went to day camp, and I exercised, ironed out details of the new house, and read and played with Beth. I met our new neighbors-to-be, and I played tennis regularly with the wife of Larry's partner at their home tennis court. It was all going seemingly swimmingly.

◆◆◆

On the ledger sheet of life, I clearly maintained a much longer list of assets than liabilities. I was married to a wonderful man who defined his own success as "taking care of people." The fact that he owned and ran a highly profitable textile business was incidental. The children and I were his main priorities, and we were comfortable and secure with the nourishment he provided.

Soon we were living in a picture-perfect beautiful, four-bedroom French colonial beige stucco house—with a slanted brown cedar-shingle roof—that could have been plucked off a street in Provence. With the experience I had garnered writing for the Chicago newspaper, I found enough confidence to establish my own consulting public relations firm, LT Communications. Through word of mouth, my business grew out of an office I'd established on the ground floor of my home. All of my life should have been guaranteed satisfaction, but the internal vacuous feeling I'd had since my mother's death, my father-in-law's passing, and the trauma surrounding our daughter's birth remained present—and growing.

◆◆◆

A short stroll from our house through a park filled with vibrantly colored wildflowers was Temple Sinai, a large Conservative synagogue in Dresher, Pennsylvania, which for years had been the spiritual home of many of Larry's relatives. As soon as we moved into the neighborhood, we became members; we enrolled Beth in nursery school, and Eric in an after-school Hebrew program. Quite quickly we took on active roles and integrated into the culture, accompanying our children to weekly Shabbat and holiday services. We hoped that by supplementing their secular educations with synagogue-based Jewish religious training, they would be provided with a critical, grounding, identity-forming Jewish enhancement that neither Larry nor I had received in our parents' homes or fostered enough in Chicago. To our delight, we discovered that being part of the synagogue experience had many benefits for us as well.

Almost immediately, I found that I really enjoyed partaking in an organized religious community and attending worship services as a regular practice. Singing prayers in synagogue was uplifting—the music, the rhythm, the cadence—and I began to notice the words in the *Siddur* (prayer book) and the *Tanach* (Bible) that held meaning for me and offered comfort. God-language was beginning to be more familiar and nourishing.

Our rabbi, the renowned late Sidney Greenberg, author of some twenty books, was a master storyteller, a brilliant homilist, a *darshan* in Hebrew, who drew equally on cartoon characters, numerology, current events at home and abroad, and scholarly works for his luminous and inspiring sermons. He always gave us a word, a *vort*, or something substantive to ponder, and his inspirational one-liners motivated us to partake in the Jewish value of *tikkun olam* (repairing the world). "Do what you can, and then a little more," he often preached. And we did.

Following services and the *Oneg,* where the congregation met in the community room outside of the chapel for a little *nosh*, and the sanctification of the day with wine, I would walk home with our neighbor, *Hazzan* Nathan Chaitovsky, the cantor of our synagogue, who was famous even in international cantorial circuits. We would sing songs and prayers together as we climbed up the hill, and he would tell me stories about the music of our tradition—the composers, the minor versus major keys, the relationship to the sacred sources.

There was also a charming *Chabad* Rabbi and his beautiful, calm, supportive wife who lived nearby, and they often invited us to their community events. Though their rituals and practices would always be much more stringent than ours, their resolute piety was alluring. We became friends, and I absorbed a lot of religious nuances from both of them by witnessing their devotion.

As time moved forward, Larry and I also found it powerfully stimulating to attend the evening classes that Rabbi Greenberg taught about current events, Israel, and the politics of the times, which he called "News and Views about the Jews." He was intensely erudite with a quick wit and wry sense of humor, and I loved listening to him.

One of Rabbi Greenberg's most appealing aspects for me was that, as the father of three daughters, he was at the fore of granting full access to the *bima* (pulpit) and the Torah to women. Like the medieval French Torah commentator Rashi, who had five daughters, he was a trendsetter pushing the community to be more inclusive of women in Jewish ritual life. Long before I had a calling to the rabbinate, he became an early mentor, encouraging me to learn how to read the Torah with its special *tropes* (musical incantations), to take additional adult education classes, and to participate more fully in synagogue community life.

Another source of inspiration was the warm and much-respected Hilda Greenberg, the *Rebbetzin* (wife of the rabbi), as she was affectionately known, who invited us to festive Shabbat dinners at their home, where the food was delicious and the conversation was geared toward the holy, like the *Shabbatot* (plural of Shabbat) in my grandparents' day. At the Greenbergs', we always talked about the Torah portion of the week and other political events having to do with the Jewish people somewhere in the world. She also gave me books to read about how to maintain a Jewish household and welcome in the holidays with the value of *hiddur mitzvah,* enlarging and beautifying them. Most of all, she stayed in touch—writing bread-and-butter notes for random acts of kindness, letters of encouragement to congregants during trials and tribulations, and congratulatory cards for life cycle events. Everyone, including her husband acknowledged her as a gifted pastor in her own right.

At Temple Sinai, Rabbi Greenberg was the brilliant academic, the Jewish texts expert. Rebbetzin Hilda Greenberg was the ultimate *eshet chayil,* a woman of valor, who helped transform a heterogenous group of two thousand congregants into a family. The compelling duo referred to their partnership as Greenberg and Greenberg, Inc., and we became fully invested into their shining synagogue business.

Bit by bit we assumed more and more aspects of Jewish life, and it felt lovely. Larry and I even helped form a *chaverah,* a Jewish fellowship group to meet with friends socially outside of the synagogue around shared Jewish interests—lectures, plays, concerts, communal dinners, and holidays.

As we developed our new lives in Philadelphia, the synagogue continued to soar as a spiritual home for us. All of our learning helped us model upright moral and ethical behavior to our children, as my grandparents had for me when I was growing up. We were now more financially solvent, so we could also travel, host charity events and parties, volunteer at the school, and sit on boards. We even helped launch a nonprofit organization, The Linda Creed Breast Cancer Foundation, named after our late friend and neighbor, a famous songwriter in the seventies and eighties.

During this time when my reawakened curiosity about Judaism continued to grow, I began soliciting professional jobs with a number of Jewish causes via my PR firm and, through word of mouth, my work morphed into a pleasant marriage between my professional pursuits and Jewish interests.

To the outside, world we looked like we had it all. And for the most part, given the necessary losses and challenges one must confront to be real in the world, we did. All that we needed. All that we wanted. Kissed by the sun! Blessed!

I was a proud, busy working and soccer Mom during this time, with hardly a minute to spare. There was so much on my plate that it seemed implausible that I could still ache for something intangible. But a part of me was discontented with the routine busyness of our lives, even though nothing was really ever routine or rote, and I was getting closer to defining what it was I was longing for. It had a name: "spirituality."

— CHAPTER 10 —

Adult Bat Mitzvah

*"Sing and rejoice, Oh daughter of Zion! For behold, I am coming
and I will dwell in your midst—the word of God."*

(Zehariah 4:2)

WE HAD BEEN BACK in Philadelphia for a couple
of years. And I was in my early thirties when I
enrolled in an adult Bat Mitzvah class at the synagogue. One
of the lamented consequences of my parents' divorce was that I
had been forced to abandon my nascent formal Jewish studies,
which had always been alluring to me. I'd missed out on having
a Bat Mitzvah at the appropriate age of thirteen when most of
my contemporaries had been celebrating. To finally have an
opportunity to recover an important part of what had been lost
in my difficult childhood felt like a dream come true.

The adult Bat Mitzvah class became a two-year process
in which the students were challenged to study prayer, Torah,
history, and holiday and life cycle celebrations with Rabbi
Greenberg and the Executive Director of the synagogue. It was
a great bonding experience for the seven members of the class,
who, like me, were all highly motivated and eager to engage with

the Jewish texts. It became a centering source of my spiritual growth at a time when I was trying to figure out my true calling in the world, a sense of meaning and purpose that as yet remained unclaimed. I looked forward to our study sessions more than anything else I was doing at the time, and my sense of enchantment with Judaism deepened.

My adult Bat Mitzvah turned out to be the most significant point of reentry into my past relationship with Jewish life, a connection that hadn't been nurtured in its fullness since my early linkage to my Orthodox grandparents, and it inspired me to move forward with my studies. It propelled me to become even more enamored of all things Jewish—concerts, speakers, books, movies, theatre, and Israel. I wondered if this might satisfy the yearning I'd started to feel back in Chicago. Judaism seemed to be calling to me through multiple arenas.

I was in a constant state of pondering about Judaism and my future goals when Larry and I took our first life-altering trip to Israel in 1983. Israel had just returned the Sinai to Egypt, forging a cold peace between the two countries, and it was front-page international news. I wanted to be in the thick of it.

From the minute we landed at Ben Gurion Airport, I was enthralled. I LOVED the sensation of the turquoise Mediterranean Sea cooling the arches of my feet as I stood in the water with the glistening waves thrashing back and forth. I loved people-watching in the charming, throbbing street cafés of Tel Aviv, a cup of *café hafuch* (upside down coffee), in hand. In addition to visiting the historical sites, I loved meeting people who told larger-than-life stories, of transcendence of good over evil, of perpetual faith and hope, reminding me that the name of the national anthem *"HaTikva,"* actually translates to "The Hope." Particularly after the Holocaust, the State of Israel seemed to be the modern-day equivalent of the phoenix emerging out of the ashes.

What was particularly poignant about the trip was that we experienced the dramatic juxtaposition of the two important Israeli commemorations of the spring season: *Yom HaZikaron*, the holiday of remembrance, and *Yom HaAtzmaut*, Israel Independence Day. A siren sounded at 10:00 a.m. in the morning of Yom HaZikaron. People stopped their cars on the highway and stood at attention for two full minutes till the blare of the noise faded into silence. A pall fell over the country. But by nightfall, when according to the Jewish calendar, a new day begins, the mood shifted upwards and there was dancing in the streets to celebrate Yom HaAtzmaut. The image of both radical scenes became seared in my mind.

As a small, young country surrounded by hostile neighbors—many of whom didn't recognize the Holy Land's right to exist—Israel seemed to pulsate with an unquantifiable urgency. There was a certain rhythm of life, a living-in-the-moment, cast-fate-to-the-wind attitude that I had never found anywhere else. The heartiness of Italy, the lush lavender landscape in Southern France, and the sense of exotic mystery in Asia had always appealed to my senses, but from the get-go, Israel felt like home, familiar and welcoming. Exhilarating, actually, even after only a few days. And most important, I was certain that I could feel God's sheltering wings close by throughout the landscapes and vistas. On our departure, I vowed I would return again and again.

Back home, I soon recognized that even though I was engaged in a plethora of secular, social, and cultural activities in Philadelphia, I was my most authentic self in the Jewish arena. Occasionally I even confronted the offhand remark that I was "obsessed with Judaism," or that I was "too Jewish."

Too Jewish? I thought, "too Jewish," like beauty, was in the eye of the beholder. But the message I was getting from some people around me was that I was not conforming to mainstream Jewish convention. They seemed bothered that my time was being spent on all things Jewish, all of the time, like the international headlines being played on cable news. Too Jewish seemed to be the opposite of societally secularly *pareve* (neither milk nor meat in kosher parlance), which can't be mixed according to biblical law concerning *kashrut* (Jewish dietary laws).

The direction I was moving in apparently wasn't neatly compatible anywhere. In analyzing how I viewed myself, I seemed to be becoming an anomaly, set apart from the pack as I had been in my youth. Externally, being labeled "other" was complex for me, but internally I was being called to be *more* Jewish. It was a conflict that needed radical reconciliation.

— CHAPTER 11 —

The Calling

"Our deepest fear is not that we're inadequate. Our deepest fear is that we are powerful beyond measure. It is our light, not our darkness that most frightens us. We ask ourselves, 'Who am I to be brilliant, gorgeous, talented, fabulous?' Actually, who are you not to be? You are a child of God. Your playing small does not serve the world."

(*Marianne Williamson in* A Return to Love)

HE CALLING TO GO INTO THE RABBINATE did not come in a loud, thunderous voice from heaven, a *Bat Kol* (Divine voice), saying, "Hey you lady, with the Prada shoes and the privileged lifestyle, come serve *Me*." Initially, it was soft and devoid of drama. The decision to make a complete and total lifestyle and professional change first manifested in little baby coos, a series of subtle voices from unlikely messengers, sounds from near and far that coalesced almost unnoticed.

The first voice came from an unlikely source—my husband, who, by definition, was not religious, contemplative, introspective, or terribly spiritual, and who liked things between us—advantaged, establishment, and conventional—just fine the way they were.

Couldn't be better. Thank you! Change demanded energy, and the effort that Larry already expended to maintain the equilibrium of work and our happy household was enough for him. It surprised me that he opened a door even a crack to an idea that would bring sweeping changes to our quotidian doorstep.

The idea surfaced one afternoon when Larry and I were on a short getaway in Bellmawr, New Jersey, while the kids were in sleepaway summer camp. We were in a hotel overlooking the ocean with a stunning panoramic view of delicate sand dunes when I turned to him in one of those intimate moments that happens unexpectedly in the context of a long marriage. "Larry," I said. "I love you so much. If God forbid anything should ever happen to you, I would never marry again."

Without a second's hesitation, he responded, "Oh yes you would! You would marry some rabbi—or become one."

Become a rabbi? Hmmmm. That sounded very cool. But me—no way! Me a rabbi? I was speechless. What was he thinking?

Admittedly, over the last few years as my desire to embrace and immerse myself in Judaism had deepened, the thought of becoming a rabbi had crossed my mind once or twice. But it was a fleeting apparition, the shadow of a pipe dream that seemed utterly out of touch with reality. Being a female rabbi, though no longer a perceived forbidden avenue, was still a rarity in comparison to the number of men in the rabbinate. Sally Priesand had been ordained as the first Reform rabbi in 1972, and Sandy Eisenberg Sasso had been ordained by the Reconstructionist Movement in 1974. Other women followed in each of their footsteps, but I didn't know much about them, or an even earlier woman, Regina Jonas, who, in Europe, had become the first woman privately ordained as a rabbi in 1935. She died in Auschwitz. Because of the lack of a personal connection, I was unable to contextualize these women in the

Jewish narrative, and I certainly couldn't imagine myself as a candidate at their level.

The rabbinate as an aspiration had originally occurred to me when I had heard Rabbi Amy Eilberg, the first female rabbi ordained by The Jewish Theological Seminary (JTS) of the Conservative Movement, speak at our synagogue in 1985, right after she was ordained. The synagogue community was aflutter with her impending visit, especially since she was a native Philadelphian and the offspring of the late Joshua Eilberg, a well-respected Democrat who had served as a representative to the U.S. Congress.

Rabbi Eilberg was charming, lovely, poised, and full of confidence, and she had the enviable ability to rattle off, on one foot, the wisdom of the ancient rabbinic sages that she had gleaned from her years of engagement with the sacred Jewish texts. She seemed to have mastered a wellspring from which to draw upon life's deepest insights and understanding, and she was radiant and erudite beyond her years. I listened and watched her in awe.

For a split second, I imagined myself in her place—a smart, spiritual woman with the ability to enact social, religious, and cultural change; a woman with a religious, moral voice in the community. But the image passed quickly. How could I possibly get to her station? Even after the two-year Bat Mitzvah experience, I couldn't write an *aleph* or a *bet* (the first two letters of the Hebrew alphabet), and I didn't know a lick of Hebrew beyond *Boker Tov* (Good morning) and *Shalom* (hello, goodbye, and peace). I couldn't decipher the Hebrew prayer book or the Torah except what I had memorized, and I was only peripherally familiar with Judaism's literary canon. I didn't know the great folk songs of our tradition beyond humming, and I surely didn't possess the skills or confidence to conduct services like rabbis and cantors or even educated lay leaders. I'd never learned much in depth about Jewish history, the Bible, or the symbolism of the holidays and the Jewish calendar year.

Realistically, what knowledge did I possess in the vast bosom of an ancient religion—Jewishly speaking? Quickly my inner doubts charged in and appeared front and center. Too late for me! I thought. Maybe in my next incarnation, if there really were such a thing.

◆◆◆

In the meantime, without any professional training, I had always maintained what Larry called "a regular unpaid caseload" of people who sought my counsel and advice when they needed support at critical junctures in their lives. I had graduated from college with a degree in English and Education. I was schooled to become a teacher, a writer, and had eventually developed into a public relations professional with my own business. Yet, my natural acumen to analyze difficult emotional situations and to help find resolutions for my "cases," perhaps born out of the myriad challenges I'd faced since childhood, was keen and desired. Many of the people I'd helped had asked me, "Did you ever think about going into counseling or doing some kind of spiritual training?"

"Isn't that part of a rabbinic portfolio?" I asked myself when those questions arose. But with a metaphorical snap of a finger I dismissed them because I didn't think I had the makings to become a rabbi, whatever those qualities might be. Looking at the long path to the rabbinate—five years of concentrated study with two semesters in Israel and clinical field work—I imagined that it would be a terrible load on me, and more important, a burden on my family. So I continued to walk the safe path of what I was already doing.

But little angelic hints continued to arise, pulling me like a magnet toward the rabbinate. Author Letty Cottin Pogrebin's book entitled *Deborah, Golda, and Me* came into my purview and resonated. In it, Pogrebin, a leading Jewish feminist and one of the cofounders of *Ms.* magazine, chronicles her self-imposed alienation from Judaism following the death of her mother. She had been Jewishly educated at the knee of her father, like the fictional character Yentl, but when her mother died, she was refused a place in the *minyan*, the prayer quorum traditionally composed of ten observant men needed to recite the *Kaddish* for her mother, the hymn praising God believed to symbolically lift the soul of the deceased. Feeling marginalized, she left the fold. After decades of estrangement from conventional patriarchal Judaism, Pogrebin reconciled with her Jewish roots and returned to the active Jewish community, able to embrace a new Jewish-feminist model where women were educated and could claim a vocal space at the table and be counted in the minyan.

Quoting Rabbi Nina Beth Cardin, one of the few women rabbis later ordained by the Conservative movement at that time, Pogrebin wrote, "We don't have to like everything we find in women's history, but we should know everything. Then we can decide which parts of our past we want to reclaim—and the rest, the unusable past, we can convert to memory." I found her insight an appealing call to arms.

Pogrebin's tales of the biblical Judge Deborah, as well as Golda Meir, the first female Prime Minister of Israel, and herself were all remarkable stories of courageous women trailblazers who had modeled a sustainable version of female Jewish leadership. I wanted to be like them—"righteous rebels," catalysts for social change, moral agents. But how? There was so much I needed to know. Was I capable of the advanced learning required? Even if I could access the necessary information, I wondered if I would be able to put the knowledge into practice at this late stage in my life. I was full of fear.

"Feel the fear and do it anyway," Pogrebin wrote in her subsequent book, *Getting Over Getting Older*, which helped me understand that it wasn't too late to pursue lofty goals, whether in my forties, fifties, or beyond. Little by little my destiny was becoming clearer.

— CHAPTER 12 —

Poland 1991

*"To remain silent and indifferent
is the greatest sin of all."*

(Elie Wiesel)

THE CALLINGS TO THE RABBINATE continued to visit me in subtle tones. Periodically, the sounds in my head would vanish. But there were times that I imagined hearing the ta-ta-ta-ta of trumpets blowing, calling: "This is it! Go for it! Feel the fear and do it anyway."

And as each unformed vision of the rabbinate materialized, I continued to cave in to an avalanche of self-doubt. Pursuing the rabbinate in my forties felt tantamount to a person in midlife seeking a medical degree without the requisite organic chemistry, or wanting to sing on the stage of Carnegie Hall without the vocal pipes. A seemingly ridiculous notion!

Days and days of ambivalent reverie became the norm. On one of those flashes when I was sitting at my desk looking out the window, I received an unexpected call from a man whom I had worked with briefly by doing PR consulting at his accounting firm. As soon as I picked up the phone, without even stating the requisite, "Hello, how are you?" he asked. "Want to go to Poland and Israel?"

The caller, Christopher, was an interesting character. A *Jew by Choice*, he had converted from Catholicism many years earlier and had a high profile within a myriad of Jewish communal causes. His demeanor reminded me a bit of my father—he was a jolly soul with good intentions, but occasionally lacking in deliverance. I was always suspicious of his offerings.

"Now that the Gulf War has ended," he continued, "it's important that we travel to Israel and show our support, particularly during the Intifada, the Palestinian uprising. I'm leading a mission. It's by invitation only. I'm inviting you. You'd be a great addition to the group. Just say yes."

He told me that we would be going to Poland first for three days, accompanied by a scholar, Dr. Michael Reiner, the creator and president of The Leadership Education and Development Foundation (LEAD), and we would be visiting Auschwitz with a Holocaust survivor of the camp. On the fourth day, the group was scheduled to head to Israel in time for Yom HaZikaron, Israel's sobering national day of remembrance, followed by Yom HaAtzmaut, Israel's Independence Day celebration—the commemorations that had so touched my soul on my first trip to Israel. This proposed mission was positioned to be a penetrating experience—deep mourning over what had happened to Poland's Jews during WWII as well as Israel's long history of human losses, followed quickly by the ecstatic festivity on Israel's Independence Day.

For almost an entire decade, I had fantasized about returning to Israel. I hadn't been back since that first penetrating trip. I longed to walk the historic ancient streets of Jaffa, Safed, and Jerusalem. I salivated for the taste of authentic falafel and Israeli salad stuffed in a doughy pita topped with creamy white *techina* sauce dripping over the sides. I craved seeing the amber sun set on Shabbat over the rectangular stones of the *Kotel* (the Western Wall), the famous structure from the time of Herod that surrounded the Temple in Jerusalem and had been destroyed in 70 CE by Roman forces. I longed to dance in a circle arm in arm with welcoming Israeli women and a sisterhood of other energized women of every age visiting from all corners of the earth. But work, children, time, and a mass of responsibilities had made it seem too difficult to return . . . until the phone call from Christopher.

The new opportunity to breathe the Israeli air after a visit to the hallowed grounds of the Concentration Camps in Poland, to become a living witness to the collective Jewish history as well as to my personal family story surrounding Bubby and Zaida and their families, seemed irresistible.

"Let me clear it with Larry," I said.

◆◆◆

Before World War II, there were approximately 3.5 million Jews living in Poland. At the turn of the century this Eastern-European country, home of my ancestors, had been full of color, vibrant with Jewish life and culture. It had served as an enormous center of Jewish spirituality and religious learning, the birthplace of scores of famous rabbis. Twelve million people in total had been killed in the Holocaust—political dissidents, people with disabilities, gay people, non-Aryans. Half of them were Jews—90 percent of the innocent Polish population. Now it was virtually devoid of Jews, *Judenfrei* as Hitler had desired, save for some five thousand mostly elderly people, who couldn't or wouldn't leave Poland out of familial or economic necessity. So few Polish Jews had survived the Holocaust. Yet anti-Semitism was alive and well, and roaring in a place that, relatively speaking, had very few Jews.

As soon as we deplaned at Fryderyk Chopin airport in Warsaw, our group, comprised of four women and ten men, was greeted with insidious swastikas smeared all over billboards in full frontal view on the streets and on public buildings. People in the airport pointed and laughed at the secular men among us, who for this occasion wore outward signs of their Judaism, *yarmulkes* (religious head coverings) and identifying necklaces as signs of solidarity with our lost ancestors.

The day of our arrival, and every subsequent day of our three-day stay in Poland, was shrouded in grayness. The general atmosphere was perennially dark, dank, and dreary, mired in unshakeable Nazi and Communist history. In preparation for our visit to Auschwitz, we met with survivors. I was moved and inspired by them; most had transcended terrifying cruelty and abominations, reconstructed themselves after unspeakable tragedy, trauma, and loss, and rebuilt successful, relatively happy lives in the aftermath of profound suffering. Their stories left us breathless and emotionally drained even before we ventured to the sites.

On the morning we were slated to visit the camp, I was nervous and doubled over with a stomachache. Was it real or psychosomatic? I didn't know what to expect, but my gut anticipated that it would be harrowing to stand on the sacrosanct ground of former death camps, now monolithic memorials to the 6 million Jews, including 1.5 million children, innocent little Shmuelys and Mendeles and Rifkas and Ruties, who might have grown up to change the world for good but were sent to early deaths on this very location. It was agonizing to imagine those little children lost, generations of talent gone.

I had always been drawn to stories about the Holocaust. I grew up reading *The Diary of Anne Frank*, the *Night Trilogy* by Elie Wiesel, and other memoirs by survivors, or friends and relatives of survivors. I'd been to Amsterdam to see the Secret

Annex where Anne Frank and her family had been hidden during the War. I'd read so many books on the subject that over time I had developed an enormous collection of Holocaust material for my personal library, and a deep connection. I also went to movies about the *Shoah*, another name for the Holocaust, and I became a bit of an amateur expert on the subject.

With so much exposure to the Holocaust, I thought that I would be as prepared as anyone could be to experience the concentration camps, to light memorial candles and recite traditional psalms and the memorial prayer at the site of the devastation, and still remain composed. I was wrong.

When we first came upon the entrance to Auschwitz with its iron arches bellowing *Arbeit Macht Frei* (Works Makes You Free), I thought it was a movie set. I had seen many pictures of this scene in films, documentaries and books. But now I was confronting it in all of its naked horror, the killing center for state-supported mass genocide, man's inhumanity to man, a chilling symbol of blind hatred turned to sinister madness. In the book *Sophie's Choice*, William Styron asks the question, "'Where was God during all of this?' The answer, "Where was man?'" Tears started flowing at the outset of the visit and continued throughout. I stood mute and raw. It took time until I could lift my feet to follow the silent group who were walking like puppets into the campgrounds. It felt surreal.

Trembling, I ambled along with the others through the rooms of the so-called "museum." I remembered reading that Hitler once said, "One day, all that will be left of these people, the Jews of Europe, will be a museum." I discussed this dire prediction with famed Nazi hunter Simon Wiesenthal once when I interviewed him in his office in Vienna. Now I saw with my own eyes that all that was left of these departed souls in Auschwitz were rooms filled with human hair turned gray from gases that had been used to asphyxiate the prisoners selected to die. Rooms crammed with suitcases filled with family pictures, heirlooms, and artifacts of unsuspecting Jews on their way to a gruesome death. Rooms filled with dead children's tiny shoes and clothing, toys, books and dolls, and tattered blankets. Rooms filled with wheelchairs, crutches, glasses, and artificial limbs because their disabled owners were not valuable to the Nazi war effort, unable to work for the "Final Solution" of the Third Reich.

Shuffling through spaces filled with pictures of nameless, naked human skeletal bodies piled twenty to thirty high, a pale numbness set in, then shamefulness at looking at the pictures of naked Jews, who, heretofore, steeped in the highly valued Jewish principle of modesty, were now exposed. Frozen in these pictures that the Nazis catalogued to be humiliating, their personal modesty and dignity were unwittingly invaded again and again. And yet, it was impossible to turn away.

In the rooms that documented the random sterilizations and sadistic medical experimentation on women, children, and most notably on twins, performed perfunctorily without anesthetics by doctors who had been trained to heal, it was sickening to look at pictures. But to hide our eyes meant not to validate or integrate the full spectrum of the atrocity. We owed more than that to the victims and to the survivors.

We stood as parched onlookers, face-to-face with the concrete barracks where lice-ridden, disease-infected half-humans had been squeezed into every squalid corner. Face-to-face with watchtowers and electrified barbwire fences that had instantaneously executed anyone who had the temerity or courage to attempt to escape the brutality and barbarism of the camps. Face-to-face with the end of the line at the train tracks at Birkenau, the point at which a turn of a thumb by Dr. Joseph Mengele, Dr. Death, meant immediate annihilation by Zyklon B in the gas chambers or by firing squad, or a stay of execution for a few lucky ones who appeared able to do manual labor. Only a small number among the thousands of European Jews survived—Jews who had been swept up in the Nazi maelstrom and arrived daily on cattle cars filled with the stench of human feces and dead bodies, corpses that had been lying for days with their open eyes staring at horror-struck family members. All the while, Paula Bornstein, the survivor who accompanied us, gave eyewitness testimony and on-site gripping narration.

Toward the end of our mission, we lit candles on the grounds of Auschwitz inside the barbwire fences. We recited Kaddish and chanted the traditional memorial prayer. Paula wept for her lost sister who had died there, and for all of the other souls who were tormented, murdered, and left to decompose like garbage in a compost pile. We wept with her and for her. It was abysmally impossible to leave and more dreadfully intolerable to stay. We lingered for as long as we could, embracing each other in the damp crustiness of the day.

The *Babylonian Talmud* reads, *"There are times in our lives when we can grasp the reason for our existence in a single moment"* (*Talmud Avodah Zerah 10b*). For me, standing in Auschwitz became the *AHA* moment that would change me endlessly, the apparent reason for my existence. The Epiphany! Prior to the trip, I had been aware of what I might see, but now that I had been a witness to the gruesomeness and the barbarity of humanity, I felt charged with a huge responsibility. I was the next generation that would succeed the few remaining survivors, now in their twilight years. I felt called to recount their stories, to become a human candle—to somehow light the way for others as an ongoing witnesses.

I shuddered with the recognition that if my great-grandparents, grandparents, aunts, uncles, and cousins had not left Poland shortly after the turn of the century to escape the pograms, I would almost certainly not have been born. I would have been devoid of the rich Jewish legacy my relatives had bequeathed me as a lifelong gift, a bloodline to my *neshama,* my soul. Like my friends who were children of survivors, I might not have had any surviving family beyond my parents. I would not have had the love and stability of my grandparents, especially in times of need after my parents separated. I would not have had memories of Shabbat, of accompanying my grandmother to shul, or the inklings of a sustaining faith.

Rabbi Dov Baer of Mezrich, an eighteenth-century disciple of the Baal Shem Tov and founder of the Hasidic Movement, once said, *"Sometimes one must look into the ashes to find a solitary spark."* A spark in the dust. Or bones in the soil. There they were—sharp, white, hard boney bits of dead humankind standing out against the black-brown mud. I was beckoned. A solitary spark summoned me.

I looked down at the variegated ground and picked up a handful of soil. Unknown gravelly voices seemed to rise above unmarked mass graves and call to me: *"Please, don't let this ever happen again. Don't ever forget us! Make sure the world knows what we went through, just because we were Jews. Say Kaddish, for us. And keep Judaism alive . . . "*

I heard my grandparents' voices above the gray horizon. "Lynndala," they said in their broken English. "We went to the new country so we would have the freedom to be Jewish, so our children could be Jewish, so you could be Jewish. So be Jewish! Be the most Jewish you can be. You can never be 'too Jewish.'"

I felt the presence of our patriarch, Jacob, who, after a Divine night encounter en route to his real life, woke up spiritually and declared, *"Surely the Lord is in this place, and I did not know it . . . How awesome is this place"* (*Genesis 28:17*)!

Beyond the landscape of ghastliness, I heard the now-silenced trumpets of lively klezmer music, and the call of the fishmonger, the town crier knocking on neighborhood doors telling of the impending Shabbat coming in, rabbis giving *shiurim*, lessons on the biblical portion of the week that taught the values of Jewish ethical living according to the sources. I heard the voices of women negotiating for fruits and vegetables in the market to feed their growing children. I heard a Bubby say to her grandchild, "Say thank you to the nice man," like my Bubby had said to me when she'd taken me shopping on Brooklyn's Pitkin Avenue before Shabbat, and a pushcart vendor had handed me a treat.

I imagined the beautiful, museum-quality canvases, masterpieces painted by talented Jewish artists, of art collectors and artists' representatives; the exquisite words of works written by brilliant poets and novelists, of bankers negotiating deals, of store owners selling their wares, of actors and actresses entertaining people in the Yiddish theatre, of bakers kneading challah to sell in the marketplace, the fantastic contributions of inventors and scientists. I heard all of the voices of lost talent in a cacophony of wasted achievement.

I also heard the distant sound of happy children in the public parks—laughter, joy, the promise of a burgeoning Jewish future. Too much had been lost already, lying beneath the cold soil. From where would the new Jewish voices emerge from our people of storytellers? Who would continue their narrative?

Full of *chutzpah* (audacity), I asked myself, "Could I be a voice of the Jewish future, the Jewish destiny?" Could I be one of the storytellers? Did I have something to give, to contribute—that is more than what I was already doing? What *was* I to do? Rav Kook, the first chief rabbi of the modern State of Israel, had said, *"Our task is to make the old new, and the new holy."* Would I be able to do even a whisper of that work?

Here in the midst of death and destruction, I heard a calling to a living Judaism. With a clump of packed soil in my palm, I closed my hand into a fist and raised it up like Scarlett O'Hara at

Tara in *Gone with the Wind*. Then I swore an oath to myself and to a Higher Power: "I am going to work in and for the Jewish community now and forever. And I want to concentrate on sustaining a celebratory Judaism, an ethical Judaism, a Judaism of meaning, an antidote to the horror of Auschwitz. This is what I've been yearning for, what I'm being called to pursue . . . I need to find the path, a means to step into my holy power . . ."

Christopher Bamford wrote in his story "The Gift of the Call" from the journal *Parabola:* "The call comes gradually or so it seems. We must be called over and over before we hear its whisperings. Then we begin to notice. Unconsciously, hesitantly, we start to listen. Incrementally our response deepens. Finally, we realize that we ourselves are the call; that call and caller are one in a life lived in obedience to the gift of the call. We come to recognize that we were called from the beginning."

The epiphany at Auschwitz was my Sinai revelation. My call from the beginning. This sacred mission to act would become the dominant imperative of the rest of my life.

I asked God to show me the way and prayed that the personal calling I imagined I heard was not just holy hubris.

— CHAPTER 13 —

Israel

*"God may it be Your Will
to place us on the side of light."*

(Talmud Brachot 17a)

𝒜FTER THE SHOCK of visiting the concentration camps, we
were all exhausted and emotionally drained. In silence, we
boarded our private tour bus and left the area. Someone pulled
a bottle of sweet Bailey's Irish Cream out of a small duffle bag
and passed it around. Even people like me who didn't ordinarily
drink, took a hearty swig as we maintained our silence, trying
to recover, while we watched the iron gates and the bucolic
countryside fade from sight.

The next morning, still depleted from the experience at
Auschwitz, we packed up and left for Israel. Five hours later, we
arrived on the sunny tarmac in the Holy Land, in plain sight
of the familiar blue-and-white flag that was emblazoned in the
middle with a large, six-pointed Jewish star, the *Magen David*—
the shield of David—waving in the wind. Pure glee lit up the
faces of my traveling compatriots, an outward manifestation of
what we were all no doubt feeling inside. It was as if, following

Poland, we needed the grounding and bright light of Israel. Home sweet home.

Our first stop was Modi'in in the Center District of Israel, midway between Jerusalem and Tel Aviv, known as the birth and burial place of the Macabees, the emboldened heroes of the Chanukah story. As a life-affirming gesture after leaving the camps, we were each going to plant a tree at the site of the revitalizing community. New life was sprouting everywhere in the spring sunshine.

Though Jews have inhabited Israel since biblical times and grew in numbers after the 1897 Zionist Convention in Basel, Switzerland, which was led by Theodore Herzl, Israel was fortified by ravaged refugees who made *Aliyah* (immigrated), coming en masse to their Homeland following WWII after their families and communities had been nearly destroyed. When the UN declared Israel's Statehood in 1948, these same war-weathered people fought valiantly against the five Arab countries that invaded them during Israel's War of Independence. That time they won the rights to a home and a language, wandering Jews no more.

After Israel's military victory in 1967 following The Six-Day War, Israelis wanted to be fortified and convey an image of strength, debunking prevailing mythology about European Jews "marching like sheep to their deaths," an image which always disturbed me. After all, how could an unarmed citizenry have been able to fight state-supported mass genocide and a criminal war machine that had an artillery of ammunition and willing accomplices? Those who could do so fought. Many joined the Resistance. Most lost their lives anyway. A triumphant Israel discredited the depiction of Jews as a weak community.

The clump of soil I had picked up to make room for the little sapling I was about to plant stood in strong contrast to the bone-ridden soil at Auschwitz, which would sprout new life no more. Here in this earth were voices of triumph over tragedy, evolving humanity, imagination, creativity—all singing in harmony, calling to me in melodious tones. Like a lusty lover, Israel beckoned, raw and naked, and I was a consenting partner.

The disparity between the two experiences was stunning. A warm feeling of love showered over me as I put the baby tree into the soil and covered its roots. The power of planting a tiny greenery where nothing had ever bloomed before, and enabling it to become a strong, resilient tree like the symbolic Torah tree of life with wide leafy branches rooted strongly in the ground, set the tone for the Israel portion of our mission.

◆◆◆

When we arrived at our hotel in Tel Aviv, after depositing our luggage in sun-soaked rooms, we sprinted to the beach to feel the sand between our toes, the water on our feet, and the crisp air on our faces. We stood on the water's edge, watching the sailboats bob majestically on the Mediterranean, appreciating the beauty of our homeland following the long, dark, and unrelenting days in Poland. After a deep breath and a whiff of the salty air, we continued the work of the mission, preparing for the next day in Jerusalem.

A visit to Yad Vashem, Israel's astonishing Holocaust Memorial Museum, became the companion commentary to the experience of Auschwitz. Yad Vashem was named after a quote from the biblical prophet Isaiah (56:5): *"And to them will I give in my house and within my walls a memorial and a name* (a Yad Vashem), *that shall not be cut off."* Comprehensive documentation of the *Shoah* in all of its aspects stands as Israel's concrete promise to never forget her dark history, even as she shapes a future as "a light unto nations."

Confronting Yad Vashem so swiftly after the encounter at Poland, paired adjacent to my studies with Rabbi Greenberg, made this experience of Israel exceedingly more profound than my first visit. At our scheduled *Yizkor* (remembrance) ceremony, I stood silently, unable to move, listening to the cantor chant the haunting memorial prayer, *El Male Rachamim* (God full of compassion), in front of the eternal light burning in the center of Memorial Hall.

Shortly after we left the grounds of Yad Vashem, we stopped at nearby Mt. Hertzl, the cemetery which stands as a bleak reminder of the cost that Israel has paid, and continues to pay for its survival in bloodshed through many wars and ongoing strife, sitting as she does surrounded on all sides by hostile neighbors. The hard truth is that each baby boy and girl who is born into the "land flowing with milk and honey" will someday be plucked out of youth's garden to become a soldier. War after senseless war had turned youngsters on all sides into ashes. Golda Meir famously said, "I can forgive them murdering our children. I can not forgive them for making murderers out of our children."

As we were departing from the complex, we came upon bereaved parents standing bravely at the gravestones of their children and shaking their heads, some crying silently, some overcome with sobs. It was excruciating to watch, yet turning away seemed disrespectful. I missed my own children in America. I wanted to hug them. I ached to feel their ribs beneath my arms.

Just as I had questioned myself at Auschwitz, the questions were forthcoming here as well. What could *I* do to honor the martyrs from the Holocaust and the fallen heroes of Israel? Would I do something? For now, all I could offer was my seeming readiness to embrace service to the Jewish people and humanity at large with the word, *Hinenei,* the response spoken by biblical characters to convey a spiritual willingness to oblige God. *"Hinenei."* Here I am.

◆◆◆

Ahad Ha'Am, a Hebrew essayist and one of the foremost pre-state Zionist thinkers, once said, "More than the Jew has kept Shabbat, Shabbat has kept the Jew." And I know for sure that one thing that's as right as daylight on a spring Friday morning, especially after surveying scenes behind prickly barbed wires, is the advent of Shabbat in Israel. All over the world, Shabbat continues as the weekly day of rest for the Jewish people, a biblical holiday devised as a time for reflection, meditation, joy, and praising God for Creation. After the revelation at Sinai, the Israelites were mandated in the Ten Commandments, *"Remember the Sabbath day to keep it holy. Six days you shall labor and accomplish your work, but the seventh day is a Sabbath to the Lord, your God."* The gift of Shabbat is considered a "delight" by the rabbinic sources. In Israel, even the most secular in society pause for a day of rest, to feel the rhythm of Shabbat and welcome her as a weekly "Sabbath bride," with personal observance, formal or informal, grand or gracious.

As we headed back to our hotel after Yad Vashem, I reminisced about the many Shabbatot we had celebrated with my immigrant grandparents who were steadfastly faithful to "the day of rest." After their deaths, I'd inherited my Bubby's silver Shabbat menorah, the well-worn candelabra with openings for five candles set into wide bobeches. Jewish women—and men, if no women are available—are commanded to light a minimum of two candles eighteen minutes before sundown to herald in the Sabbath. My grandmother always lit the five candles in this special menorah that was believed to have come from the Old Country. After her passing the responsibility fell to me, but I had been only quasi-committed to the practice until we joined Temple Sinai.

For a time, my grandmother's candelabra served as a *tchotchke*, a quiescent decoration on a shelf, a reminder of the grandparents who'd loved me unconditionally and had offered me safety and stability as a child in crisis. When Larry and I married, we had emulated the customs of our American parents and had lost touch with my grandparents' lively traditions. We'd eaten dinner in restaurants on Friday nights and gone to movies. We'd felt little sense of the celebratory or restful aspects of Shabbat, even in Chicago with my friend Sheila organizing Jewish holiday get-togethers and maintaining some image of ritual connection to the religious aspects of Jewish practices.

Lighting candles on Shabbat had returned to my sensibility through an unlikely source in Philadelphia—our son, Eric, after he learned about Shabbat in the synagogue's Sunday school program. One day when he came home, he asked, "Mom, why don't we ever light Shabbat candles?"

"No reason, Eric," I said. "We'll do it this week." And suddenly, without any contemplation, discussion, or debates, we began lighting candles as a family and have continued to do so ever since. Bubby's candelabra became an active ritual object once again, spreading its glow throughout our dining room. As I became increasingly more active in the synagogue and my Jewish inner life deepened, I was grateful for the example my grandparents had bequeathed to me, happy that our son had suggested reviving the action that they had modeled, pleased to be passing the blessing on to my own developing family.

And there in Jerusalem with Shabbat nearing, I was flooded with memories. In anticipation of the holiday in the Holy Land, our group made a scheduled stop inside the sensuous open-air market, *Mechane Yehuda,* where the flurry of activity, like the Pitkin Avenue of my youth in East New York, was concomitant with the impending Sabbath. Organizing for Shabbat, enhancing and beautifying it, is a key traditional value, and the Israeli masses are suffused with the spirit. And so were we, as we stuffed our bags with flowers, fresh figs, and *rugelach* (little sweet rolled pastries).

Laden with treats, our group arrived at the hotel for a rest before setting out for our communal dinner near the Wall. Exhausted, I was nevertheless too hyped-up to nap. As I peered out from my room's Juliet balcony, I noticed the sun, still vivid and blazing. I changed into a bathing suit to take a quick swim in the hotel's pool, imagining it to be a symbolic cleansing from Poland, like a ritual bath, a *mikveh*, used for purification purposes.

I dove precipitously into the pool's water, surrendering to the cool, refreshing sensation, and swam the breaststroke, which my father had taught me so many years earlier, and the crawl, exerting myself vigorously and continuously for twenty or thirty laps until I lost count. Fatigue set in, but I couldn't stop swimming for a long, long time, pulling the water apart with my cupped hands. Breathless, I stayed in the pool until the skin on my fingers and toes shriveled, until the cold air caused goose bumps to appear on my exposed skin and the little hairs on my arms to stand up, and until I was too exhausted to do anything except succumb to the mystical powers of Shabbat in Jerusalem.

Nowhere can I remember a more dazzling human spectacle than Shabbat at the Kotel—the Western or Wailing Wall, long revered as one of the holiest sites in the world, and once again under Israeli governance since the Six-Day War when it was captured from Jordan. With the radiating orange sun settling in the west over the sand-colored Jerusalem stone, and the sky splattered with vibrant hues of gray, hot pink, and lavender, it looked like an artist's palette.

Hasidic schoolboys with payos descended the hillside from their *Yeshivot* (study schools), high on Shabbat, singing with pubescent changing voices and dancing fervently, their feet barely touching the ground. Proud, joyous men in traditional black silk garb with *streimels* (round fancy hats made of fur) were swept up in the music and magic with them, forming a human chain of celebration. It was impossible to watch and stand still at the same time.

Shabbat is one of those liminal moments, an anthropological concept that comes from the Latin word *limen*, meaning "threshold." It defines the ambiguity that occurs on occasions when it's indistinguishable between where one situation ends and the next begins. The transitional time between one day and another, the end of the week and the commencement of Shabbat, is a holy liminal moment.

Just as it is hard to discern the exact, precise second that a bride and groom are transformed to husband and wife under the chuppah, the wedding canopy, it is almost impossible to know when the last rays of sunset give way to the moon and stars of the holy Shabbat. The rabbinic sages defined this liminal time as *Bein HaShamashot*, between the suns, and it is implicit that this hazy, numinous time is where God, in the feminine form of the *Shechinah*, hovers close to hear our prayers.

Standing in the Southern quad adjacent to the Wall, our group observed the faithful and the not-so-faithful men and women praying on separate sides. The humble as well as the emboldened leaned close to the Wall, their foreheads pressed against it, eyes closed and lips moving. Supplicants from all over the world were submitting messages into the cracks of the rectangular stones, hoping to feel God's anchoring presence—grasping for healing and petitioning God for peace. *Shabbat Shalom.*

I watched as my male colleagues approached the Wall, observing with wide-eyed awe as they began dancing with strangers, giddily caught up in the Shabbat frenzy. The women also seeming to feel compelled to rejoice, joined hands, forming circles, dancing together, friends and strangers alike in Shabbat joy, which according to Jewish eschatology, is a taste of the euphoria to be found once again in *Gan Eden* (the Garden of Eden), constructed in faith to be the "World to Come."

Some of the women were standing on chairs looking over at the men's side to watch the *shigayon* (craziness) of the men dancing as though they had fire under their feet. Before the Six-Day War in 1967, men and women wandered together freely in the area of the Wall, which was part of occupied Jordan's territory. After the War, when the Wall was returned to Israeli hands, the Orthodox Rabbinate designated the entire area a kind of outdoor *Beit HaKnesset* (a synagogue) where men and women must be separated during prayer according to a strict fundamental rabbinic interpretation of early laws. The arrangement is a continuing source of great political consternation for many women who are represented by the Women of the Wall, and others who champion the cause, petitioning for the rights to egalitarian, pluralistic prayer space, and opportunities for women at the Kotel, such as the right to read from the Torah, to wear a tallit and to pray with impunity. As a feminist and member of a liberal stream of Judaism, I identified with the mission of equality at the Wall. It is symbolic of the parity for all that should be the prevailing force in a democratic, pluralistic Jewish State. Nevertheless, I surrendered to the moment, temporarily suspending my exasperation in deference to the glory of Shabbat, and started moving.

As I danced with the other women, I felt enveloped in sheer bliss. I promised myself that if I ever became a rabbi, I would be helpful to Jewish women and concentrate on women's issues. My eyes welled up with tears. This is the antidote to Auschwitz, I thought. Thank you, God for this gift of Shabbat in Israel.

◆◆◆

After an evening of eating, singing, and dancing late into the night, the rhythm of the Holy City shifts on Shabbat morning. There's a quiet stillness in the air. Our mostly secular group, given the option to spend Shabbat morning "at leisure" after a long, extended dinner, went their separate ways.

Some people attended services at the famous Great Synagogue, where the all-male choir sings the traditional songs like a heavenly retinue. Another contingent slept late, regrouping, reflecting, and recovering from the trauma and lack of sleep in Poland. Others met for a typical sumptuous Israeli breakfast buffet before heading back to the Wall in daylight under a blue sky.

I took a casual morning walk near the foreign embassies in the sunshine with two male friends who had never been to Israel before, and we marveled at our discoveries behind every curved corner. The flowers cascaded from the hillside, resplendent in vivid tones of orange, yellow, and indigo. The sweet smell of spring honeysuckle permeated the air. I was happy in the moment with my new buddies, to whom I imagined I would be bonded forever. As we strolled the streets my heart whistled.

Later that day, at the conclusion of our *Havdalah* ceremony, marking the end of Shabbat, Michael Reiner, our scholar-in-residence, and his beautiful blue-eyed American-born wife, Arona, an accomplished and admired painter, hosted a party for us on their three-tiered, tile-lined deck overlooking the Judean Hills. The city lights twinkled in the distance. An important Israeli guest was invited to sit at each table and share stories, evoking the salon culture of the nineteenth-century where patrons and artists exchanged ideas and conversation. It was a delightful night, cleverly orchestrated for us to become familiar with various aspects of Israeli society, passionately conveyed directly from the mouths of Israel's pioneers and contemporary movers and shakers.

I spent time with Arona in her studio, where she painted in the European surrealist tradition of Dali and Magritte. Self-defined as secular, Arona told me that she was spiritually troubled by the fallout for women resulting from the biblical story of the Fall and expulsion from the Garden of Eden, and the repercussions of framing Eve as the seductress sinner who is blamed for the loss of Paradise. Her paintings include zippers, buttons, and seams, symbolically repairing the narrative to elevate the image of women in society, and shift the yoke of responsibility for evil in the world, particularly in religious sectors.

I found her fascinating, charming, talented, and thoughtful, and I was mesmerized. We talked for hours about how the country simultaneously inspired and troubled her, and we discussed what it means to contemplate universal themes in a place like Israel, which is unique unto itself. How—when you are this close to the core of life and death—religion, art and history meld into one. What would it all mean for me as I moved forward with thoughts of the rabbinate?

◆◆◆

Our sojourn in the Holy Land whizzed by like a video on fast-forward. On the long plane ride home, I had a chance to ruminate about the trip and play back the powerful images in my head over and over. I wondered how this little country managed to survive all of its social, religious, and cultural challenges—the *intifada* (Palestinian uprising), the water shortages of the time, the disagreements between the *datim,* religious, and the *helonim,* secular, in society, the Ashkenazim (Eastern European Jews) and the Sephardim (Middle Eastern Jews). How would they absorb more than a million new *olim*, immigrants, expected to make *Aliyah* (move permanently to Israel) by 1993? With so many existential threats, would there ever be peace?

Despite its challenges, I thought, Israel stood proud and strong—a mother country welcoming her children to suckle at her breast. It was a distinct voice among the millennia of previous Jewish voices calling me to service. I had a lot of figuring out to do.

— CHAPTER 14 —

Reentry

"To be or not to be is not the Jewish question.
How to be and how not to be is the Jewish question."

(Rabbi Abraham Joshua Heschel)

OST-POLAND AND ISRAEL, how to be and how not to
be, became my spiritual dilemma. I knew empirically
that I was changed. It was difficult to reenter my routine life with
family and work. My head was filled with the miasma of *what
next?* Even without much formal Jewish religious training, I was
keenly aware that Judaism has survived because it is a religion of
action and transmission—a philosophy of learn and teach. After
lessons garnered, Jews are expected to be motivated into service.
I continued to engage with my enquiring mind: What have I
learned? What must I teach? In broad strokes, I asked myself
repeatedly, what is it that I am being called to do?

The Zachor Mission was designed partially to develop and
foster leadership in the Jewish community. Soon after I returned
from the trip, the Human Resources Department at the Jewish
Federation of Greater Philadelphia contacted me and suggested
that I begin working as a volunteer for one of its constituent

agencies, the Jewish Community Relations Committee (JCRC). Three Holocaust-related programs under its auspices felt especially pertinent after the mission. I was recruited as a writer for the annual ecumenical Philadelphia *Yom HaShoah* (Holocaust Remembrance) program, based on the knowledge I gained on my trip to Poland. Held outdoors on the Benjamin Franklin Parkway in the heart of Philadelphia, the event unfolds in full sight of sculptor Nathan Rapoport's dramatic Holocaust memorial sculpture, the first in the United States, erected in memory of those who perished during the War under Hitler's regime. The citywide program attracts thousands of survivors and supporters, including the mayor, local celebrities, and many politicos, and I was delighted to be part of the creative team. More important, my involvement with the event enabled me to amass trust from the survivors, a group who by design is cautiously suspicious of outsiders—that is, those who were never entrapped in camps, hidden during the War, or directly descended from someone who was.

In addition to writing for the Yom HaShoah program, I was also appointed a judge for the annual Mordecai Anielewicz creative arts competition. The innovative program—named for the youthful hero of the Warsaw Ghetto Uprising—was open to Philadelphia public high school students who had studied a Holocaust curriculum and were moved to create an artistic response to the learned lessons. I was blown away by the talent and thoughtfulness of the young participants, whose contributions would become youthful witnesses, vehicles for the next generation to offer light against hatred and injustice.

I also volunteered to join the ongoing Youth Symposium on the Holocaust, a highly effective high school program that brought survivors into the classroom to tell students their personal stories and answer questions about their experiences during the War. I served as a moderator, moving the program along, caring for and giving emotional support to students and survivors, and fielding the questions. It was an important pedagogic tool for teaching tolerance and diversity to kids who would shortly leave the protection of their homes and face strong outside peer influences in college or at jobs. The lesson of "the power of one" was front and center.

For the survivors, many of whom suffered from "survivor guilt," it was a way of assuring a personal legacy. Their stories would live on in the hearts of young people, and their family and friends who had perished during the Shoah would be remembered in light and love.

In 1994, my experience with the JCRC put me into position to become an interviewer for Steven Spielberg's Survivors of the Shoah Visual History program. The organization was established after the famous director completed his 1993 Oscar winning film, *Schindler's List*. On typically bitter, snowy winter days during the filming in Poland, survivors would approach Spielberg wanting to talk to him and share their stories of loss and survival. Overwhelmed with requests, he felt an urgent need to preserve remembrances of the Holocaust before the survivors died. He had the technology and resources.

My work for the USC Shoah Foundation gave me access to a fragile people who were willing to share the pain of their wartime experiences with me. It was a difficult task to be a vessel for survivors' excruciating experiences, but I was honored to assume the responsibility of *witness* to the sacred testimonies. I was privileged to be a partner in creating a remarkable living testament, even gathering testimonies from some parents of friends who, prior to the taping sessions, had never exposed the secrets of their past.

For my labor I received a certificate of recognition expressing gratitude: "For your dedication and commitment to ensure that generations will never forget what so few lived to tell," and a letter from Steven Spielberg praising me for my efforts in "creating a better tomorrow." Inadvertently, I had become an oral historian, and it prepared me for my next transition, the new direction that my life was subtly beginning to assume.

◆◆◆

For many years, the editor of the *Jewish Times*, a weekly Philadelphia newspaper covering topics of Jewish interest from local, national, and international Jewish-related sources, had been trying to convince me to write a family column for the newspaper. I kept turning him down, citing deadline pressures and the anxiety of having to explore new ideas on an ongoing basis in the midst of all the other commitments I was trying to juggle and manage—sometimes not terribly successfully. But after the Zachor Mission, he prevailed upon me again to write an account of the trip that he wanted to publish as an incentive to inspire others to make the journey. How could I refuse?

On Thursday July 11, 1991, with an article entitled, "From Auschwitz to Jerusalem," a firsthand account of our trip to Poland and Israel, my column was launched, sporting the byline, "Lynnda Lewis Targan." Subsequently, I began writing a monthly piece entitled *"All in the Family,"* with total editorial freedom to pick my own topics. It evolved into a warm and fuzzy, 750-word epigrammatic column about family life that explored lively issues, like holidays and human-interest topics relevant to its predominantly Jewish readership. It put me in touch with a whole new group of people, a vibrant audience who communicated with me long before social networking became the phenomenon it is today. Many stories later, the paper was subsumed by *The Jewish Exponent,* and my monthly column was picked up as "A Woman's World," the first ongoing column in that paper written by a woman. Writing about my kids, my family, and friends, as well as other tales that people pitched to me, provided a window into my own life that was both expansive and illuminating.

◆◆◆

In the years that followed the Zachor Mission, I journeyed back and forth to Israel at every opportunity. I enrolled in Gratz College's Hebrew immersion program and supplemented my learning by attending classes for a month at Israel's famous Ulpan Akiva in the coastal town of Netanya. During my stay I studied with amazing teachers and fraternized with an international student body. I met new and interesting people, attended colorful outdoor craft shows, and ate gobs of falafel, hummus, and chopped Israeli salads. In the late afternoon I drank coffee in the cafés and chatted in nascent Hebrew with anyone who had the patience to listen to me struggle to put a sentence together. For a while, my life in Israel was *rak Ivrit* (only Hebrew). Later, our family participated in a synagogue mission to Israel with Rabbi Greenberg when our daughter, Beth, became a Bat Mitzvah on the top of Masada, the ancient desert fortress near the Dead Sea.

On one of those visits, I had an opportunity to meet Danny Siegel, the founder, fundraiser, and presiding spirit of the Ziv Tzedakah Fund. Prompted by a *Midrash* (a rabbinic explication of part of the Hebrew scriptures), that teaches to bring charity to Israel insures a safe journey accompanied by angels. Danny began by soliciting friends, a dollar or two here and there, and quietly making a difference in the lives of needy recipients in Israel by dispensing funds to "mitzvah heroes," who would allocate the money. Through the years, "Ziv" had supported a wide spectrum of deserving, offbeat, important charity work, and Danny had become so modestly influential and inspiring that he reaped the nickname, "The Pied Piper of Tzedakah."

"Come along for the ride with the Ziv Tzedakah Fund," he invited me. "It's a good one."

"Next time I travel to Israel, I want to visit your charitable endeavors. Can you make that happen for me?" I asked unreservedly.

"Done."

We shook hands as I looked into his eyes, and I started talking to him, as though he were a psychiatrist.

"You know, I always have a marvelous time in Israel. But I mostly leave feeling sad. Very sad. Melancholy even. I can't wait to see my husband and my family, yet I find it sooooo God-awfully hard to reenter America after being here. Does this happen to you or anyone else you know?"

Without missing a beat he said, "You feel the way you do because you don't study enough. You're not linked intimately enough with the Jewish texts."

"What do you mean?"

"You're doing a lot of work in the Jewish community— great things! You have a presence, a unique style, the ability to create powerful changes and leave a legacy in the world. But," he challenged, "you need more academic Jewish substance. Learning is the key to empowerment in the Jewish community. Jewish texts open the channels to connection."

I had never heard such advice before and had never explored or really understood how I could gain systematic, formal access to the sources. I tried to process his observation quickly, the adrenalin galloping clippity clop.

"How can I make that happen at my age, forty-five, knowing nothing—*bubkas, nada, klum?*" I asked.

"The great Israeli Rabbinic Sage of the second century, Rabbi Akiva, started his studies at age forty," he responded. "You probably know more than he did at his age. It's not too late for you, too. You're smart, and you have a lot to give to the world as well. You could even be a rabbi . . . Go for it!"

Pow! He'd hit the rabbi nerve again. Rabbi Akiva was an old, wise, and respected teacher, about whom there are many famous and inspiring stories. At age forty, prompted by his wife, Akiva began learning the *aleph-bet,* the Hebrew alphabet, studying along with his young son. He said, "If a rock, though extremely hard, can be hollowed out by water, how much more so should it be possible for Torah, which is compared to water, to change my heart, which is soft. I will begin to study it, and try to become a Torah scholar."

To become said scholar, Akiva left his family and traveled to Lod for twelve years. After coming home for a brief visit (one in which it's reported that he didn't even see his wife), he returned to Lod for another twelve years of study. He was isolated with his Torah, committed exclusively to his learning and teaching, and, subsequently, held up as a model of sacrifice, righteousness and knowledge for all eternity. He became legendary in the amount of Torah knowledge he amassed, and in the heritage of the 24,000 disciples that he'd inspired and influenced with his beautiful lessons.

Was Danny really comparing my potential to Rabbi Akiva? What a far-flung idea, I thought, to imagine that I might ever attain even one millionth of the knowledge or the *yichus,* the status, of a Rabbi Akiva figure.

Women have always needed female rabbinic role models, and sadly, there weren't many. You can't be what you can't see, it's been said. Clearly my situation was dramatically different from this famous Sage. Rabbi Akiva wasn't responsible for putting food on the dinner table, or doing household chores, chauffeuring children to classes, being a soccer Mom, sewing buttons on pants, and taking care of sick parents or screaming toddlers. Rabbi Akiva studied, and when his eyes were bloodshot from reading and his neck cranked from bending over the sacred books, he studied some more. No break. No rest for the weary. No time to make Purim costumes.

At this point, I was already five years older than Rabbi Akiva, well into midlife, and deeply entrenched in family and work responsibilities. But the poignant conversation I'd had with Danny left me with an important message: I needed to study. What to do? How could I make it happen?

Since graduating from college, I had taken numerous adult education courses, many of which had been Jewish-themed, but I had not been enrolled in a formal education program for more than twenty-five years. My memory wasn't what it used to be, and I knew from past experience that doing well on standardized tests was hardly my forte. The volume of disciplined scholarship required to attain an advanced degree in Jewish studies seemed as daunting as competing in back-to-back triathlons. To do so, I would need to punch up my Hebrew, which is in itself a lifelong process; understand the intricacies of our holy Torah with its Five Books of Moses, Prophets, and Writings; become skilled at *cantillation,* the musical system of notes for chanting the Torah during synagogue services; and make the volumes of liturgy from the various *Siddurim* (prayer books) as familiar as my index fingers. I would have to learn all about the post-biblical sources, including rabbinic commentaries, like the Mishnah, Talmud, Midrash, and *halachic* (legal) writings, which created and governed the laws of the Jewish people, and, by the way, were often written in Aramaic, another language I didn't know. I was exhausted just thinking about the sheer immensity and degree of difficulty of the vast trove of material that I would have to master before even setting foot on the formal rabbinic journey.

There were also a lot of gaps in my experience that stemmed from not having had a formal Jewish education growing up, or not attending a Jewish camp such as Camp Ramah in my youth. And even with all the recent studying I had been doing, I still didn't own the catchy songs, the how or the why of most of the religious rituals, or the nuances of thousands of years of Jewish history. How might I ever harmonize desire and reality?

There's a Talmudic lesson that teaches, *"Every blade of grass has its angel that bends over it and whispers, 'Grow, grow.'"* Maybe, I reflected, Danny was my angel, like Larry and Letty, and he was telling me in the most compelling voice yet to "grow." And I knew that for growth to occur, I had to create a fertile internal and external environment.

◆◆◆

A week after I returned from Israel and the meeting with Danny Siegel, I invited a friend of mine, Nick, a professor at Temple University, to meet me for lunch. I sat across the table from him at the restaurant, buttering my roll with tears dripping down my face. I confided how much I missed Israel, how hard it was for me to reenter life in America after having been there. I relayed the conversation I'd had with Danny Siegel, and told him that I felt stuck.

"I need to grow," I said, channeling the angels. "I have to study and learn. When I was in Auschwitz, a few trips earlier, I even had a fleeting vision of becoming a rabbi."

He just listened, nodding his head like an empathetic father for the hour that I jabbered on while I was picking at my salad.

A few days later Nick called and said, "There's someone I'd like you to meet."

— CHAPTER 15 —

School Days, School Daze

*"Know that what is impenetrable to us really exists,
manifesting itself as the highest wisdom
and the most radiant beauty."*

(Albert Einstein)

*T*HE IMAGE OF ME BECOMING A RABBI, part of a chorus of new Jewish voices keeping Judaism alive and well, continued to show up in my dreams. Israel had stolen my heart like a soulmate beckoning: *"Take me away with you—let us hurry"* (*Song of Songs*). The memory of Larry telling me I should become a rabbi, the vision of Rabbi Amy Eilberg standing on the bima in my synagogue years earlier, Letty's books, Poland, working with Holocaust survivors, my reveries, and now Danny's conversation all made a compelling case for me to, at least, explore the possibility of new possibilities. The rabbinate?

Dr. Laura Levitt, the woman that my professor friend Nick had brought into my consciousness, became the lead in the pencil connecting the dots. She was a new professor in the Department of Religion at Temple University and was about to teach a graduate course in Holocaust Studies.

"She had just received her PhD in religion and a Women's Studies Certificate from Emory University," Nick told me on the phone by way of introduction. "I hear she is very smart, someone with a fresh perspective. She could be a great mentor for you. Here's her direct line."

He was excited and, as it turned out, right.

Dr. Levitt, I surmised from a short introductory phone call, was keen and likeable, someone who could teach me life lessons beyond academia, even though she was quite a bit younger than me.

So, like the legendary Nachshon who was purported to have dipped his toe into the Red Sea, causing it to part when the Israelites left Egypt, I took a first step into the unknown waters. By enrolling in her Introduction to the Holocaust class, which cost $850—almost twice what a year's tuition had been when I was an undergraduate student twenty-five years earlier—I was making a commitment to swim in uncertain seas.

Dr. Levitt did not disappoint. Between my voracious reading, participating in the JCRC programs, interviewing survivors for the Shoah Foundation, and listening to eyewitness accounts, I thought I had amassed some prior knowledge on the subject of the Holocaust. But what Dr. Levitt presented in the way of concentrated Holocaust material—books by survivors, liturgy, theology, literature, and poetry—went way beyond my purview. I was a slow reader, and she was a demanding, tough taskmaster with high expectations. She assigned volumes of reading and writing for the twice-weekly class, which filled me with anxiety as I simultaneously maintained my business, served on boards, and took care of my family.

I was treading water, to be sure, but I loved the stimulation and the company of my bright, thoughtful classmates. Periodically, a fellow-student, an African American Baptist minister, asked us to clasp hands in prayer, "to ask the Lord to help us assimilate the knowledge we are required to absorb." I was down with that. And down with learning more about my own religion's prayer customs.

One day, Dr. Levitt leaned over my desk while I was sitting alone waiting for the class to begin, and whispered quietly. "Lynnda, I've been thinking about you. In my opinion you should study with other Jewish people. We don't have a formal Jewish Studies program at Temple yet, so you probably won't find everything you need at this religion department. You should tuck more Hebrew under your belt to gain more proficiency with the texts. It might be a good idea for you to take Hebrew classes at the Reconstructionist Rabbinical College (RRC). Actually, I was wondering if you had ever considered becoming a rabbi?"

"It's crossed my mind," I answered.

◆◆◆

If timing is everything, it was clearly my time to begin moving ahead on a beckoning path. At the suggestion of Dr. Levitt, I enrolled in a master's program at Gratz College in suburban Philadelphia, the oldest independent college of Jewish studies in North America, where at one point in my career, as president of LT Communications, my public relations firm, I had been the Director of Public Relations and a consultant for its capital campaign.

Simultaneously, at Dr. Levitt's suggestion, with permission from Gratz College, I was able to take courses as a nonmatriculated student at RRC that would count toward my master's degree, with a possible eye towards a future rabbinical program. The rabbinical seminary was near Gratz, and unlike the other liberal seminaries that were housed in New York, Cincinnati, and Los

Angeles, RRC was an astonishingly convenient twelve minutes from where I lived.

I was excited about the opportunity, and I wanted to make a good impression on the first day of school in my first class. Not knowing what to expect, my anxiety level kicked in big time. I discovered that the popular adage "dressed for success" was very subjective. My late mother's spirit had been in the air earlier that morning, coaching me to look my best. She was a woman who applied makeup to her face every morning before leaving the house—even to take the trash to the outdoor bins. With the scoliosis she'd had as a child, which had left her back curved, she also worked hard to find the right clothes to fit and flatter her body, and she had exquisite taste. Consequently, she became quite the renowned fashion expert. For a time, she even owned and operated a small clothing boutique in a popular neighborhood beauty parlor where people sought her advice as THE style maven. For better or worse, she passed the fashion penchant on to my sister and me.

When I arrived at school, I sashayed through the doors of the old house, now utilized as a seminary, dressed up in an outfit that might have served me better in a job interview for a corporate position, or for posing in a photo shoot on one of the back pages of *Vogue* for midlifers. I wore a black tailored pantsuit, with stylish shoes and bag, and a gold necklace with matching earrings. My face had the full complement of makeup and my manicured nails were professionally lacquered in crimson red. Boy, was I naïve!

Despite my good intentions, I was a standout on my first day at RRC—and not in a good way. My demeanor, which was the truth of my being, wasn't consistent with what I was noticing as I approached the classrooms. Looking at the student body, I began to feel uncomfortable in my own skin, and real or not real, extremely conspicuous. In general, the student body at

RRC appeared casual, dressed mostly in jeans or comfy baggy pants and tops, not necessarily matching. It only took a quick glance around for me to realize that my fashion getup was as out of place as a ball gown at Woodstock.

As time passed in the day-to-day, clothes weren't the only issue that seemed to separate me from the pack. Most of the students at school who talked to me had spent years pursuing multiple advanced degrees at prestigious universities, whereas, aside from the two recent graduate classes I'd taken at Temple, I boasted only a BA in English/Education from the commuter state school I had attended a quarter of a century earlier. At this point in my late forties, having not studied in a serious way for decades, I worried that my brain was no longer functioning as sharply as it had back in my yesteryear.

What also set me apart was that, despite my nascent studies at Gratz, I had virtually no Jewish academic background, and only the minimal Hebrew I had picked up by attending Ulpan Akiva years earlier and working privately with Tamar, my loyal and capable tutor. The other students all seemed exceptionally conversant in most of the Jewish disciplines—Bible, Jewish history, philosophy, liturgy, Talmud, and mysticism. Their retention and the way they strung ideas together in almost fluent Hebrew amazed me. And scared me. Would I, could I, ever be part of this conversation in any language?

RRC was also an in-your-face political hotbed. It was open early on to ordaining gay and lesbian rabbis, while the other seminaries dragged their feet. One gay woman described the ambiance at the school to me as "a comfortable lesbian womb." It was the 1990s, and I seemed to be walking on eggshells most of the time, trying to understand the requisite political correctness, and hoping to be respectful. Maya Angelou famously said, "When you know better, you do better." I realized I had a lot to understand to get better at being sensitive to many things if I was to survive in the prevailing climate.

Furthermore, most of the students I engaged with at that time identified themselves as very left wing on virtually every topic, including Israel. Right-wingers that I knew outside of school expressed dismay at the institution for being perceived as a community of "Palestinian sympathizers," who in their words, "ignored the fact that suicide bombers on buses and in the streets were constantly murdering innocent civilians."

"What are you doing at THAT school? Where is your loyalty?" they asked.

"They're good, thoughtful, caring people, with robust minds," I answered shrugging my shoulders. Fending off barbs coming from all directions had me ducking a lot.

At the core of the uneasiness about everything else was the fact that I didn't fully comprehend the philosophy of Reconstructionism. What was it really? I had spent the last several years *davenning* (praying) at a Conservative, mainstream synagogue with my family. The Conservative Movement was tied to *halacha,* strict adherence to Jewish law, but not as strict as Orthodoxy and unique in its practice. The Reconstructionist Movement had been around for years, and it seemed to be a hybrid of sorts, a smattering of *Hasidism,* Jewish Renewal, tradition, and modern thought. Its principal Jewish tenets were open to liberal interpretations, governed by one of its most important credos: *"The past has a voice, not a veto."*

I sensed an unspoken framework of in/out at the school. Who was out of the closet and who was in? Who was on the left-wing side of politics and who was out? Who had a voice and who remained silent? Who was invited to attend community time and who was not? Who was kosher and who was not? Who was a vegetarian and who still ate chicken and meat? Who davenned at traditional services and who attended alternative

Reconstructionist services and *minyanim* (plural of minyan)? Who was a matriculated student and who was not?

Most of the time, I felt clearly OUT of the loop. Even on those rare days of clarity when I was inside the conversation, I was out. My husband felt uneasy and out as well, often expressing how much he didn't fit in. As time rolled on, he started to distance himself from that part of my life, and I was troubled by the crevasse that studying at the school seemed to create between us.

By design, the rabbinate is not a family-friendly profession, with the majority of the work happening on the Sabbath, a time in both the secular and religious worlds that's usually designated for family togetherness. The rabbinate presents conflicts that force clergy members to make difficult choices between professional obligations and family and personal needs, and much of it happens in the public eye. I thought a lot about how I was going to keep my primary relationship intact and settle the big balancing decisions going forward.

Yet on a day-to-day basis, there was a great deal to champion about the school. The people were generally kind, thoughtful, interesting, smart, talented, and inventive. Students and teachers all seemed to look at Jewish life in a cutting-edge way and ask poignant, relevant questions about rituals and practices. They were liturgically imaginative, inventive, and musically gifted. Individuals were constantly adding new meditations, songs, poems, and other writings to the body of the traditional liturgy, which were at once fascinating, uplifting, and daunting.

Community was a big priority. The RRC polity accepted social-action challenges to create a better world, in the name of *tikkun olam*—repairing the world. Despite outside criticism, it was bold and brave in confronting thorny religious and political issues, including women's roles, gender equality, and intermarriage.

I worked very hard to accelerate my knowledge, spending countless hours preparing for lessons and trying to figure out how to find my voice within the community. Gratz College, which is pluralistic, was an easier environment for me to be myself. RRC seemed to be in another stratosphere. I constantly asked myself: Who am I here? Where do I belong?

Reb Nachman from Bratslav, the grandson of the Baal Shem Tov, the founder of the Hasidic Movement, taught that God puts stumbling blocks on a person's journey to verify that she really wants what is upcoming. I felt like I was stumbling a lot. Did I really, really want to be a rabbi after all? Could I maintain this pace and this level of insecurity for the time it was going to take to complete the process? I thought I wanted to commit to a life makeover, to be in the rabbinate, but at my age was it worth it? If so, did I actually fit into this particular institution?

After two years of part-time classes where I still felt mostly "out" of the RRC community, more like an observer than a participant, I realized that I had carved out a wee niche for myself. Though I struggled to define my *raison d'être* at the school, I had made some lovely, supportive friends, and I was grasping new ideas and concepts.

And beyond my doubts, people were now constantly telling me that the rabbinate was my calling, and I was beginning to accept that it might be THE moment to take the big risk and apply for formal admission. If I didn't pursue the calling, how would I ever understand the sensations that emerged when I saw Rabbi Amy Eilberg, read Letty's words, or picked up a bone-ridden clump of soil in Auschwitz? How would I ever know what God's purpose was for me?

I devised a plausible plan—wait a year to apply for full-time study, when our daughter, Beth, had left for college and the timing would be better for my family. Eric had already been out of the house for years, working on his own, and with Beth gone there would be less demand on the mothering part of my life, and fewer difficult choices to make. I would somehow figure things out for Larry and myself and find my space at the school. In the end I might also corner my unique place in the rabbinate.

◆◆◆

Meanwhile, I continued to meet remarkable souls on my journey. Most of my teachers at RRC were geniuses, great storytellers, passionate and romantic about Judaism. One of my early teachers, unlike any other I had known, was a well-touted young theologian named Dr. Shoshana Sunshine (not her real name). I wanted to study with her and was delighted when she granted special permission for me to join her class as a nonmatriculated student.

The subject was feminine hermeneutics, and under Dr. Sunshine's tutelage I learned a new exegetical method of parsing Jewish sacred texts through the lens of women's experiences. She brought tales of Jewish women to the fore, elevating their status, not by replacing the men's positions, but by moving men and women side by side as foils for one another, equal in status. Centuries of women had been mostly ancillary to the study of Torah and the ratifying of Jewish law.

Dr. Sunshine introduced me to the narratives of courageous women in the Bible and Talmud and recounted modern stories of immigration—where women had worked to establish emerging synagogues—and of social and cultural services for Jews in early America and Israel. Their worthiness next to men shone in a new light. Mary Anton, Emma Lazarus, and Henrietta Szold became familiar names, as did contemporary Jewish writers like Leslea Newman, Binny Kirshenbaum, and Rebecca Goldstein.

I was a child of the feminist movement of the late 1960s and 1970s. Back then, in an effort to educate myself about contemporary women's issues of the day—reproductive rights, domestic violence, maternity leave, sexual harassment, and equal pay for equal jobs in the labor force—I had attended "consciousness-raising" sessions. I took the requisite assertiveness training for women of my generation and read the books that ignited the feminist movement: *Sexual Politics* by Kate Millet, *Outrageous Acts and Everyday Rebellion* by Gloria Steinem, *The Feminine Mystique* by Betty Friedan, *A Room of One's Own* by Virginia Woolf, and *The Women's Room* by Marilyn French, among piles of other eye-opening feminist literature like *Ms.* magazine, which had been launched in the early 1970s, with Letty as one of its founding mothers.

Now in the mid-1990s, Dr. Sunshine provided a course packet full of astounding source material that opened the gateway to an avant-garde system of integrating feminist stories into Judaism, a serious departure from where I'd traveled before in Jewish text study. I saw my own feelings and emotions reflected in the tales of women, and for the first time I identified with strong Jewish public female role models who had made a difference beyond shaping *matzah* balls in the kitchen. I was attracted to Dr. Sunshine's "radical" thinking on the subject and knew that my point of view, which now had shifted, would become critical and transformative. Again I noted, if I ever became a rabbi, I wanted to make sure that women enjoyed full access to the sacred texts of our rich tradition, that they learned the names and deeds of valuable Jewish women role models who had paved the way for future generations of women's advancement, and that contemporary women could claim their worthiness within the tradition, have a voice, and feel valued.

Dr. Sunshine's educational methodology was also a source of wonder. One morning she started the class by stating matter-of-factly: "It has come to my attention in this mixed class of men and women that the men—as they always do in mixed settings—are talking longer and louder and more often than the women. In a class on feminist hermeneutics where we are open to new ideas about gender roles and inclusivity, let's all pay attention to this social dynamic in our classroom. Women must have their voices heard, and it is essential to be conscientious about monitoring the process.

"Therefore," she continued, "when you speak, put a check at the top of your paper. Halfway into the class if you have too many checks, *ztimztum* (retract)! Please give others a chance to talk. If you have no checks, it's time to express yourself. Make a contribution. We want to hear what you have to offer."

I was gobsmacked. Dr. Sunshine's pedagogy seemed an ingenious approach to a problem I had never identified before, even as a former high school English teacher. Now I was one of the students with no checks on my paper, unaware of my voice, afraid to share. I had never thought about the dynamics of expressing myself in a mixed-gendered crowd, but I vowed that I would take careful notice from here on in—especially since I was hoping to enter a traditionally male-dominated profession.

The more I was in her company, the more Shoshana, as she preferred to be called, fascinated me. I learned that prior to landing at RRC, she had been on a long spiritual journey, having evolved primarily from a Baptist background before her conversion to Judaism.

A few years earlier she had come out as a gay woman at The Jewish Theological Seminary of the Conservative Movement, where she had been studying for the rabbinate. After she revealed her sexual orientation, the administrative powers informed her that she could earn her PhD in Jewish philosophy, but she was no longer welcome in the rabbinic program.

Since women had not been accepted into The Seminary's rabbinic program until 1983, change had come slowly in all directions. Until March 2007, when a split decision altered the school's century-and-a-half-old policy, The Seminary would not ordain openly gay rabbis, even brilliant, talented women like Shoshana. Although there was already a sizable student body of gay and lesbian students in the rabbinic program who called themselves "The Incognito Club," they remained undercover to the administration. The practice was akin to the U.S. armed forces' policy of "Don't ask, don't tell." You could be at The Seminary as long as you weren't "out." It seemed to Shoshana to be a hypocritical stance for a religious institution whose mission it was to train truthful, moral, righteous, religious people to become leaders in the world.

Despite her rabbinic career being derailed, Shoshana chose to stay in The Seminary's doctoral program. Eventually she reestablished her footing at RRC. Many people in rabbinic circles saw Dr. Sunshine as a rising star in the spiritual marketplace, and when she arrived at RRC, in addition to teaching, the president of the college slated her to head up the nascent "ethical center," a baby of his that he was anxious to birth. I wanted people to know about her too, so I interviewed Shoshana for my regular monthly column at the *Jewish Exponent*.

Much to the chagrin of the *Exponent*'s publisher at that time, and much to the delight of the powers at RRC who were happy for the positive publicity, I had been writing periodic articles about my experiences at RRC for a couple of years. The *Exponent* was pretty much a right-wing arm of the Jewish Federation of Greater Philadelphia, and I was a quasi-liberal voice. The editorial board back in the late 1990s viewed RRC as too radical, too left leaning, and too alternative to be featured prominently in its pages, which were reserved mostly for the movers and the shakers in the community, i.e., those who supported the Jewish Federation and its associated agencies.

As a columnist, however, I had some leeway to write feel-good pieces about any subject of my choosing, and when I wrote about the college, I usually featured a personality from the community as a vehicle. The articles about the school offered a window into the scriptures of progressive Judaism, and allowed me to share my newly acquired body of Jewish material.

The interview with Dr. Sunshine took place in mid-December 1996, and because Shoshana was my teacher, I did something I never did before. I gave the article I wrote to her to edit before I submitted it for publication. She was thrilled with the piece, offered no comments, trusted me, and sent me off with her blessing. When the article was published the following Thursday afternoon a week later, I winced when I saw it.

Unbeknownst to me, my editor had put a curious headline on the article. It blared, "Feminist Founds a Center for Liberal, Egalitarian Judaism." It wasn't at all what I had expected.

I called Shoshana immediately. She seemed pretty unruffled by the headline, and she reiterated that she liked the article. She told me, "It's fair and accurate, and you did a good job." End of subject for her in terms of editorial review. Unfortunately, it was only the beginning of a problem for me at RRC because it was not the end of the subject for the school. Quite the opposite.

When I arrived at school a few days after the article had been published, a friend of mine who taught there said, "The president is furious with you."

My heart sank. I knew that the headline on the article might be conceived as controversial, but the content of the piece was very flattering to both Shoshana and the school.

As I walked through the corridors en route to my class, someone from the development office cornered me. Fuming, she asked with piercing eyes, "Who gave you permission to write about the school?"

"No one has ever said a word to me about publishing my flattering articles before," I replied. "Everyone knows that I'm discreet, nonjudgmental, fair, and not interested in writing negative pieces about anyone or anything." *L'shon ha ra*, or gossip, is vilified in our tradition, and I prided myself on steering clear of it. "I'm a columnist, and I write nice stories about nice people, places, and things. Good stories, helpful stories," I continued. "I want my articles to uplift people or inspire them to learn something. I thought I was writing content that RRC would love."

"You had no authority to write this article," the woman hurled back at me, looking directly into my eyes, her eyebrows furled. She lingered for another moment, then pivoted on her heels and walked away, mumbling under her breath. I was speechless. The situation was worse than I had imagined.

My heart racing, I immediately ran up the stairs of the old house where the college held classes, and I asked for an appointment to see the president. He saw me standing outside and ushered me in right away.

"I hear that you're upset with me about the article," I began.

"Well," he answered with a blank expression on his face, "I know that you would never do anything to hurt the institution, but this article should not have happened."

"Why?" I asked.

"Don't you think the headline was a little incendiary?" he answered.

"I didn't put that header on the article," I said.

"And it didn't strike you that the headline could be unflattering for the college?" he asked, his eyes narrow and cross.

"I didn't put the headline on the article," I repeated. "I admit that it wasn't what I had envisioned, but if you read the article, you would see that it was very flattering to Shoshana *and* the school. It showed that I'm proud to be going to a school that would name someone like Shoshana Sunshine to head up the ethical center at RRC. After all of the ethical issues she was forced to negotiate in her life, she seems like a natural—an expert on ethical issues from the front lines."

The president stared at me and I continued.

"I was eager to give her a forum and a place for the college to toot its own fearless horn." I pulled out a copy of the article and read aloud the concluding words I'd written: "'The ethical center is a text-based operation informed by biblical, rabbinic, medieval and contemporary texts, as well as feminist insights,' says Sunshine. 'We're using halacha in a way that teaches but does not command. The center wants to be the voice of liberal, egalitarian Judaism on ethical issues. It has great potential to guide, support and enrich men and women with dignity as we all grope to do the right thing.'"

I had tried to paint the vision of the ethical center to my readership in the best possible light. Instead, the school felt that the headline made them appear *too* alternative, and therefore, perhaps not appealing to mainstream Judaism. How had my good intentions crumbled and fallen like a sandcastle at the turn of the tide? It was a holy mess.

I spoke quietly to him. "I'm in the middle of applying to the college for formal admission," I reminded him. "Should I just withdraw my application?"

"No," he said. "Keep the appointment for the interview, and we'll see what happens."

"I'm so sorry," I said, newspaper in hand. "I never meant to trouble anyone here. I've grown to love being at the school, and this whole incident is so very upsetting to me."

"I know your intentions were good," he said, "but it was wrong what you did."

"I'm so sorry," I said again, and left the room while he stared at the ground.

As I fled down the steps, I knew that from here on out I would be looked upon as a mole, a talebearer, one who would share secrets sacred to the community. I had worked so hard to be trustworthy and accepted, and now it all appeared to be vanished.

After my discussion with the president, I perceived a definite change in how I was received at the school both by teachers and administrators. As I walked around the halls, attended classes, and ate in the lunchroom, I tried to ignore the negative vibes hanging in the air like stalactites in a cave. But I couldn't escape the feeling of being increasingly marginalized. If I'd felt "out" before, there were no words to describe how "out" and exposed I felt now. Despite the chilly atmosphere, I still planned to apply to the rabbinic program as the president had suggested. I hoped that the process would be fair—and that the column fiasco wouldn't define me.

◆◆◆

In March of that year, three months after the article appeared, I was summoned for the requisite college interview, the final step in the long application process. I had written a candid and reflective spiritual journey, filled out the lengthy application answering myriad questions about my personal life, secured an official stamped transcript from college and graduate school, and gathered teacher recommendations that were glowing. In that packet was a gratuitous letter written on my behalf by a beloved and well-respected dean of the college who had rotated off the admissions committee that year. In effusively flattering language, he told the admissions committee that I would be an excellent candidate for the rabbinic program and eventually a superb rabbi. It was an important endorsement, one that I had hoped had the power to influence the entire admissions process beyond the Shoshana Sunshine article. It didn't.

When the Israelites are about to receive the Torah at Mt. Sinai, God says to Moses, *"They shall wash their clothes and be ready" (Exodus 19:10)*. Washing clothes was a ritual that signified cleansing, a change in status, a spiritual uplifting, a defining moment. I approached my imminent interview with those instructions in mind, again channeling my late mother who had taught me that appearance wasn't everything, but changing my clothes did matter.

On the day of the interview I dressed in a well-tailored, simple, nondescript black suit. It had a long skirt that skimmed my ankles and a matching three-button fitted blazer pulled down below my hips. I wore a single strand of white pearls on my neck with small matching pearl earrings and comfortable, sensible, low-heeled, black patent pumps. Looking at myself in the full-length mirror, I thought I appeared the appropriate blend of style and modesty.

After I was invited into the conference room at the school, I sat at a long wooden oval table across from several members of that year's admissions committee, all of whom I knew personally. The president of the school was there, as well as one of the deans, a couple of my teachers and a member of the board of directors. They all looked serious and were poised to ask tough questions. I expected that going in. One didn't pick up a rabbinic degree like a tuna hoagie at Subway. Rabbinical students require a big investment of money, time, attention, and nourishment by both teachers and administrators before they can be launched out into the world as spiritual leaders. The decision makers would be asking themselves, "Is she worthy of our time and mentoring? Would she serve the community well as a rabbi?"

I was nervous, but I imagined that the committee would try to put me at ease, even as they would be strong in their questioning. That didn't happen either.

The board member, a JCRC colleague of mine, began the questioning. "You wrote in your application that Judaism is 'a dance of Torah.' What does that mean?"

"Well, I just used it as a kind of metaphor for the partnership of humanity to the sacred word," I responded.

"But why did you use the word 'dance?'" she continued.

"It was poetic," I said. "I'm a writer."

"But why 'dance?' What's dancing got to do with it?" she pressed on.

Stunned by her combative tone, I gave a few more words of explanation. "It takes two; it's about partnership and engagement. Torah study has a certain rhythm."

My voice dropped off.

This was not a good beginning.

A dean asked, "What's your theology?"

My *theology?* "On one foot," as the sages say—meaning extemporaneously, with no preparation.

The Reconstructionists have a unique and amorphous view of God—a God that inhabits this world and, especially, the human heart. I was trying to understand the Reconstructionist theology, but I hadn't fully integrated it into my own beliefs, and to this day I still haven't. I had faith in my own views on God that worked for me, and still does.

"I know that God is good," I began. "I have a kind of Kushnerian theology." (A popular philosophy gleaned from the bestselling book *When Bad Things Happen to Good People* by Rabbi Harold Kushner.) "I believe that when God created humanity with Free Will," I continued, "it meant that God gave up some control. God left the possibility for people to have the freedom to make choices which had consequences, and enabled a certain amount of randomness in the world."

I continued my soliloquy rapid-fire while the admissions committee sitting around the table stared at me doe-eyed.

"God doesn't sit up there on some gilt-encrusted throne saying, 'You didn't call your mother today, Zap! Now you're getting a bladder infection. Oh, you didn't come to synagogue on Saturday morning on time. Hmmm, that little fender-bender in your new car might be the perfect reminder . . . You cheated on your wife, Zap, Zap! Now you better check out that little dark spot on your ankle and see if it isn't a melanoma. Punishment for your indiscretion.'

"Some things happen by chance and some as a result of the choices we make. It's God that helps us get through the tough times, and wants us to feel grateful for the good times. And I don't think there's a *quid pro quo* according to God, that if we do something hurtful or shameful, whether intentionally or by accident, God says, 'Now there, Zap, you lost your job so you can learn the lesson of humility through homelessness.' God helps us find shelter and solace in our waywardness, and then we probably will learn some lessons along the way. In hindsight, in spite of what we have to endure, with God as our guide we will rise above our challenges to find the light.

"What I've learned is not to ask the question, 'Why?' of God. Life is not consistently fair and doesn't always make sense. There are no guarantees that we get what we deserve or deserve what we get. But we must move on with our wounds and our losses, like Jacob did after wrestling with the angel, and find the joy in our new reality.

"All of this is to say that my theology is a work in progress at this point. I am hoping that after five years of advanced study, my theology will continue to evolve over time, that I'll be able to garner some new insights and then bring those observations to the spiritual outlets." *Amen*, I thought.

The room was silent like a tomb. My mouth started to go dry like parchment, cracking at the corners. I needed a drink of water.

It says in the Talmud, *"The Divine test of a person's worth is not theology but life" (Bava Kamma 38)*. It was obvious that the admissions committee had not reflected much on that ancient teaching with regard to my prior life experiences. Or so it seemed.

"What about your Hebrew?" someone asked breaking the quiet. "You wrote down in your application that assimilating Hebrew is one of your weaknesses."

"It's coming," I said honestly with a smile, now trying to hide my growing anxiety. "I attended one Ulpan immersion program in Israel, and I've been working with a private tutor."

So they ask about my weaknesses? Okay, fair, I thought. Would they then ask about my strengths? Would they want to know what kind of contribution I hoped to make to the community at the school? To the Jewish community? To the world? Would they ask me how I envisioned my rabbinate?

They didn't.

I added another point about my Hebrew: "I'm going to Israel this summer and I'll be studying at Hebrew University in Jerusalem. It will be all Hebrew all the time. It will be a completely immersive experience. I'll be fine by the fall," I said confidently. And I sincerely believed I would be.

They thanked me for my time, and I thanked God that the interview was over. I was underwhelmed by the process of the meeting, but the outcome was out of my hands. For good or ill, I needed to move on to the everyday. *Que sera, sera.*

◆◆◆

Two weeks later on a Sunday afternoon, my husband, Larry and I were at the airport in Las Vegas after spending a long weekend with close friends, celebrating his fiftieth birthday. Larry, my most devoted supporter, was always behind me, no matter what, "the wind beneath my wings," as the song goes. Now it was his turn to be the center of attention. School was in the back of my mind, buried below the immediate experience of hearing Rod Stewart in concert singing "Maggie May."

When I called home before boarding the plane back to Philadelphia, Beth told me that a small letter had arrived from the college. She knew I was waiting for news.

A small envelope portended *bad* news—no matriculation materials, no welcome packet. . . . Should I wait and read it to myself or just let my daughter deliver it straight up? I chose the latter.

"Could you read it to me, honey?"

She began, "Dear Lynnda: We were pleased to have the opportunity to meet with you and discuss your application to the Reconstructionist Rabbinical College."

Good start. My daughter continued reading. I could tell with the next breath that her voice was starting to waver. "After careful evaluation and deliberation, the admissions committee has decided against your admissions to the rabbinic program in the College."

Against? They were "against" me? I heard my daughter say that the school had invited me into their master's program, but not into their rabbinic curriculum. My body stiffened, then went limp.

Larry, standing nearby, knew by the look in my eyes, that had immediately welled up with tears, that it was not good tidings. Happy Birthday to him down the old craparoo.

In a monotone voice, my daughter kept reading the letter which continued with words to the effect, "You are doing such a fabulous job with all of your amazing work that the committee felt that you would better serve the Jewish community in your current capacity," or something like that. But I had stopped listening. I had zoned out after I heard the word "against." *Against* is not a happy or inviting word. Why would they be against me? What might their explanation be? I was totally confused.

"Mom," Beth said, responding to my silence. "I think it's better if you read this for yourself when you get home." My poor daughter had been the unwitting messenger of bad news—she, who would be leaving for college in a short time, didn't know what to say. "You don't belong there anyway," she prompted, trying to ease the blow.

That was probably true, I did not fit there, and never really had. However, if I wanted to be a rabbi where did I belong? Unlike how Groucho Marx once said, "Why would I want to be a part of a group of people who would have me?" I thought now, who *will* have me? Is this the end of my efforts to become a rabbi? To follow my calling? To live the life of service I imagined? Oy.

◆◆◆

Standing in the Las Vegas airport, even in my immediate shock and grief, I knew the following to be true: If you don't get into Harvard or Yale or Brown for your undergraduate studies, you can apply to the University of Michigan, Penn State, Colby, or any number of the 2,000 other admirable American colleges. Eventually, some institution of higher learning will accept you and your tuition, even if it's a community college that serves as a launching pad for a transfer to another school. You can still pursue your dreams, start your career—like I did back in the day—and ultimately become what you want to be. Not so for a woman pursuing rabbinical studies.

There were very few available seats in rabbinical programs—ten to fifteen in each incoming class in each of the THREE other liberal rabbinical seminaries that I knew admitted women at that time. The competition was fierce. People who were selected for admission were scrutinized almost like the Torah itself.

Candidates had to be perceived to be able to go the distance, like running back-to-back uphill marathons in wind and rain. School is five or six arduous full-time years of intensive study—in Hebrew and Aramaic—replete with thousands of years of data in courses ranging from history to liturgy and literature and counseling, to name a few, while you hold down a field-work job, and attempt to take care of your individual and family's needs.

Jewish tradition looks at rabbis as "ministering angels," who are expected to have enough refined magnetism to bring Divine sparks into the world. Any contender must be mature enough to become a counselor or a pastor who can offer advice and solace to others in their sacred moments of transition—in celebration and tragedy. The rabbi must set an example and be able to preach something wise from our Jewish wisdom that connects the symbolism of meaning and purpose in the spiritual sphere to life in the contemporary real world.

I quickly ran down the list of my alternative options. Not good. *None* of the other liberal schools that I might apply to for admission for the following academic year were personally ideal. For starters they were outside of Philadelphia, in New York, Cincinnati, and Los Angeles. Commuting on top of all of the other school responsibilities seemed daunting and practically impossible.

All of the seminaries required a year of study in Israel, and that would mean I would have to go alone. Larry was the primary breadwinner in our marriage, and with thirty-six employees and two children to support through college, an extended leave of absence was not in the stars for him. Retirement was somewhere over the rainbow. Separating from Larry for a year, give or take the few times we might be able to cross the ocean to see each other, leaving him in our newly empty nest alone, was untenable. I loved the idea of living in Israel, observing the weekly Shabbat and holiday cycle over a whole Jewish calendar year, but I couldn't imagine trekking off for so long and so far away without my husband. A few years prior, when I had been in Israel studying for the summer session at Ulpan Akiva, I'd had a meaningful time for a month. But a year apart? No way.

The Conservative and Reform seminaries, though both excellent institutions, posed political, religious, or personal challenges that I could not reconcile at the time. But in talking to aspiring rabbis, I became aware of a fourth, lesser-known, unaffiliated, pluralistic seminary with leanings toward the touchy-feely Jewish Renewal Movement. It didn't have an Israel requirement and attracted a diverse student population, mostly second-career people. Like the others on the East Coast, it was in New York. But, I reasoned, many students before me had figured out the commuting challenges. Couldn't I?

My worry was that this "alternative" school, whose official name I didn't even know, might be too alternative. Did it have enough *yichus*, stature or legitimacy in the Jewish community, for me to sign up for over five years of my life in its classrooms? The school had been around for almost fifty years, but it wasn't academically accredited. Did it matter? Was it worth pursuing?

Theoretically, one can study for the rabbinate with a private teacher and eventually receive *smicha*, the laying on of hands by a rabbi that says you know enough to be called a "Teacher of Torah in Israel." As you stand before a *beit din*, a court of at least three rabbis, the process is approved and witnessed. But I didn't know of any rabbi with whom I could study for smicha. And there are a roster of compelling reasons and advantages to studying at a seminary. The journey is in many ways an isolating experience. A seminary, similar to a twelve-step program or Weight Watchers, breeds achievement and success because it brings together willing members with a shared mission in a like-minded community. A variety of teachers expose students to new ideas that give birth to ingenuity and help them find their leadership voices.

The realization that I hadn't been invited into the rabbinical program at RRC was an existential crisis, like an earthquake in my soul measuring 8.0 on the Richter scale. The aftershocks of defeat came rumbling in, boom, boom, boom.

Nothing made sense. My career plans, my aspirations, my intended path to study Judaism and serve God were dashed like a grounded-out cigarette, the red glow extinguished. There I was, standing in the middle of the Las Vegas airport, Sin City, holding a public telephone in my hand, rebuffed, like the fallen from the flock, my mind reeling and free associating about my limited options to become a rabbi, the clinking sounds of coins from the slot machines kerplunking into tin cups in the background. It was like the theatre of the absurd as my destiny to become a rabbi hung in the ether.

I boarded the plane home from Las Vegas and cried a river of tears I didn't know I could produce until we landed in Philadelphia. My husband, sitting next to me was quiet and stunned, and not knowing what to say or do, took my hand and held it tight for five straight hours.

— CHAPTER 16 —

The Appeal

"I charge you, be strong and resolute."

(Joshua 1:9)

TWO DAYS LATER, I clawed my way out of catatonia, looking like a *shmata*, a rag, and with puffy eyes I ambled out of bed and back to school. It was only March, and I had to be at RRC until June, continuing to face the administration that was "against" me and hadn't offered me acceptance into the rabbinic program, and the rabbinical students who now knew the news of my status. It was awkward and humiliating, but I had no choice because I needed to complete the classes I was taking to earn credits for my master's degree in Jewish studies. Without the requisite grades, I wouldn't be able to transfer my credits to Gratz College and graduate on time. I'd lost so much already, and I was determined not to fall apart and forfeit everything else I had accomplished in my pursuit of the degree and the rabbinate.

But it was tough. At school, I was more "out" than ever. I imagined that people were always looking at me askance, that I was being judged, as if I had the scarlet letter "L" for "leper" etched on my forehead. Just like the lepers in the Bible, I felt quarantined from the community, existing outside the camp, in the *galut,* exiled.

It was torture walking up and down the halls every day, feeling like an unwanted failure in a place that appeared on every level to devalue me, and apparently didn't think I had the qualities to become a rabbi. Did I?

The whole fiasco had fed my insecurities big time. Day-by-day, and sometimes hour-by-hour, I had to push through the heartache to show up at school and focus on my work. It was extremely trying and a real test of fortitude.

There's an old Yiddish saying, *"Man troct, v'Gut lacht,"* which means, "We make our plans, and God laughs at them." God laughs because God has other plans for us, which are not necessarily consistent with ours. God doesn't even necessarily reveal those plans until it's in God's time to do so.

"Okay, God," I asked, my arms outstretched and eyes heavenward like Tevye questioning God's motives for poverty in *Fiddler on the Roof.* "What's so funny here? Please let me in on the joke. I'm not laughing! In fact, I can't remember experiencing this kind of agony since my mother died almost twenty years ago.

"What are your plans for me? Could you please send me one of those signs and wonders you're so famous for, like parting the Red Sea, so that I have a path on which to proceed? Thank you!"

◆◆◆

There were a few sympathizers at school and, as I started recounting the interview process and all that had transpired, I learned that there had been rabbinical candidates in the past whose candidacy had been rejected, but who had reapplied to the school at a later date. After they had fixed what needed to be fixed, or strengthened their applications in "weak" areas, they were accepted and given another chance to emerge as a rabbi with the school's imprimatur. I wondered if this might be a possibility in my case.

I also wondered whether there was a formal appeal process whereby one could revisit the decision of the admissions committee and reverse their ruling for the forthcoming semester. Perhaps if I knew the truth about their decision, I could change the course of things.

After years of hard work, I decided I had nothing to lose if I went to talk to a few of the people on the admissions team to see if there was information I could learn about the narrative surrounding my rejection, something the members might say that would provide a speck of clarity or offer a granule of solace or hope or understanding. Unfortunately, the answers I received were vague, not forthcoming, and unhelpful.

"You were weak in stating your rabbinic goals," one of the committee members shared.

"I don't remember you asking me about my goals," I replied. Silence.

One of the deans told me that I had "it," but hadn't presented "it" well.

When I asked what "it" was, she shrugged. I was sure that if they couldn't define "it," I certainly never could. And no one uttered a word about the article.

As I reported the conversations to my closest non-rabbinic friends and family, they offered lots of support and wide-armed hugs. They were behind me in my quest for the rabbinate, and they ached for my loss. Many attempts were made to assure me that I was valued for all of the other goals that they reminded me I was achieving.

"You'll move onto something else," they told me. "Look at your many talents and options . . ."

But I didn't want to move on to something else. I wasn't looking at other options. I was hooked on the idea of becoming a rabbi, even as the reality had begun to feel less and less probable.

There's a well-known rabbinic teaching: *"Do not pacify your friend at the time of her anger, and do not comfort her while her dead lies before her" (Avot 4:18).* I feared that the dead dream of the rabbinate might be lying before me like a decaying body on a funeral bier, and I was inconsolable.

I tried to do a mental inventory, a reality check on my current circumstances. How could I *"turn mourning into morning"* as *Psalm 30:11* says? I was earning a master's degree in my late forties; I was running a house and mothering two children, one of whom already had finished college; I was managing a successful business, and I was being a spiritual partner in a sturdy marriage, that we always nurtured back to a healthy place when we had differences. And we had strong family ties. I was a writer, an oral historian, a community activist, and a philanthropist. I took care of people, cultivated friendships, and contributed to the world with a loving and open heart and a generosity of spirit. Wasn't all of that enough to fill a life portfolio?

Plenty for some. But for me personally, I felt that I still had work to do. I had a calling to follow. I wanted to stay true to the path, even though one rabbi friend once told me, "You only choose the rabbinate when there is nothing else you can do."

"Nothing else I can do?" I thought. Her words reverberated again now. The reality was, there was nothing else I could do but pursue the calling to the rabbinate because the pulse of it was in my bloodstream. It had become a life force and to ignore it at this juncture was impossible.

It says in the Talmud, *"Act while you can, while you have the means, the strength" (Shabbat 151a).* Though I knew empirically that my RRC days were over, I decided to meet with the lovely dean who had written the letter on my behalf to thank him for his efforts, and to see if he had any further guidance or consolation to offer. He was a burly man, cuddly looking like a big teddy bear, bearded, with kind, friendly eyes and a hearty belly laugh. I sat across from him in an oversized upholstered chair in the middle of his office.

"I'm sorry," he said. "There was no one on that admissions committee who went to bat for you. Everyone was kind of lukewarm on your confirmation and there wasn't a person who sounded a rallying cry on your behalf. I might have done it had I been there, but . . ." His voice trailed off. "In the end, none of them could image you as a rabbi."

"*Image* me as a rabbi?"

I tried to process what I had just heard. In my mind I couldn't stop repeating the phrase, "*image* me as a rabbi. *Image* me as a rabbi*." The superficiality of the words stung and kept shooting back and forth in my head like a boomerang. Thwack, thwack, thwack. Could he really be saying I wasn't accepted into the rabbinic program because I didn't look like a rabbi? It was okay to earn a master's degree at the school, to be a teacher, perhaps, but not a rabbi—because somehow I didn't adhere to whatever the standard image of a rabbi was? Dear God! REALLY?

"What is the image of a rabbi?" I asked in disbelief with the words half-caught in my throat like a fishbone.

Even in those days, the Jewish community at large had come a long way from when the stereotypical Hasidic male rabbis, with their requisite beards and payos, were valued as the ultimate authorities, the sole arbiters of Jewish Law and custom. Women were increasingly part of the fold, raising new and creative voices. Many were famous. The image was changing and yet the dean, a modern, left-leaning rabbi dressed in jeans, had just relayed that the admissions committee at a liberal seminary did not invite me into the rabbinic program because I didn't fit the image of a rabbi.

"What about the old proverb, 'Don't judge a book by its cover?'" I continued incredulously, my heart racing. "Surely this applies equally to men and women?"

"It's hard to say what the image of a rabbi is," the dean answered calmly, ignoring the pithy adage I had quoted. "It's visceral. I mean, you know, it's funny, but the committee felt that . . . well you don't look like a rabbi."

I don't look like a rabbi? I don't look like a rabbi? The words continued to adhere to me like sand on wet skin.

I was speechless. I knew African American rabbis and Asian rabbis, male rabbis and female rabbis, gay rabbis and straight rabbis, old rabbis and young rabbis. But the dean was telling me that I was rejected from the rabbinic program because *I* didn't look like a rabbi. Whatever that meant? Were they thinking I was outwardly too put-together? Did they think I didn't appear serious or smart enough?

His response made it as clear as Baccarat Crystal. In that instant I knew that it wouldn't matter if I turned into Ben Yehuda, the father of modern Hebrew on the spot, or dressed in tattered garments like the modest and poor first-century Rabbi Hillel, who sat on a scholar's roof listening to the rabbinic lessons through a skylight in the frigid cold. The matter at RRC was done. I could hear *Taps* playing in my head. *Day is done . . .* I was done. My sought-after place at this seminary's table was going to be filled by another person—someone the key players at the school had "imaged" as more of a rabbi.

OMG! RRC was out of the option column! Just as my daughter had asserted upon reading the rejection letter, I wasn't a fit for them, and it wasn't a fit for me. I was going to have to walk away with my self-worth torn asunder. As I left the dean's office, I wondered what kind of spiritual work I might have to do to heal from this situation and get back on the path that now seemed not just hopeless, but impossible.

◆◆◆

The days became longer and longer, like White Nights during a Russian summer, as I continued to finish up my classes at RRC. Aside from performing requisite tasks at school, I retreated into my own little cocoon, trying to spin out through the feelings of doom and gloom that precluded my hopes for the rabbinate.

To add to the misery of loss, around the same time, the newspaper where I had been working for seven years began having financial difficulties. I found out through whispers down the lane that they were poised to lay off all of the freelance columnists—only no one ever called to tell me that meant me, too.

Instead, I learned of the editorial changes by accident. I had written an article, which didn't appear one month as scheduled. I called my editor, a friend, who said the paper had been losing advertising revenue, and, as a result, there were space issues. He assured me that my article would run the following month.

But the next month came and again my article was missing from its place. Concerned, I called my editor a second time. Then he gave me the crushing news that due to "budgetary restrictions," the publisher had made a decision to use only staff journalists to write articles going forward. Poof, just like that, with no advance warning, the column I had been writing as a stringer for almost seven years was *kaput*. My public forum, my creative writing outlet, a community dialogue, the sacred connection between a writer and her audience, my press pass, my contacts, prestige—all gone. Like a pedestrian caught in a sudden downpour of torrential rain without an umbrella, I was totally unprepared. The writing job loss combined with the realization that I wasn't going to stay at RRC was another thrum on the head.

By this time I had lightened my client load in my PR business, thinking that I would be attending rabbinical school full time while I worked on my master's degree. If I wanted to make my PR business viable again, I would have an enormous amount of rebuilding to do, and it was, frankly, no longer my passion, or the journey I was seeking.

In addition, Larry and I were about to face the new reality of an empty nest as Beth left home, and even though we were very close, our marriage would inevitably undergo shifts and changes. How would we negotiate the requisite transitions? There were lots of questions, many gaps, and what felt like too many unknowns at one time.

All of the hours of studying and careful planning for the rabbinate, the maneuvering I had done to prepare for the time when my kids would be out of the house now seemed for naught. I was fragile, confused, and frightened about the future. Completely cheerless.

Fortunately, other factors coalesced to keep me chugging along while I fought through the most recent avalanche of losses. First, and foremost, I identified myself as a survivor. With resilience, faith, and grit, I had survived my parents' divorce, my father's wife's mistreatment, the loss of my mother, and the deaths of other close friends and family members. I had suffered miscarriages and two premature births, and there had been a number of issues with my children as they'd grown up that had turned my mothering hair white. But I had transcended tragedies, traumas, and losses, and always managed to bounce back, healthy and on my feet, like one of those inflatable punching bag toys that pops upright after each swat. And deep, deep down in the raw I knew that if I failed at something, I was not an ultimate failure.

I struggled to keep everything in perspective. I recognized that, although my hopes for a career in the rabbinate might have received a fatal blow, I was not facing a fatal illness, as some of my friends were. I would recover . . . I would advance . . . I would grow . . . I would have a life. Maybe it would not exactly be the life I'd thought that I would have—in "the afternoon of life," as Carl Jung called it—but a good life, nevertheless. It would be meaningful and purpose-driven, somehow.

Slowly, I regained my footing. Prayers for clarity were revitalizing. Optimism, the *ayin tovah* I had cultivated, began to creep back in. I might not have had a choice about where I went to rabbinical school or whether I would ever become a rabbi, but I accepted that I had a choice about how I would handle my disappointments, and if I would move forward with a strong will and a can-do attitude. I recognized that if I failed at something, I was not a total failure. A friend said to me, "You can either rise and shine, or rise and whine." I really, really, really wanted to whine, but whining would only perpetuate my pity party with me as the pitiful one. Pity was an unsustainable option.

— CHAPTER 17 —

Meanwhile

"God does not ask us to do extraordinary things.
God asks us to do ordinary things
extraordinarily well."

(Rabbi Sidney Greenberg)

HIGH SCHOOL GRADUATION was looming near for my daughter, and I was busy planning a large outdoor garden party to mark the milestone, tenting our backyard for family and both her friends and ours to honor her. I planted flowers in large clay pots on the deck and gussied up the house, fixing odds and ends that had been neglected while I had been working and going to school. The graduation festivities provided a cheerful respite from my lingering unknowns hanging in the nethersphere. I was still deciding whether or not to move ahead with my plans to study Hebrew in Israel for the summer semester. The Ministry of Tourism in Israel ran television ads showing scenes from various sites in Israel, the voiceover beckoning, "Shalom. Welcome to Israel where history began. There's a little bit of Israel in all of us. Come find the Israel in you . . ."

There was so much of Israel in me already, and I perpetually yearned for more. Pictures taken of me in the Holy Land always made me appear ten years younger. I felt content there, strengthened in spirit, soulful, elevated, and there was the lingering feeling of God's hallowed presence soaring close. But if I weren't on the path to the rabbinate would the summer be better spent elsewhere? Should I still go to Israel or plan something different?

As the days unfolded I realized that if I went to Israel, I would inevitably have a lot of time to think, to pray, to sit in silence beneath the golden light shimmering on the ancient Jerusalem stones of the Old City. I could study and grasp new wisdom from brilliant teachers, meet new companions, fraternize with old, supportive Israeli friends in outdoor cafés while we drank honey-sweetened dark, strong, black Turkish coffee in short cups. God and I would have some serious talks, and possibly I would find my way again. Larry encouraged me to go.

◆◆◆

Before I left for Israel, I scheduled an informational meeting with one of the deans at The Jewish Theological Seminary in New York City. Set on the Upper West Side of Manhattan, near Harlem and close to Columbia University, the complex is awe-inspiring. The Seminary had been established in 1886 as the academic and spiritual center of Conservative Judaism, even before the Conservative Movement evolved. Its initial focus was on training rabbis to minister to the children of the massive waves of Jewish immigrants from Eastern Europe and the Pale of Settlement on Russia's western border. When they arrived, their children—first-generation Americans, like my parents—wanted to be "American." A new brand of assimilated Judaism arose, and leadership had to be developed to articulate the new generation's self-definition and understanding. JTS took this on as their mission. In the biblical narrative, the burning bush represents the location where Moses was appointed by God to lead the Israelites out of Egypt and into Canaan. The Conservative Movement adopted the unconsumed bush as a symbol of their undertaking to produce strong rabbinic leadership.

Among its assets, The Seminary boasted a world-renowned library, replete with volumes of treasured, sacred texts and rabbinic writings, many recovered by British scholar Solomon Schechter in the famous Cairo Geniza, where sacred ancient books and ritual objects were buried with respect, and not burned. The holdings were treasured worldwide. Besides Schechter, JTS boasted a legacy of venerated scholars, personalities, and teachers as well as distinguished alumni, such as Louis Ginzberg, the Lithuanian-born Jewish scholar (1873–1953), who was an author and professor at JTS for over fifty years, and even today is recognized as one of the foremost respected *Talmudic* and Jewish scholars. He was also a contemporary and friend of Henrietta Szold, the founder of Hadassah and a myriad of other social service agencies, who studied at JTS in the academic classes almost a century before women were admitted to the rabbinic program. With all of its prized academia and vibrant cultural zeitgeist, I decided it was worth checking out—even though I wasn't convinced that I could fit snugly into rabbinic training there either. But in my mind at that time, it made more sense to me than pursuing the program in the Reform Seminary, Hebrew Union College.

A couple of my rabbinic friends who were JTS graduates made phone calls and wrote letters of introduction for me. When I met the dean, he reached out and shook my hand as he ushered me into his office with a sweep of his left arm, pointed toward a leather chair, and motioned me to "make myself comfortable." After a few minutes of Jewish geography, in which I also told him about my upcoming trip to Israel, he began asking personal and pointed questions.

"You *daven* at a Conservative *shul* I hear, with our friend Rabbi Howard Addison, and before that Rabbi Sidney Greenberg, of blessed memory?"

"Yes," I said. "I took many courses with Rabbi Greenberg, and later when I expressed an interest in the rabbinate, he presented opportunities for me to *leyn*," read Torah. "He also gave me tips on preparing for sermons and talks. After Rabbi Greenberg retired, I studied rabbinic literature with Rabbi Addison every Shabbat after services. We became friends, and he was another champion of my cause."

The dean continued, "And I hear you are a protégé of theirs . . ."

"Protégé! Well, that's very nice," I answered. "My goal is to live up to the confidence they apparently had in me."

"Do you keep kosher?" he asked me, beginning the checklist of necessary religious qualifications needed to be considered for admission to the prestigious JTS.

"Of course," I answered without hesitation. Many years ago, when I had first started my studies, I had changed my kitchen, first because I wanted teachers, rabbinical students, and others who kept kosher to feel comfortable eating in my house. Hospitality in a Jewish home is salient among the highest of values. Slowly, I had embraced *kashrut* myself and came to acknowledge it as a way of living as though I were a sojourner on God's land—food from the land being one of its gifts. Since that shift in my home and my heart, I had continued to maintain the dietary laws to the best of my ability inside my home, at other people's homes, and out at restaurants.

"Tell me," he resumed, moving down the ritual checklist, "Do you put on *tefillin?" Tefillin* or phylacteries, are comprised of two small leather boxes, containing verses of scripture, which are worn on the forehead and the "weaker" arm as a reminder of God's commandments. For many years, this had been the elite province of men, and though I'd learned how to correctly put on tefillin and had inherited my grandfather's set, I was not comfortable with them yet as a regular practice.

"I'm warming up to them," I answered. "And I have my grandfather's."

"When you get to Israel, put them on every morning and see how you feel," he recommended. "Notice if it changes you in any way. This is an important ritual." I nodded, thinking about how I would feel in Israel, donning tefillin in secrecy while the Orthodox rabbinate, which has agency over Jewish religious life cycle events and practices, still excluded women from wearing them.

"What about driving on Shabbat?" he asked.

"I don't drive to the mall or anything like that, but I do drive to synagogue and to lunch at someone's house or a life cycle event," I answered honestly. Ancient rabbinic law forbids using electricity and traveling long distances on the Sabbath.

"You can't drive at all on Shabbat if you become a rabbinical student here," he followed up quickly.

This hit a sensitive spot. With the advent of suburban and urban sprawl, the Conservative Movement made an accommodation regarding the law restricting driving on Shabbat. Under the new ruling, one could drive on Shabbat, but only to a synagogue, the one closest to home, then back again. This new decision didn't apply to the rabbinical students, however. They were expected to maintain exemplary standards beyond the letter of the law while at The Seminary.

"I understand," I replied, even though I wasn't sure I could abide by that ruling, or that it made sense for my life. My entire level of observance seemed well below their standards.

"Lynnda," the dean said, "All things being considered, we'd love to have you here at The Seminary. We have a *mechina* program, an extra year of preparation that will help you if you need it. Go to Israel, study Hebrew, put on your tefillin, and call me when you return. We'll talk again."

I thanked the dean for his time, and we left his office together, my head swirling with rules and regulations, but also good vibes and gratitude for the warmth he had shown me as we walked through the majestic, sprawling campus.

JTS presented itself as a beautiful but daunting religious and academic environment. But for all of its scholastic and cultural strengths, it still didn't seem to be the perfect match that I was seeking. Even though I belonged to a Conservative synagogue, there were certain aspects of the Conservative Movement that didn't harmonize with the Judasim I wanted to practice and share with others. As much as I longed to become a rabbi, I wasn't sure that JTS was the path to take either.

I was reminded that The Seminary had made a landmark decision to accept women into the rabbinical school in 1983, but still, many men in the Movement were not thrilled with women being ordained at JTS, and the school maintained separate minyanim, an egalitarian one for men and women praying together, and one for men and women separated by the *mechitzah*—the partition that ostensibly kept men from being distracted from their commanded time-bound prayers by seeing women or hearing their voices praying nearby.

Even with the advent of women's ordination, 30 percent of Conservative congregations at that time still banned women from public Torah reading in mixed settings, and from being counted as part of the quorum needed for public prayer. It was a challenging time for both men and women at JTS, and I wasn't sure I wanted to be part of the necessary growing pains. More than that, I was beginning to recognize that I was a bit of a post-denominational hybrid. I enjoyed various aspects of all of the denominations and didn't find comfort in one size fits all, in categoric acceptance of every aspect of any particular denomination. But post-denominationalism or pluralism was a category unto itself, and not necessarily a popular or comfortable one either, presenting an entire galaxy of new religious dilemmas. Thoughts were spinning. Who was I in all of this uncertainty?

As I was leaving the building with the dean, we came upon a female rabbinical student who was sitting at a rectangular wooden table, her papers and books spread out all around her. The dean introduced us, and I sat down to talk to her. After the dean said goodbye, she asked, "Are you thinking of coming to The Seminary?

"I'm exploring my options," I told her. "How do you like it here?"

"It's the hardest thing I've ever chosen to pursue, but I love that I'm in the rabbinic program. It would be great if you would consider coming. We could use a few more women in these halls."

"How is it here for women?" I asked.

"Not bad—not as good as it could be, but it's getting better on most fronts," she acknowledged.

"I'm going to Israel for the summer," I said to her. "I have a lot to ponder. Let's keep in touch. It was really nice to meet you, and thank you for making me feel welcome. Good luck."

I heard she died before she was ordained.

— CHAPTER 18 —

Israel Summer 1997

*"Sometimes our light goes out, but is blown into flame by an
encounter with another human being. Each of us owes the deepest
thanks to those who have kindled the inner light."*

(Albert Schweitzer, MD)

J LEFT FOR ISRAEL the following week. With all of
its myriad problems—religious, cultural, political,
situational, and all of its ensuing quirks and rifts—I adored the
country, particularly Jerusalem. As world-renowned Israeli-poet
Yehuda Amichai once wrote, *"This is the city where the vessels of my
dreams are filled like oxygen tanks for deep-sea divers."* I desperately
needed to inhale the Jerusalem oxygen to breathe normally again
after my recent disappointments. On the day I arrived, I knew
that my summer in Israel would prove to be exceptional.

I checked into a unique guest house/hotel called *Mishkenot
Sha'ananim*, outside the Old City walls. The neighborhood,
which I knew well and loved, was known as *Yemin Moshe*, literally
the "right hand of Moses," and it was easily identifiable by the
sturdy windmill that stands as a noted landmark on the top of
King David Street. Down the beautiful Jerusalem stone steps

past the windmill there was easy access to the Zion Gate and the Old City, and a relatively quick route to the Western Wall.

The original two rows of houses in *Yemen Moshe* were built at the end of the nineteenth century and had developed into a cultural center, a home for visiting actors, musicians, artists, teachers, rabbis, and writers, including Philip Roth, Jonathan Safron Foer, and Nicole Krause, as well as Israeli authors like Amos Oz, who had written literary masterpieces while sojourning in the cozy quarters. Israeli author and peacenik David Grossman was in residence when I moved in. I'd heard that it was an interesting place to work and study, and as a by-product, a place for battered souls like myself to heal from life's wounds.

My apartment was lovely—charming, and the perfect combination of Old World and modernity, with pleasant amenities like powerful air-conditioning, which kept the rooms cool in the blazing hot Israeli summer, and updated appliances in the kitchen. But the best part of the apartment was the *merpeset*, the coveted long public balcony space, lined with reading chairs that from my perch on the hill overlooked the famed Sultan's Pool. Beyond the immediate setting was a sweeping view of the walls of the Old City. A brilliant book I had read years earlier, Gaston Bauchelard's *The Poetics of Space*, spoke of the "titanic importance of setting." The indoor and outdoor space in *Mishkenot Sha'ananim* would be my "nest for dreaming," a shelter for imagining, my space for reading, writing, studying, and praying. It was a precious gift.

Picturing the smorgasbord of interesting experiences before me—including studying at the prestigious Hebrew University and upcoming visits from my daughter, who was in Israel with a friend for a month teaching English as a second language, as well as an upcoming minibreak with Larry—I exhaled with a long, full breath and said to myself, "*Y'hiyeh tov.* This will be good. Thank you, God, for bringing me to this place at this season!"

I prayed spontaneously that Jerusalem's magic would provide a healing balm, that I would have the power to overcome my present circumstances and take the necessary steps towards discernment and growth.

I began unpacking immediately, putting my clothes in the closet in the bedroom, my alarm clock next to the bed on the lone wooden night table, the few books I brought into the bookshelves in the living room.

Soon after I began organizing, Beth and her friend Niki showed up at my doorstep looking to hunker down. They oohed and ahhed about my apartment, which stood in stark contrast to their living conditions in the poor section of Jerusalem in Katamon where they were working.

For the past several days the "kids" had been sleeping on mattresses on the kitchen floor in a dingy apartment where bugs "the size of antelopes" roamed as free as if they were in Yellowstone Park. "Wow, Mom!" Beth said. "You even have a shower stall that doesn't need a shower, and towels that cover more than your pubic area."

"Our entire skuzzy place needs to be imploded," added Niki.

They started to peruse the fridge for nosh like mice in the night. Young and full of humor, they were super fun to be around. I looked forward to spending some time with them in the coming weeks.

◆◆◆

Later, my dear friends, tour guide and cookbook author, Judy and her husband Bob, an ABC news editor, whom I had known from my many prior visits to Israel, came to welcome me to the guest house, delivered a few thoughtful staples and took me out to a homey restaurant, where we ate a beautiful, simple lunch of salad piled high with crunchy seeds and vegetables. As the three of us strolled by the park adjacent to my apartment, with the scent of wild rosemary bushes wafting through the air, I looked up and there was a familiar face—a young friend and fellow student from RRC, Rutie Gold, who had recently arrived with her new husband for a year of study. Instead of being reminded of my rejection from RRC, I was thrilled to see her, and we agreed to get together for Shabbat the following week. It turned out to be a very serendipitous encounter because Rutie held the key to information that would prove pivotal to my career and my life.

◆◆◆

That night, I was excited to be invited to my friends Arona and Michael Reiner's house for a welcoming Shabbat dinner. After we had first met during my trip to Poland and Israel in 1991, we had remained close. I'd observed Shabbat come together in their home many times during my previous visits. Like the Shabbatot of my childhood with my grandparents, the flurry of daily activity gave way to a more sensual and spiritual way of being. The abundance of great food beautifully presented on pleasing tableware, the recitation of traditional Shabbat prayers, the singing of joyous songs, the naturally slower Shabbat pace and the air of rising spirituality—which according to Jewish tradition comes forth from the extra soul, the *neshama yetira*, that we all gain when we allow Shabbat to enter us physically and spiritually—were part of the early memories I cherished. In Israel, I had always noticed that even secular Israelis like the Reiners bowed to the mellow rhythm of the country, slowing down, shutting off, welcoming in a quiet way of being.

At a certain hour, Arona would relinquish her paintbrushes, leave her canvas, and transition into her role as cook and hostess. The smell of the food that had started simmering while she was painting wafted exquisitely through the house. Everything she did to prepare for Shabbat had her signature artistic flair, even the way she cut tomatoes for a salad. Before we were ready to eat, Michael cupped their children's heads, one at a time, and blessed them.

After we took our places at the table, Michael raised the family's large, ornately decorated silver *Kiddush* cup and led the singing of a rousing chorus of the traditional Kiddush, and the *motzi*, before eating the challah. After the full complement of blessings was recited, we all enjoyed a delicious, sensuous, and joyous dinner together. The food was always *ta'im m'od,* very tasty, marvelous.

That day and Shabbat evening represented a new beginning for me—the resolution to make each day in Israel mindfully a good one. I left the Reiners' glowing with the spirit of Shabbat and friendship. I slept peacefully, tired from the long trip, the active day, and the little tastes of the Sabbath wine that the Reiners' served, grown in one of the burgeoning vineyards in the Galilee. *Yhiyeh tov,* I thought. Yes, things will be okay.

— CHAPTER 19 —

Hebrew University

*"These are the things the fruits of which a person enjoys in
this world, and the stock of which remains for a person in
the world to come: honoring one's father and mother, charity
and making peace between a person and a friend; but the
study of Torah is equal to them all."*

(Mishnah Peah 1:1)

MY CLASSES BEGAN on a Sunday morning at Hebrew University on Mt. Scopus, Sunday being the first day of the week in Israel, a regular work day after the Sabbath break. Established by Jewish intellectuals who roamed the streets of the area looking down at the spectacular view of *Gei Chizayon*—the Valley of Vision, one of seventy names ascribed to Jerusalem—Hebrew U was officially declared open by Lord Balfour in 1925 and has educated hundreds of thousands since its inception.

When I arrived at the beautiful campus, I felt a jumble of emotions, excitement to finally be able to dig deep into Hebrew, the *Holy Tongue*, a language I found rich and intensely nuanced, mixed with apprehension about my ability to learn fast enough. I was placed in intermediate level classes, which seemed perfect—not a beginner, but a review of the basics and then a lot more ... not too stressful and appropriately challenging. The fantastic staff and teachers at school were enthusiastically upbeat, always smiling, full of joy, buoyed by their mission to enlarge the circle of Hebrew speakers in Israel and around the world. *Boker Tov*, good morning, they chirped in sing-song voices as they welcomed the diverse student population that walked through the doors.

My fellow students were a group of highly motivated foreigners of all ages from all over the world. Some people came to study as part of an advanced degree program, others wanted to learn Hebrew to be able to converse with their Israeli grandchildren, whom they visited periodically after their children made *Aliyah*. There were even many nuns in my classes, eager to learn Hebrew to be able to read and interpret the word of God in the Bible in its original language, with all of its brilliant shades of meaning.

There were Russian immigrants, who brought violins to classes but very little knowledge of Judaism, which during Communist rule had existed only surreptitiously under the radar. There were also Ethiopian immigrants, dressed in colorful native print garments with shiny silk turbans on their heads, who had immigrated to Israel with knowledge of the Jewish religion and its rituals as practiced in their respective communities, but no modern Hebrew or job skills to bring to their new home. Each group had added a new flavor to the multicultural landscape of Israel, but they needed to be fluent in Hebrew to assimilate fully into Israeli society and find employment. Like me, they were struggling through transitions.

My Hebrew immersion classes began at 8:00 a.m. and continued until 1:00 p.m., and for me the five hours passed like quicksilver. We worked from workbooks and Hebrew newspapers, sang the golden-oldie Israeli folksongs in Hebrew as a mnemonic device, and spoke about our lives to one another—all in Hebrew. It was stimulating and exciting. I was happy being at school. And soon my ear caught the rhythm of the fast-paced Hebrew, and my passive Hebrew repertoire became activated and expanded.

With new confidence in my accent and the requisite rolling of rs, I was able to order cucumbers in the market and coffee and pastries in the cafés. I asked directions of Israelis walking on the street, most of whom weren't terribly patient and often responded in English. Not helpful. But I persevered, delighted when a fluent Hebrew speaker would respond to me in the native tongue.

After my first week of studies, Rutie Gold and her husband, Noam, hosted me and Niki and Beth for Shabbat dinner. We said the traditional prayers together, and enjoyed a great homemade meal with some of Rutie and Noam's other friends. After dinner as we were sitting down in the living room, Rutie pulled me aside.

"I've been thinking about your situation a lot," she said. "I'm so sorry about what happened to you at RRC. What a *balagan* (mess)! I do think you have what it takes to be a rabbi, Lynnda, and if you won't consider reapplying to RRC, where they'd be foolish not to accept you again, there's another rabbinical school in New York that many people like very much. It's called the Academy for Jewish Religion (AJR). Its model caters to second-career midlifers like you. And it is truly pluralistic."

"I've heard it mentioned a few times," I answered. "But I don't know anyone who's been ordained from there."

"I do," Rutie responded. "And they were very pleased with their experience."

"Hmmm . . ."

"AJR's been around for a long time," Rutie continued, "but since it's not attached to any movement or denomination it isn't as well known as it should be. You might settle in there perfectly."

I actually had considered the Academy as one of the options I'd ticked off after receiving the news of my rejection from RRC, but I'd dismissed it at that time because its reputation seemed slightly amorphous. An endorsement coming from Rutie, however, gave it more gravitas.

"It's a good place. You ought to mull it over," she continued.

"Okay, I'll check it out when I get home," I said, hoping that I didn't appear too dismissive.

◆◆◆

Back at Hebrew University, I made a young friend, Rachel, who was a few years older than my daughter, Beth, and mature for her age. A recent college graduate, she was starting law school in the fall on a full scholarship. She was smart and funny, and we arranged to study together after classes.

Many days we walked in tandem from the campus through the neighborhood of French Hill and into the heart of the city to eat lunch. We sat in restaurants and cafés completing our homework together, bantering for hours, drinking *café hafuch*.

Rachel's sister was also living in Jerusalem for a year while earning her PhD in Middle Eastern literature from the University of Michigan, and on many Shabbatot we would get together with them and their friends, all women younger than me, but who like me were evolving, forging new paths. They were different than how I was at their age, with so many more options, and it was a privilege to eavesdrop on their conversations while they were figuring out their lives and developing their personal and professional personas. Our conversations made me think about women, identity, and how important it is to know how to tap into our power to help each other and promote equality in the world.

At times during the summer I would amble over to the Old City to my friend Mira's store. Mira, a modern-Orthodox woman who didn't cover her hair and wore pants, was slightly younger than me. She and her handsome husband, Yossi, and their four gorgeous children lived in a stunning, spacious Old City apartment, and owned a brightly lit, small store filled with out-of-the-ordinary Judaica (Jewish ritual items), and beautiful Israeli-inspired jewelry, handicrafts, and ancient coins.

I sat on a backless three-legged high wooden stool for long periods of time after my classes ended and helped show merchandise to the customers. I shared the history and story behind the extraordinary lifelike diorama dolls that Mira offered for sale, made by my friend, Holocaust survivor, Magda Watts, who lived in the south of Israel in Eilat. I also tried on expensive colorful red, blue, and gold stone bracelets and pendants made of opalescent green Roman glass and other beautiful jewelry that was too expensive for me to own. Mostly, Mira and I engaged in thought-povoking talks. She knew I was struggling, and she tried to reassure me that I was meant to be a rabbi, even though in her world, women rabbis didn't exist, according to halacha.

"You have something special," she would say to me. "*Hashem* (a name for God) works in mysterious ways. Be patient, *motek* (my sweet). *Savlanut!*"

Savlanut is the Hebrew word for patience, but it also carries the linguistic root of struggle or burden. I felt burdened by rejection, the apparent loss of a lofty goal, and the fear of the unknown. It was hard trying to be patient, to wait for a sign about which direction I should take.

From time to time Mira and I walked together to the nearby kotel, a place that at once makes me cry with pleasure and pain because of women's ongoing struggle to pray there, wear a *tallit* (prayer shawl), or read from the Torah. It never made sense to me that women were discriminated against, fined, sent to jail, and even abused by the Orthodox rabbinate that had likened the entire outdoor area to a synagogue, where men and women needed to be separated by a *mechitza* for purposes of prayer.

But despite my disappointment about the politics that keep men and women separate at the Wall, and the province of the Orthodox rabbinate controlling life cycle events all over Israel, Mira and I, like many women in the "women's section," still found solace praying at our designated area. We wrote notes on tiny pieces of paper and crammed them into the small crevices between the stones, already overstuffed with thousands of petitionary notes from women pouring their hearts out to a just, merciful God. All around us, faithful women dressed in long skirts and kerchiefs on their heads, prayed fervently, with their cheeks against the wall, to get pregnant, or to heal their sick children, for safety in their homes, for ailing parents, for daily sustenance, for peace in Israel and around the world.

In general, I prayed for continued good health for myself and for my family. I prayed for ongoing strength; I prayed for peace, and I prayed for clarity, serenity, and patience. In full view of the Wall I vowed again to live in the moment, to enjoy the summer, to learn voraciously, and to feel grateful for my children, my husband, and my closely knit extended family, as well as for my awesome opportunity to learn in Israel.

In addition to my formal studies, now and again, late in the day, I wandered over to the German Colony to learn Torah with Danny Siegel, who had first told me, more than six years earlier, that I would feel more connected to Israel if I explored the depths of the rabbinic sacred texts. Danny spent his summers in a sun-filled apartment, directing a group of United Synagogue Youth (USY) interns that he was prepping to be emissaries for his humanitarian work.

Whenever I left Danny's study sessions, I felt elevated by his sense of compassion. His text-based teachings always shifted my mind away from my own issues, and challenged me to look at my situation through the lens of empathy for others less fortunate. Transformation through learning was exactly the message he had offered me the first time we met, and it continued to resonate. Particularly in Jerusalem, which is often likened to a mother responsible for disseminating moral and ethical teachings, Danny's lessons for living were inspiring and worth pondering.

I also discovered that on Tuesday evenings the Israel Museum was open late, and I went to the famous repository periodically after classes to catch a new exhibit or revisit an old one. Sometimes I wandered by myself and occasionally I joined friends or fellow students to examine the Dead Sea Scrolls or to stroll along the adjacent Billy Rose Garden.

And almost every day all around Jerusalem there were free lectures in a variety of venues on interesting topics taught by contemporary scholars, such as charismatic Israeli author Avivah Zornberg, who wrote, among other erudite books, *Genesis: The Beginning of Desire*. Experiencing her unique teaching style was like being present in a master class in rabbinic literature much like, I would imagine, an aspiring opera singer would cherish being in a Master Class with Maria Callas.

Of continuing interest to me were the many *shiurim* given on the weekly *parasha*, the Torah portion of the week, taught by scholars, poets, and educated lay leaders. I listened intently for moral, ethical, spiritual, cultural, and historical messages inside the lessons, which would instruct and inspire me. I searched the lessons voraciously for my own truths, my own wisdom, my own enlightenment, as I listened to tales of the biblical characters who had been looking to find personal meaning and purpose in their journeys. What was I to do with this knowledge I was gleaning? Would it spur me to action? Where was I actually heading?

◆◆◆

During that summer a number of my American friends came to Israel, and we often connected. One of my most cherished visitors during those weeks was my friend Vera, who I'd known from high school. We'd met in Philadelphia three years after she and her family moved there from Israel. Vera's parents were Holocaust Survivors, and Vera had been born in a Deportation Camp in Germany shortly after the War. The family had moved to Israel when she was sixteen months old, then later decided to join many of their survivor friends in the United States. Family and motherhood aside, Vera and I were simpaticos on Jewish causes, Holocaust issues, and the importance of Israel in the world. She was brilliant, well-organized and zen most of the time. I loved being with her, especially in Israel, where her fluency and my developing Hebrew skills surprised people.

One stifling hot day when there wasn't a hint of wind in the air, we were on our way to Mira's store in the Old City, when a jewelry shop owner named Ezra, sitting on a stool outside his store, beckoned us to come inside. Israeli men are generally known to be flirtatious, with a kind of devil-may-care, live-for-today attitude that comes with being surrounded by hostile neighbors, subsisting with almost daily terror incidents somewhere in the country, and a legacy of fighting wars. Vera and I glanced at each other, bemused.

Peering in at the upscale golden jewelry in Ezra's beautiful store, we knew right away that the merchandise was beyond our budget, and even though we were parched, we initially resisted his invitation to come into his heavily air-conditioned shop for a glass of iced tea. But the gentleman persisted, simultaneously persuasive and charming, and we were so thirsty from the intensity of the dusty heat that we shrugged and crossed the threshold into his store.

As soon as we settled in, savoring the thirst-quenching drink, he began relaying the story of a large golden ring that he held between his thumb and index finger. He said, "This ring tells of a parable that is attributed to the son of King David, the wise and venerable King Solomon, who built the Temple in Jerusalem. The King, feeling discontented and sad, asked his advisors to find him a ring he had seen in a dream.

"The King said, 'When I feel satisfied, I know it won't last. And when I don't, I am afraid my sorrow will go on forever. Find me the ring that will ease my suffering.'

"Eventually, one of the advisors met an old jeweler who carved into a simple band the Hebrew letters *gimmel, zayin* and *yud.* 'What does this mean?' asked the advisor.

"The jeweler answered that the three Hebrew letters were symbolic of the expression *Gam Zeh Ya'avor,* which means, 'This too shall pass.' The King's advisor was delighted to have found the ring that King Solomon had seen in his dream, and hurried to bring it back to him in his kingdom.

"King Solomon was overjoyed with the find. When he read the inscription on the ring, his sadness turned to joy, and later when he read it again, his joy turned to sadness. Studying the inscription on the ring he suddenly grasped an essential life lesson—that both sorrow and joy are often connected to each other, like euphoria and despair at either end of the feeling spectrum, and that each will pass with time.

"King Solomon discovered balance and equanimity with this new wisdom. Forevermore, he was able to face both sorrow and joy, knowing that whatever the circumstances, *this too shall pass.*"

Ezra, his eyes wide and smiling, concluded his animated storytelling: "And this very ring, that I am holding, is a replica of the same ring that changed King Solomon. And if you buy it, you will look at it every day, and you will be a better person for it."

"Bravo," I said, clapping my hands. Ezra's tale was another confirmation that everyone in Israel is an amazing storyteller, colorful, interesting, and part of our ongoing rich oral tradition.

We didn't buy the ring, but we did buy the *shpiel* (the story). *Gam Zeh Ya'avor.* This too shall pass.

The parable made me have confidence that my current situation would turn around, too, and I knew in my veins that I would be okay. I recognized in that instant, how much my mood and outlook had lifted since I had arrived in Jerusalem only weeks earlier. Little by little, I had been turning the pages of the most recent negative chapters of my life, and moving on.

The high-pitched energy and abundant spirituality in the Israeli air had made me feel energized and more at peace, and the malaise of rejection had evanesced into a serenity that I was just beginning to identify. Without being conscious of the process, I had somehow established the inner climate of gratitude that I was seeking, and I felt truly blessed. Even joyful.

But all too soon I would experience the flip side of the lesson in King Solomon's mythical ring—my joy was about to turn to mourning, and the oasis of tranquility that I had created during my healing sojourn in Israel was about to crash and burn.

— CHAPTER 20 —

The Bombing

*"The whole world is a narrow bridge.
The main thing is not to be afraid."*

(Reb Nachman of Bratslav)

I HAD ONE MORE WEEK TO GO before finishing my classes at Hebrew University, when Beth and her friend Niki finished their work and took up residency in my apartment. After a month working in Katamon, they looked like refugees from the underbelly of the third world, sweaty and weighed down by sloppily packed duffle bags filled with dirty laundry. We had seen each other periodically over the past few weeks, and we had planned that after I finished my studies the three of us would make Israel our playground for another week before the girls headed back home to the States and off to their respective colleges.

"Soooooo what are we doing today? And what about tomorrow?" my daughter asked as she plopped onto the couch.

I went into the kitchen to gather some cold drinks, wondering when I had become the certified camp counselor for two young adults in a foreign country, and how their agenda of endless free time was going to reconcile with my school responsibilities.

"We're bored with Jerusalem," Beth moaned. "It's too hot! We want to go to the beach."

Bored? I thought. With Jerusalem? A city overflowing with museums, archeology, theology, history, daily lectures by top scholars, tony shops packed with stunning ceramics and glassware? The *shuk*—the marketplace? Aromatic cafés for people watching and talking politics? My Jerusalem pastimes evidently held no fascination for Beth and Niki, who had respectfully labeled me a nerd. Anyone who wants to become a rabbi must be. They stared at me, obviously hoping I would morph into the Messiah of good times, starting now.

"We'll find a fun activity for today," I assured them. "Tomorrow, sleep late while I attend school in the morning. When you get up, go to the Y and work out or take a run in the city. By the time you shower and change, I'll be finished with classes, and we can meet in the shuk, Mechane Yehuda, on Jaffa Road and have a falafel or *shwarma* (lamb, chicken or turkey sliced from a vertical rotisserie) for lunch. How does that sound?"

The indoor/outdoor shuk, established at the end of the nineteenth century on a vacant lot owned by the Sephardi Valevo family, was one of my favorite places in the world to spend an afternoon. I loved sauntering among the crowds, aisle by narrow aisle, eyeing the fragrant bouquets of vibrant-colored flowers tied with satin ribbons, their scents mixed with the aroma of ripe fruits and vegetables, fresh spices, and brined olives marinating in barrels. Vendors hawking their wares shouted loudly in colloquial Hebrew at the passersby.

Beth and Niki were less than enthusiastic. I could tell as they looked at one another and rolled their eyes. "Okay, then what?" they asked.

Then what? Hmmm . . . I thought.

It was clear that they were primed for a change of venue. Tel Aviv with its beaches, trendy shops, and young vibe would have fit the bill, but I was obligated to my daily classes in Jerusalem, and Tel Aviv was an hour away. I couldn't just leave, and I didn't have the headspace to plan anything past the next day.

"Let's just meet for lunch tomorrow and we'll go from there," I said coolly, trying to stifle an inner anxiety. "Does that work?"

I felt caught in the proverbial working mother's dilemma, which apparently was pervasive even with adult children. Yes, I was thrilled to see them, but I was beginning to wonder how I would be the Mom and still get my assignments done satisfactorily. Guilt if I do; guilt if I don't. What to do? The pressure seemed to be mounting exponentially.

"I guess that works," Beth conceded, for the moment.

"We'll figure it out," I assured her. "Okay?"

"Fine."

◆◆◆

Having settled the next day's agenda with the young ladies, I attempted to peruse through my Hebrew lessons, but the moment I glanced up, I saw discontented faces across the living room. Beth and Niki were itching like poison ivy to get out of the apartment. There was a do-it-yourself jewelry store that they liked on *Emek Refaim*, a popular street in the nearby German Colony. "Would you like to go to the bead store?" I asked, capitulating to their desire for an activity. "Totally," they both answered almost in unison. I stacked my homework papers in a pile and off we went.

In the midst of beading bracelets, a friend they had met in their program called Beth on her cell and invited her and Niki to Tel Aviv the next day, volunteering to take them to the beach and act as their tour guide. It was like a call from an angel. Euphoric over the invitation, the girls could barely knot the string on the beaded bracelets they were designing.

I called Shlomo, a kind and trustworthy local driver I'd employed all summer, and arranged to have Beth and Niki picked up at the guest house in Jerusalem the next morning and dropped off at their friend's in Tel Aviv. At the end of the day he would bring them back to me in Jerusalem.

A perfect solution, I thought—for tomorrow at least. I would live in the moment like the Israelis, and only worry about the day after the day after . . .

◆◆◆

The next morning, which was sunny and beautiful, I awoke early and tiptoed upstairs into the bathroom that was adjacent to the girl's bedroom, careful not to wake them up. With their plans solidified, I showered, dressed, and went off to school on Mount Scopus. I was feeling calm.

On that particular day the five-hour lessons at the university flew by more quickly than usual. With the girls busy in Tel Aviv, I lingered later at school to catch up on homework. Shortly after 1:30 p.m., I began hearing the ominous sounds of ambulance sirens seemingly edging close to the area near the university.

Though Jerusalem had been relatively quiet since my arrival, the foreboding sound of multiple sirens was all too familiar to Israelis who had of late been experiencing the terror of suicide bombers blowing themselves up in multiple "soft targets." Buses, malls, outdoor cafés, and open-air markets filled with innocent civilians were fair game for Palestinian terrorists to attack in this most recent spate of violence since the intifada had ended in 1991 and devolved into the Gulf War.

Hadassah Hospital was across the street from the university campus, and the few people left in the building with me spotted the ambulances headed in our direction, careening fast around the corner.

"*Piguah! Piguah!*" (terror incident) shouted one of the teachers who had been listening to the *Hadashot*, the daily radio news that Israelis keep in constant earshot. Some kind of terrorist incident had occurred, and from what the teacher could discern, it seemed like a powerful bomb had been detonated in the shuk, in Mechane Yehuda.

Dear God, the *shuk*! If Beth and Niki hadn't gotten a serendipitous invitation to go to Tel-Aviv, we would all have been there together, probably standing at a little joint innocently enjoying a lunch of falafel or chips and shwarma. We might have been killed!

I sat, transfixed, with a handful of students and teachers as the radio news stations confirmed that two Palestinian suicide bombers carrying bags loaded with explosives and nails had each detonated a bomb in quick succession in the shuk. There were countless fatalities and dozens of serious injuries. The terrorist organization Hamas was claiming responsibility, and it was reported that their sympathizers were dancing with joy in the streets of their cities.

Sirens outside the window blared louder and louder like a swarm of angry bees, and my heart pounded loudly in my chest. I closed my eyes. It was too close.

My mind started racing with questions: Did the girls actually go to Tel Aviv this morning? Could their plans have changed and had they somehow ended up in the shuk, thinking that they would call me when they arrived? Teenagers, after all, were often motivated by whimsy.

I picked up my rented cell phone to call Beth. The phone was dead. I tried to reach Shlomo to confirm that he had taken

Beth and Niki to Tel Aviv as arranged. No dial tone.

When terrorist attacks occur in Israel the phones go down quickly and service remains spotty for an indefinite amount of time—which was caused by too much pressure on the circuitry even for the techno-savvy "start-up nation." Immediately, I felt disconnected. And frantic!

Activity began to ramp up around the halls of the school. Students were talking and gesturing wildly, eager to hear from loved ones, to know more. To find out what hand fate had dealt our Israeli brothers and sisters this time.

With no rhyme or reason, in a few minutes the phone lines hummed again, and I dialed Shlomo. He answered right away.

"Shlomo, Shlomo! It's Lynnda," I said, my voice quivering. "Did you take my girls to Tel Aviv this morning?"

"*Ken,* yes, I peeked dem up early dis morning at da guest house and took dem to da frrriend. Dey told me dey were going to da beech," he answered in his heavy Israeli accent.

"Are you sure?" I asked hysterically, almost screaming over the continuing sounds of the sirens outside the door where I was standing. "Do you know there's been a piguah in the shuk?"

"Ken, yes, I heard about de bumbs."

Because terror attacks were a frequent reality of everyday life in Israel during those years, families really were in a constant state of alert. When people said "goodbye" to each other in the morning, they shuddered to think that this goodbye might, God forbid, be goodbye forever. Tension was the norm, a way of life. *Shigayon!* Craziness, as they said in the City of Peace.

"I took da girls to da friend," he repeated. "Don worrrry."

Tears started to rise and my muscles relaxed a bit as I confirmed Beth and Niki's safety, but the constant whirring of sirens was unsettling. What about everyone else?

"What time are you supposed to pick them up?" I asked Shlomo.

"Dey will call me later in da afternoon, and I'll bring dem bek to you. I'll call you when I hear from dem. Don worry," he repeated again.

"*Todah* (Thank you). *Todah Rabbah Shlomo* (Thank you very much). *L'hitraot.*" Israelis don't say "'goodbye"—in a note of optimism they declare, "We'll see each other again."

"*L'hitraot,* Leenda. Don worry," he repeated a third time, trying to reassure me like a caring father.

Confirming the safety of the girls was momentary comfort. Contemplating the grim reports of the innocent dead and wounded made me queasy. Not knowing how the news of the incident was being disseminated back in the U.S. became another concern. America would wake up to pictures of death and destruction in Jerusalem, and with downed phone lines, loved ones would be unable to know the fate of their friends and relatives. I kept trying to communicate with Larry on my mobile so he could hear my voice before seeing the newsreel. But it was already too late.

Eventually, Larry told me what had been happening on his end. He had woken up early, he said, and gone into our basement gym to work out. As he flicked on CNN, he saw the headline: **Bomb in Jerusalem Market!**

The last he had heard I was slated to meet the girls there. Instantly, he called my cell phone and the robotic voice on the other end of the line intoned, "All circuits are busy. Please try your call again later."

Panicked, he watched the scene on the television unfold. Members of the *Chevre Kadisha*, the Jewish burial society, were busy picking up strewn body parts and small pieces of flesh from the ground and all over the debris area with gloved hands, in keeping with strict Jewish law dictating that all body remnants be buried. The on-air correspondent in the field was reporting the earliest details of the incident, speaking fast, as images of the bloody carnage at the market were projected onto the screen.

CNN's account echoed what the Israeli radio stations were reporting. Two bombs had gone off in quick succession. The first bomb exploded amidst a huge crowd causing multiple fatalities and injuries. As bystanders moved in and circled around the victims to help, the second bomb was detonated—there were 16 confirmed dead and 178 injured. In a few fatal seconds, innocent civilians who were marketing on a fine summer day or meeting their kids for a casual falafel or shwarma, were dead or forever marred.

Larry noticed a woman that he thought to be me on a stretcher holding a bloody towel to her face. He searched the screen for the girls, while Robin, Niki's mother, who lived across the street in Philadelphia, saw the same gruesome news footage and started banging on our front door.

The two of them tried to call me again. Nothing. They stood on either side of the TV, hovering close to the screen, hoping for some information, horrified as the unknown death toll and injuries continued to mount.

"Please God!" he said aloud. Though not much of a prayer person, he told me he thought of the cliché, "No atheists in foxholes," and how untrite it felt to say it.

Larry put my cell number on speed dial and, that time, I answered it on the first ring. When he heard my voice, he started to cry. I started to cry when I heard him crying, knowing how hard it is to be uninformed and desperate for information when something terrible happens far away.

I thought about our time together in Israel the week before when he had surprised me for my birthday by coming to visit for a long weekend. For four days we were like young lovers, energized, spiritual and sexy, safe in each other's arms. Now I felt alone, scared and vulnerable, with my daughter and her friend in my charge. I wanted my husband next to me and he wanted to protect me.

"Are you okay? Are you in the market?" He was asking questions and talking rapid-fire, hoping not to get cut off. His voice was quaking. "I've been trying to call for more than a half hour. Robin's here. I thought I saw you wounded on a stretcher. Where are the girls? I can hear the sirens in stereo. Are you scared?"

"I'm at school, ready to leave," I responded trying to speak above the din of sirens. "I'm fine, and the girls are in Tel Aviv. Shlomo picked them up and took them to the beach. We're all fine, sort of. It's appalling what happened here, so excruciatingly painful and senseless."

"Have you talked to any of our friends there?" he asked.

"No, I haven't. The phones . . ."

I didn't think that anyone I knew had been headed to the shuk that day, but in a small country like Israel, everyone knows someone who knows someone. It was impossible not to be impacted by the grim event. Larry ticked off the bleak statistics being updated on CNN, the airwaves transmitting the news overseas faster than I could retrieve it from the locals. The incident was being termed an *ason*, in Hebrew, a disaster. That much was indisputable.

"Don't worry," I said trying to mollify his fear the way Shlomo had tried to assuage mine. We both knew that the saying, "Don't worry," was a vacuous statement, but I couldn't stop myself from giving breath to the empty words. Perhaps speaking them would also have a soothing effect on my wired-out nervous system.

"I'll try to call you later when the girls get home," I told Larry. "*If* I can get through. Meanwhile, just know we're fine. We're okay."

"Yes. I love you."

"I love you too," I said, smacking kisses into the phone.

◆◆◆

There was a surge of activity in the classrooms and hallways of the school. Students continued moving at a frenzied pace, eager to hear from loved ones and know more details about the incident, to find out what hand fate had dealt them this time.

Many students left the building, others were milling around the radio, waiting for more official news. I thought about Beth and Niki, their disrupted Israel experience with a near miss in the market, sick at heart about the victims and their families. Their names and ages were now being identified—Shmuel Malka (44), Valentina Kovalenko (67), Gregory Paskhovit (15)—giving a sense of humanity to the tragedy.

After I hung up with Larry, I tried to collect my thoughts as I heaved my backpack over my shoulders and made my way down the street towards French Hill alone. Almost every pedestrian I passed, both Israelis and foreigners, had their mobile *pelephones* appended to their ears trying to communicate most likely with friends, colleagues, and family members, while attempting to sort through the mélange of grief. I called my Israeli friends, Mira, Arona and Michael, and Judy and Bob and I checked in with Rutie. They were all, thankfully, safe.

Outside it was hot and humid, characteristic of the stifling Israeli summer temperatures, but I hugged my arms tightly in front of my chest to contain a shiver. When I arrived home at the guest-house complex and passed the front desk, Ronit the concierge asked me if I was all right. I nodded my head silently.

"This is what we live with," she said, hurt and grief in her eyes as she raised her arms upward. I gave Ronit a lingering hug.

It was a sobering truth. Since Israel's Statehood had been declared in 1948, the young nation's history had been threatened by constant random violence. I could acknowledge a diverse political narrative, compassion for innocents, but in death's shadow in the aftermath of today's bloodbath, I felt unmitigated empathy for the Israeli people, defending their right to exist to others who hated them.

Over the years, after many wars and hundreds of attacks, the Israelis had learned how to gird themselves quickly, to clean up the scene of an attack, fix the broken glass, mop the dried blood off of the ground, bury their dead, say Kaddish, light candles, sing quiet songs campfire style, and get back to "normal" living, "business as usual." Their resilience was legendary.

"*Ayn Brayra*," they always said. "We have no choice. We will go on. We won't let the bastard terrorists destroy us. What kind of people send their children out on suicide missions to die killing innocent babies? Fuck them. We're still here."

Golda Meir, former Prime Minister of Israel was often quoted as saying, "We will have peace when our enemies love their children more than they hate ours." But on that day after all of the death and destruction, peace seemed like a whisper in the wind, a remote transient dream.

◆◆◆

When I was reunited with the girls that evening, I held them close. "God was watching out for us," I noted, sniveling, but it bothered me to say it. Hadn't God been watching out for the 16 people who died and the 178 people that had sustained ghastly injuries in that day's attack? Where was God in this terror nightmare? The only answer for me was that God apparently was in humanity's Free Will. I believed in the triumph of good over evil in a Godly good world. So? God must be in the rebuilding. In the bravery and courage. What other explanation could there be?

The girls wanted to go back to the United States immediately; they no longer were interested in sticking around for what had morphed into a high-stress situation. After listening to their concerns and their earnest desire to leave, I changed their two El Al tickets so they could head back the next day. Both of them welcomed the news with general relief. Then, suddenly faced with leaving me, Beth became conflicted.

"Come home with us," she entreated. But I wasn't ready to leave. I had my course work to complete. It felt wrong to head out, *chic chock*, fast, as the Israelis said, without suitable reflection and closure. For the girls, it was a fight-or-flight response and a different dynamic. They knew where they were headed. I did not.

"Go," I said. "If you're miserable and frightened, it's okay. I'll be home next week. We'll have a lot of time to play and finish up your shopping before you leave for college. I'll be fine, honestly. Go. It's the right thing for you to do." I said the words, but was not totally convinced that I was telling the truth.

When I informed my Israeli friends that the girls were leaving, they lamented about the perceived disconnect between Israeli and Diaspora Jews—that is Jewish people who live outside of the land of Israel. One friend said, "During the intifada, from 1987 till the Madrid Conference in 1991, we were completely abandoned. No one came. I remember thinking that if I was living abroad this would be the time that I WOULD come to Israel and show support. And now that terror is in the air again, Diaspora Jews run away and go home. We feel pain, fear, anguish and panic, but we don't flee. We are *home,* and we must stay here. What's more, I think *all* Jews should come to Israel to support us as a collective force in these uncertain times. If people leave and tourism goes down, the terrorists win. This can kill us as much as their fucking bombs. Like *Psalm 27* says, '*Hazak v'Ha'amatz.*' We all must be strong and courageous."

It was an excruciating dilemma, especially when my friends from New York and Philadelphia called and begged me to come "home." I could hear them choking back tears with every syllable they articulated.

Beth and Niki moved into my room for their final night, and huddled close, a girl on either side of me, their heads under my arms as I stretched wide to cradle them. It was a restless night for all of us, and bittersweet.

◆◆◆

Shlomo picked Niki and Beth up at 4:00 a.m. After I lost sight of Beth's tear-stained face in the car, I crawled back into bed and pulled my knees up under me in a fetal position, my cheek resting on the soft pillow. I began questioning my decision to stay. Maybe I should have gotten into the car with them, I thought. The meta-question of where I was going and what I was doing with my life now loomed large. If I left now, I wouldn't be able to take the exam, so I wouldn't receive a grade for the course—that felt so wasteful after all I had sacrificed. And my next steps back in the U.S. were still uncertain and unresolved.

When I had arrived in Israel two months earlier, I had been steeped in grief. I had traveled to Jerusalem to reclaim my identity, to heal, to recover from rejection and loss, to seek wisdom and clarify a new direction. And now, alone in a bed in darkness, almost six thousand miles from my beloveds after a brush with a violent terrorist attack, I suddenly had an amazing epiphany. I realized that, even though hard questions lingered, I no longer felt overwhelmed with sadness and hopelessness about the future.

Barefoot and wrapped in a chenille throw flung loosely over my nightgown, I went outside to stand on my balcony and look out over the scarlet-lit Old City, glistening majestically as the first sparks of dawn shot through the sky. I hated to leave this spectacular setting. Even in the wake of so much horror, fear, and heartache, I could sense that my heavy heart had evanesced into a receptacle of deep gratitude in Israel. I seemed to have been gradually fortified on my spiritual journey.

I had loved studying at the university, and I considered my time in attendance a unique opportunity to learn at an international prestigious institution, garnering wisdom from the excellent, ebullient teachers on staff. I had sat at the heels of remarkable scholars and masters, the same ones who had written the books piled on my nightstand, and I'd had the privilege to absorb some of their well-won acumen. I was grateful to be studying with worldly students and spiritual seekers like the nuns, hailing from as far away as Toga and China. Visiting archeological sites, I had relished the opportunity to experience history where history was seeded.

As a result, my academic progress was indeed quantifiable. My Torah and Hebrew skills had improved exponentially, my vocabulary had expanded, and I was chatting away almost like a native speaker, albeit at a much slower pace. I had enjoyed my stay at the famous guest house where generations of imaginative guests, writers, and recognized scholars had shared the same creative space. I adored being able to catch up with my Israeli friends, to sit with them in restaurants and cafés, sipping coffee and eating sweets, sharing savory casual Shabbat dinners and lunches, daydreaming and people watching.

I thought about the new people I met, like Rachel and her sister, who had changed my worldview and would become important connections over the years. I remembered the teas and concerts I attended with other sojourners who had passed through Israel during my summer of transition; I thought about little moments of joy and the loveliness of the day-to-day in Israel that I relished in the moment and also in current retrospect.

Whether ambling in the footsteps of human history, visiting newly uncovered excavations, praying at the Kotel, or sitting alone under a pomegranate tree, I was grateful for the Divine connection that I had fortified in Israel. I realized that I had stopped feeling overwhelmed by sorrow about my recent challenges, and instead I now acknowledged that I felt loved and blessed. I had found some peace and solace within myself, and I was gaining the necessary faith to know that I would land upright, just as others had counseled at the time of my departure from RRC.

My future in the rabbinate was unclear, but my defeatist attitude had shifted to one of *Ken y'hi ratzon*—May it be God's Will—and *Y'hiyeh beseder*, everything will be all right. Israel had become the transformative agent in the drama and shaping of my life, and I was okay—more than okay. Even if I didn't find my way back to rabbinical school, I knew empirically that I was on the path to being an open spiritual vessel. Certainly, God had some grand plan for me that I would fulfill in wonder.

— CHAPTER 21 —

Moving On

*"Slow growth is the surest guarantee of success.
For the perfect fruit, we need a slow ripening—
sunshine as well as rain, failure
as well as success."*

(Henrietta Szold)

TWO DAYS LATER, when I descended the stairs of the
plane and touched American soil in Newark after the
long flight from Israel, I sighed. Israel behind me, a darkness
of doubts crept in as I anticipated confronting the reality of
my home situation, which had remained unchanged—I was
still a reject from rabbinical school, my newspaper column
was defunct, my PR business was dead by design, our family
dynamic was reorganizing with the youngest of our two children
moving six hundred miles away. The nuclear family texture had
changed when Eric had gone off to college, but now Larry and
I were facing the unknowns of the clichéd empty nest. I hoped
that the glimmers of courage I had felt a few days ago at dawn
on my Jerusalem balcony would sustain me with renewed vigor
as I confronted the constellation of issues.

Larry was waiting for me at the gate. He had driven through the night and still managed to greet me with flowers. "You can never have too many friends or flowers," he said, repeating one of my credos. We hugged each other and held on for a long time before we picked up my duffle bag off the cart together, found the car in the lot, and hoisted it into the back seat.

The one-and-a-half-hour drive from Newark to suburban Philadelphia was quiet, almost silent. The motion of the car rocked me back into a sleepy state as the opalescent sun rose against the sky's blue background. Traffic began to mount.

I knew that Larry had been freaked out and lonely with Eric living on his own and half of his small family so far away, especially when bombs started exploding. In addition, his business situation had zapped a lot of his time and energy, and he no doubt was anticipating the loss of college-bound Beth's animated presence in our house with trepidation. I knew he was happy to have me home as a partner for company and moral, spiritual, and physical support.

Beth greeted me sleepily at the door when we pulled into the garage, just as she had since she was a little girl whenever she heard the heavy metal door automatically ascend before the car entered. She buried her head—with uncombed hair—into my chest. We ate breakfast and talked a little.

I looked around the first level of the house; it was generally in pretty good shape. A few things were out of place, but it was not the disaster area I'd envisioned it would be. I was the one bringing the mess.

◆◆◆

After catching up with Beth and Larry, my first order of business was to check in with my advisor, Dr. Rela Geffen at Gratz College. Much to my surprise, she was waiting to hear from me;

she had news: "Lynnda, I was looking over your records, and I see that you have taken so many courses that four more, and a completed community internship, would earn you enough credits to receive a second MA here at Gratz."

WOW! A second master's degree! I was surprised. My goal had been to go on to rabbinical school and earn an MA in Hebrew Letters by virtue of graduation. The rejection from RRC had thrown a monkey wrench into that idea. Would a second master's degree help me toward the rabbinate? What did I need to know, and how could I make it happen?

The more I contemplated what she told me, the more it seemed like an entity worth pursuing, at least in the short run. I loved my teachers at Gratz, the pluralistic student body and stimulating days filled with Jewish learning. I was happy there, and the not-so-unreal reality was that perhaps I wouldn't become a rabbi. Perhaps God had other plans for me. I had to allow myself the freedom to conceptualize the possibility of Option B.

If all went well, I would count two master's degrees on my resume. The credentials would certainly help make me more marketable as a teacher, a Jewish educator, or a Jewish communal worker who might make a difference in the world. It wasn't my first choice, but it was an acceptable alternative. I could still investigate the efficacy of simultaneously taking a couple of courses at the Academy for Jewish Religion, the pluralistic seminary in New York that had been twirling around on my radar screen since Rutie had raised it as a viable prospect.

I signed on to the additional program. I would take two courses in the fall and two in the spring, and I would earn the second MA by June. Not too shabby. I had only to find an acceptable internship after we dropped Beth off at school.

◆◆◆

We tearfully settled Beth into her college dorm at the University of Michigan, and Larry and I flew home and plunged into our new phase of life. The house seemed unusually hushed. We missed Beth, but we also found out quickly that having just the two of us in our own private space—while it was a quieter way of being—was an acceptable, and even welcome change. After a workday, we had only our schedules to manipulate, no one to report to except each other, no one insisting on dinner at a certain time. We had lots of freedom to reconnect with each other on a deeper level beyond doting parenting. We were suddenly able to develop new interests and cultivate fresh ideas and pursuits that we hadn't had time to explore with children in the house.

I began to think seriously about approaching the Academy for Jewish Religion. Though it wasn't a household name yet among the pantheon of great Jewish seminaries, I learned that the Academy holds the unique distinction of being the oldest independent, pluralistic seminary in the world, dating back to its launch in 1956 when it was a small, emerging institution. Totally unique in its pluralistic mission from its inception, it continued to be a progressive "still small voice" in rabbinical quarters. The early founders of AJR envisioned a meeting place, a *Maqom Torah* (a holy space of Torah learning), where every serious, "seeking" Jew and every dedicated spiritual leader of the Jewish people would strive to find his or her most authentic route to the rabbinate without arbitrary denominational boundaries.

For much of its early years, the Academy remained an open secret in the Jewish stratosphere, with a unique student body and a rich, diverse faculty, representing every stream of Judaism, and it was avant-garde in embracing the transdenominational approach to Jewish learning. Its motto—*The Torah has seventy faces*—reflects the diversity of the Torah, the plethora of acceptable interpretations, and the pluralistic nature of the student body and faculty. Only recently has the transdenominational approach gained a measurable degree of legitimacy in mainstream Judaism, whereas AJR has always been at the fore.

Perusing its modest promotional materials, I noted that the Academy worked vigorously to create and foster a unique and varied approach to Judaism, imbued with a respect and love for all of the voices of the Jewish tradition and community, garnered from the entire body of the denominational movements. I learned that it was informed by an important passage of the Talmud, "*Eilu v'eilu divrei elohim chayim*" (*Eruvim 13b*). "These words and these words are all the words of the living God." Early rabbinic voices are recorded in the holy sources, and often they serve as multivocaic commentary for each other.

AJR's history and programs were—and still are—based on the fundamental conviction that for Judaism to reach its highest ideals, its study and practice must be inviting and inclusive. Therefore, over the years, the Academy has attracted a diverse populace of aspiring rabbis, cantors, scholars, and professionals, who both support and challenge one another in a spirit of openness and respect. While the various denominational movements continued to serve large segments of the community, an increasing number of Jews, congregations, institutions, and communities, including a significant population of unaffiliated Jews, have been known to look to AJR for its spiritual leaders— rabbis and cantors alike.

I called a couple of current AJR students and graduates who confirmed that the Academy operated on the assumption that Judaism is greater and richer than any particular denomination or movement, and that Jews and Judaism are enriched by ALL the denominations of Judaism—past, present, and future. They shared that students, who are immersed in studies for approximately five full-time years, emerge inspired, well educated, transformed, and prepared and ready to integrate and teach the interconnectedness of Jewish knowledge, spirit, thought, emotion, and deed. It all sounded intriguing from the student population, but I needed to investigate AJR for myself. Was the Academy THE place I was looking for? And would there even be a place for me in the alternative place?

I wrote a query letter to the dean, and we set up an appointment to meet. I thought that if there were good vibes in the environment, I might sign up as a nonmatriculated student and take a course or two on Tuesdays. It would be convenient, even fun to commute with Larry to New York on the same day that he typically bought fabric and called on customers. I could test the waters, meet the players, and judge whether or not the Academy for Jewish Religion might be a fit for me, and I for them.

◆◆◆

On the day of my scheduled meeting at the Academy, I woke up at 5:30 a.m. after only a few hours sleep. A natural night owl, this was way too early for me to be moving with any purpose, much less feeling prepared for a significant day that might change my entire life. I dressed myself wearily in a long black short-sleeved cotton T-shirt dress that I had bought at J. Crew to wear for the occasion. I tied a blue-gray cardigan sweater loosely around my shoulders. My clothes were consciously much less formal than the outfit I had chosen to wear on my first day at RRC. Now hyperaware of image perceptions, I wondered if these clothes might be *too* informal. I shrugged as I looked in the mirror and ambled groggily into the car with Larry before I'd even sipped coffee.

It was a silent fifty-minute ride to Trenton, New Jersey, from our suburban Philadelphia home. We found parking in the crowded adjacent lot, and boarded the New Jersey Transit express train at 6:50 a.m. If everything went according to schedule, we would arrive in New York before 8:00 a.m. It was quite a grind. I wondered how Larry had managed to do this exhausting routine for so many years, and I questioned that, if the Academy turned out to be a good place for me, would the commute wear me out?

◆◆◆

When we arrived in New York, Larry immediately sauntered off to his appointments in the garment district, and I headed uptown to a friend's midtown apartment to visit and chat in anticipation of my appointment.

Sleep-deprived as I was, when I hit the New York City streets I became energized. I felt the adrenaline rush of business, fashion, and culture as I walked past Times Square, the neon billboards high above me, advertising Broadway shows and all kinds of products ranging from food to fashion to cigarettes. The streets were crowded and people were moving fast on their way to work. The city was alive. My body tingled. I was poised to uncover more layers of Manhattan's history than I'd ever experienced before.

Besides the many secular prospects in New York City, there is a palpable spirituality that exists alongside the veneer of raging consumerism. New York's metropolitan area is home to the largest Jewish population in the country. Synagogues, kosher food, and Jewish bookstores were plentiful all around the city, particularly on the Upper West Side where men and women securely wore outward signs of their Judaism—Star of David necklaces and *kippot*. Apartments had the requisite *mezzuzot* (small decorative cases that hold pieces of parchment with biblical verses) on the outside of their doorposts. New York was also a comfortable home to important rabbinical seminaries. I wanted to dive into the deepest part of the spiritual grid, head first, like the cutaway dives my father had taught me as a child.

After coffee with my midtown friend, I walked along the cobblestone pavement that ran parallel to Central Park West. The trees were still full, lush and green, and it was warm outside. There was a breezy hint of the weather about to change and the imminence of fall. I approached the Society for the Advancement of Judaism (SAJ), a four-story building on West 86th Street where AJR held its classes. I took a deep breath and crossed the threshold into the historic building. Ironically, it had been founded as the first Reconstructionist Synagogue by Rabbi Mordecai Kaplan in 1922, the same year that his daughter Judith became the first ever Bat Mitzvah. Was this an omen or an opportunity to find that AJR, a pluralistic seminary, was housed within the Reconstructionist flagship building?

◆◆◆

Taking the steps quickly, I reached the third floor and was greeted by a delightful, smiling, curly-haired woman named Miriam, the school's cheerful receptionist. "Oh, you must be Lynnda," she said, as she extended her hand to me.

"I have some material for you to peruse," she continued. "Will you be coming to AJR this semester? It's such a wonderful place—the most special community and everyone loves studying here. I commute two hours each way from Stroudsburg, Pennsylvania, just to be in the midst of this extraordinary environment."

"I don't know," I answered, startled by the candor of the question, dancing inwardly at the possibility that AJR might be the next step on my spiritual journey. "We'll see if all of the stars line up."

"If they're supposed to line up, they'll line up, don't you worry," she said, looking me squarely in the eye, a twinkle in hers.

A few minutes later Miriam led me into the office of Rabbi Sami Barth. It was a small, windowless room filled with heavy books that were "arranged" indiscriminately on wooden shelves and strewn on the desk and in piles on the floor. Papers and files were randomly spread about.

At first glance, Rabbi Barth appeared a bit disheveled like his office. He was dressed casually in a short-sleeved, blue-striped shirt, which was gently slipping out of the waistband of his khaki pants. He wore a small multicolored kippah fastened haphazardly to the side of his wild mane of ruddy, straight, long hair that met and matched his long, full, red beard. His cherubic face was set off by an enchanting smile. Even before he said a word, I thought, "Isn't he charming?"

He removed a pile of books that had been lying, slanted, on a chair in front of his desk. He then patted my wrist and led me to sit there.

"Well, very nice to have you here today. Please call me Sami," he began. A transplanted Brit, his clipped accent was immediately inviting, his speech almost lyrical. "So, you want to be a rabbi?" he asked.

"I've been thinking of moving in that direction," I answered, leaning forward.

"You live near RRC," he said. "Why not go there?"

Pow! There it was—two lines into our first meeting, and he'd cut straight to the chase. I was a goner.

"Not a fit," I replied. "I don't identify as a Reconstructionist."

"What are you?" he asked. "How do you identify Jewishly?"

"I'm kind of a hybrid," I answered. "I don't know exactly where I belong on the Jewish denominational spectrum. I've davenned at a Conservative synagogue for decades. I like the liturgy. I'm attracted to the social action segment of the Reform movement, the piety of the Orthodox, the insights of the great Kabbalistic mystics, the teachings of the Hassidic masters . . ."

"Grr-reat!!!" Rabbi Barth answered, banging his hands on the top of his desk as he stopped me in midstream, articulating the word "great" in two syllables.

"You've heard something like this before?"

"Yes! That's why we exist! There are many people at the Academy who are attracted to one denomination and pieces of another, just as you stated. For a variety of reasons they have found a home at this seminary rather than someplace else."

"So I've been told," I said. "That's why we're talking!"

"We have a lot of second-career people here, like you," Rabbi Barth continued, "who are involved with us because we do not require full-time attendance. You'll be studying with doctors, lawyers, dentists, psychiatrists, dancers, actors . . . you name it. Many of our students are already prayer leaders, *shlichei tzibur*, in their own communities, acting as rabbis and cantors. They are coming for the pedigree, the paper, the *smicha* (rabbinic or cantorial ordination), to make it official and for the chance to study with great scholars from all of the Movements."

"Awesome!"

"You can take your time fulfilling your course requirements, according to your own schedule, seventy points in all, a total of ten semesters, five years if you elect to study full time. Now mind you, lots of people do attend school full time, but many don't. It's your choice. We like consistency, but if you have a job, you can maintain your income, support your family, and study with us. We're quite family-friendly at the Academy."

He continued without taking a breath. I was mesmerized.

"We also don't require a year of study in Israel like other seminaries. We encourage people to study in Israel—it's the best place to live and learn en route to becoming a rabbi—but since our student population is heavily geared toward the second-career person, we recognize that it's not doable for everyone. And why shouldn't they become rabbis or cantors just because they can't leave their families for a year? In this day and age with two-career families, it can be quite unrealistic. And we think the Jewish community may be depriving itself of its best new leaders if seminaries aren't more flexible."

"Indeed!"

"The Academy recognizes its strengths. We have fantastic students here and amazing teachers. Because we are pluralistic and transdenominational, there is a plethora of choices running the gamut. Picking classes is like picking delicacies from a Chinese menu—some from column A and some from column B—all leading to a sumptuous kosher meal of Jewish wisdom to train today's leaders effectively to serve in the Jewish community and the community at large. We want to train our rabbis and cantors in the most authentic and respectful way possible, serving *Klal Yisrael* (inclusivity of all Jewish denominations). You'll love the *gestalt* here."

"Wow, no doubt," I answered, my heart fluttering with excitement as he ended his soliloquy. This man did not need sales training. "Sold!"

"You just came back from Israel, I see," Rabbi Barth said pensively, stroking his straggly beard as he looked down at my resume, changing the focus of our conversation from the school to me personally.

"You studied Hebrew at Hebrew University," he noted. "And finished Level Three. Brilliant!"

"I audited the course," I said. "I never took the final exam and didn't receive an official grade. I left shortly after the bombing in Mechane Yehuda when my daughter and her friend bolted out of the country."

"No matter," he continued. "If you weren't keeping up, Hebrew U would have placed you into another level. They don't play around there. They're pretty serious about their Hebrew classes."

"I did keep up," I said, "but I just wanted to be clear."

"You are, perfectly. And I see you have an MA from Gratz College. Very good! And other graduate level courses. Marvelous! There's an excellent likelihood that you can get some credit for your course work here and have to take fewer classes to complete our rabbinic requirements."

"That's wonderful!" I said, beaming a little inside. "I'll be working on another MA at Gratz and fulfilling a community service requirement the next two semesters. I'd like to take a course or two here before I apply. Is that possible?"

"Yes, it is certainly possible," he said, standing up. "All you have to do to join us is pass our Hebrew entrance exam, and you can take courses with our rabbinical and cantorial students. I'm sure coming from Level Three at the Ulpan at Hebrew U, there will be no problem."

A Hebrew exam? "What kind of Hebrew test?" I asked warily.

"Nothing to worry about. Nothing to worry about at all."

"Can I possibly see some examples?" I asked.

"Surely, here you go," he said, taking a sample test out of a drawer. "We study all of the biblical and rabbinic texts in Hebrew and Aramaic. We expect a certain level of proficiency. You'll do perfectly fine. I'm confident of it."

I looked at the exam. A feeling of terror coursed through the sinews inside my body. Hives began to erupt on my skin. Yes, I probably could pass the test. Handily, actually. But what if I didn't? Could I take it again and again like a driver's license or the bar exam until I passed? The thought of flunking the exam and being humiliated at the very least, or even rejected from AJR before I even had a chance to be admitted, felt too risky to contemplate.

"You mean I can't even study as a nonmatriculated student without passing the exam first?" I asked.

"No, I'm afraid it's our policy. You have to pass the test first."

Who knew? No one had given me the heads up about an entrance exam. My heart sank fast. Kerplunk! Another challenge! Another hurdle! I had not counted on this issue being raised. It was not on my agenda. I had imagined that I would be accepted after the interview, as I had been at RRC, with no language or academic requirements. I was so disappointed. I could sense immediately that AJR was a benevolent place; I felt good in the space, and I wanted to move in immediately, pull up a comfortable chair, and sit at the family table. But now it appeared that it wasn't going to be that easy.

Taking even one course at the Academy this semester was apparently not on God's agenda. The old Yiddish proverb was twittering again. *Man troct, v'Gut lacht.* I'm making plans and God is laughing. He must have other plans for me—and apparently, quite a hearty sense of humor. It was an unexpected difficulty that an alternative school, unknown to the masses, had stringent rules, boundaries, and higher admittance standards than I had anticipated. Good for them! But it was a mixed bag for me at the moment.

Quickly, I devised a substitute plan. I would work with my beloved tutor, study for the exam, and take it sometime in the near future when I was confident and ready. Yes, I was almost certain that I could pass the exam on the spot, but I was 100 percent certain that I couldn't handle another failure that might mean the final kibosh on the rabbinate for me.

"Sami," I said, "If it's alright with you, I'm going to take a little time to make sure I pass this exam. I'll be back in touch as soon as I feel more prepared. Okay?"

"Of course, it's okay," he said. "I think you would do fine with the exam, but you have to feel comfortable."

As I turned to leave, he said, "Wait one minute, there's someone I'd like you to meet before you go."

He disappeared for a brief time, and when he returned, he was accompanied by a petite, angelic-looking woman with smooth, pale skin and blue-geen eyes, the color of opals. She was wearing a long, flowing print skirt and a midlength colored tunic vest over it, with flat shoes on her feet. Her head was topped with a large round colored kippah, shaped like the ones worn by the ancient priests, which fit snugly over short, wispy blonde hair. Smiling broadly through wire-rimmed glasses, she moved slowly and purposefully toward me.

"This is Rabbi Shohama Weiner," Sami said to me. "She is an esteemed alumna of the Academy and is now our venerated President." She was in fact, I learned later, the first female president of any rabbinical seminary.

"Lovely to meet you," she said taking my right hand in hers and covering the top of mine with her left. "Please call me Shohama."

"I'm very honored to meet *you*," I said, smiling, feeling as though I was in the gentle reassuring hands of one of our treasured biblical matriarchs.

"Lynnda just came back from Israel and she would like to study at the Academy with us," Sami explained. "I tried to tell her to make an appointment to take the Hebrew exam, but she's not quite ready."

Shohama's eyes never left mine, her smile was sweet and welcoming.

"I'm going to study a little more, then make the appointment," I said quickly. "Hopefully next semester." As I said the words a feeling of panic gripped me, rooted in a sense of wasted time. I was forty-nine years old, and I wasn't getting any younger. Did I have the ability to pass the Hebrew test? And if I did would I like studying there? Would they like me? Would my studies work out?

"Lynnda, I've seen your query letter and your resume," Rabbi Weiner said. "You are the kind of person we like to have at the Academy. It's an important choice to study to become a rabbi. It's a lot of work and it takes a loooong time," she said, stretching out the word, "long." "You take your time doing what you need to do to prepare. It will be in your time and in God's when you make a decision to study for the rabbinate. We'll be here waiting for you."

— CHAPTER 22 —

Swing Time

*"The Torah suggests life is a choice of two paths: one of fire
and one of ice. If one turns in either direction
she will be harmed. What shall she do?
Let her walk in the middle."*

(Jerusalem Talmud, Chagigah 2:1)

I LEFT THE SAJ BUILDING with an armful of papers,
sample exams, and some support material from the
Academy. Why didn't I take that damn exam right then and
there? I berated myself. I could have passed the test before I went
to Israel, I thought. With a summer immersion semester under
my belt it was likely a no-brainer. The powers at AJR seemed to
like me. Now what were they thinking? Would they judge me
unfavorably because of my hesitation, envisaging I wasn't serious
about my studies, my spiritual quest, my career, my desire to
be a rabbi, to serve? Did *they* think I was a frothy dilettante?
Would they be able to "image" me as a rabbi? I was in a state of
high anxiety—feeling excited about the school, but nervous that
I might have blown a critical opportunity.

◆◆◆

Shortly after my trip to New York, I started my new courses at Gratz College. Simultaneously, I was offered an internship at the American Jewish Committee (AJC), to work at the local office in Center City Philadelphia. My job was to assist with an oral history project that was to focus on the lives of prominent Philadelphian women who had made an historical impact on the development of the local Jewish community, one of the oldest and largest Jewish communities in the world. In turn, the community had a far-reaching influence on the destiny of the Jewish people. As a journalist and former interviewer for Steven Spielberg's Shoah project, I was excited about the opportunity to facilitate a repository for people's stories and contribute in some way to the preservation of local Jewish history. It would be a busy schedule, but I was determined to compartmentalize the tasks without forsaking my goal of the rabbinate. I made arrangements with Tamar, who had been tutoring me periodically in Hebrew after my experience at Ulpan Akiva, to meet two or three times a week in order to really amp up my Hebrew and work on texts that would give me the necessary confidence to pass AJR's entrance exam. If I passed, I could start my journey at AJR the following year.

Tamar was an excellent and demanding teacher, and a lot of fun. We agreed that during our sessions we would speak, *rak Ivrit*, only Hebrew, which would inculcate and enhance my knowledge of modern Hebrew as well as the Rabbinic Hebrew we studied in texts. As we began the process of preparing me for the exam, we broke down the long rabbinic discourses into manageable assignments. I enjoyed our system of decoding the texts. Not only did I learn the requisite Hebrew, but I had the opportunity to delve into biblical, Talmudic, and liturgical passages that were new and interesting to me and to Tamar, who had grown up as a secular Jew in Israel. I was busier than a chef stirring six pots with two hands, but the mixture was coalescing with visible progress.

◆◆◆

At the beginning of January, right after our family had arrived home from a winter-break vacation, I made an appointment to take the Hebrew exam at AJR. With no production or fanfare, I passed it easily! Two days later, I was registered for four classes as a nonmatriculated student. They were all offered on Tuesdays when Larry and I could travel together back and forth to New York. It promised to be a challenging day every week as it required a lot of energy and concentration, but I was as thrilled with my acceptance to the school as I would have been if I'd won the Powerball multi-million-dollar lottery.

I also enrolled in two final courses at Gratz to finish my requirements for my master's in Jewish liberal studies, which was shaping up to have a concentration in rabbinic literature. I was also required to write a thesis. Six courses, traveling back and forth to New York, writing a thesis, and hours spent interviewing and training interviewers for AJC's oral history project zapped all of my time and lots of energy. I was sleep-deprived, but joyous in my pursuits and delighted to be engaged on so many levels with my Jewish studies.

◆◆◆

I began sitting in on classes at the Academy in January 1998. It was considered the "spring semester," but it was still in the dead of winter and the weather was miserable—cold, snowy, and icy, which added another challenge to commuting from Philadelphia.

On my first day, Sami and Shohama greeted me warmly. I quickly bonded with the other students, fellow "spiritual seekers" from all walks of life, and who were like-minded about spiritual self-reinvention and welcoming to others on the rabbinical journey. From the get-go, I felt at home, comfortable in my element, and elated to be delving into ancient texts with fabulous teachers and smart, engaged students—all of whom were helping me elucidate rich material.

Students and teachers typically sat around an oval table, seminar style, in a comfortable room, with so many books spread out in front of us that it was almost impossible to discern the table was made of oak. Preceding the era of technology, when everyone came to school with a smart phone or a laptop, people recorded lessons on small cassette recorders which they listened to later, hoping to preserve every nuance of the lecture, or share it with an absent student. Others, like me, wrote furiously in lined notebooks, to which we would refer when preparing for future classes and written exams, or writing papers.

There was no "in" and "out" at the Academy. If you studied there, you were "in." Politics took a back seat to politeness, *derech eretz*, and even though the pluralistic nature of the school and its commuter community might have made it a breeding ground for dissension, quite the opposite was true. Everyone from the administration to the teachers to the student body was kind, accepting, and inviting. People treated each other equally with sensitivity and caring. AJR stressed reverence over "rightness." No one could endlessly hijack the classes with too much opining. No infinite sermonizing, soapboxing, or lecturing was tolerated. When someone was talking, we were expected to listen. We could differ—even the ancient rabbis in the *Batei Midrashim* (study halls) argued with each other in a noisy process called *pilpul,* "pepper" in Hebrew, since disagreements on a point of law could become quite hot. Their rabbinic disputes resulted in the formation of precedent-setting legal and ethical Jewish standards for the decentralized Jewish community. The model for the study halls at the Academy was the Talmud, an expansion of Jewish biblical law that was finalized in the fifth or sixth century of the Common Era. It records all of the rabbinic opinions in the discussion along with the names of the rabbis who stated them, asserting everyone's voice as valid.

The teachers at the Academy were its chief assets. The budget being small, there were only a few professors on permanent staff. The rest maintained adjunct status, and had been culled from a rich pool of teachers embracing every denomination. One of my first teachers, Dr. Miriam Klein Shapiro—or Miriam as she preferred to be called—was an observant Conservative woman with her own brand of subtle piety. She was the mother of five children and the daughter of Rabbi Isaac Klein, the much-touted author of *A Jewish Guide to Religious Practice,* a seminal work of the Conservative Movement as a comprehensive guide for home and synagogue use. Miriam was a scholar in her own right, and a kind, modest, and generous teacher who smiled constantly, and seemed to be floating around with a halo above her head.

From the moment I took a seat in her class, I loved her. I wanted to be like her—educated, steeped like rich, smooth tea in Jewish learning and practice, loving, cheerful, and happy with her lot. I wished I had come from the kind of family in which she had been raised, where family traditions were supported by Jewish formal education for girls and boys alike. Like a child sitting on the knee of her mother, my own mother long gone, I looked to her to provide me with text-based lessons for righteous living.

In Miriam's session, we began by studying the "Writings" section of the Hebrew Bible. With a unique spiritual sensitivity, Miriam made the biblical characters like Ruth, Esther, and wise, old King Solomon come to life as though they were sitting in the front of our room on a panel, sharing their inner musings. Miriam made connections to the liturgy, the holidays, and life cycle events, pulling the stories together in a comprehensive way that wove a rich tapestry of tradition and practice together with practical rabbinics. And she had amazing insights into the biblical women who had captivated my early fascination with feminist Jewish studies, challenging us to think out of the box.

Each of us was expected to come to our sessions prepared, having mastered the material thoroughly in advance. I read the homework assignments many times before I felt ready, not wanting to appear stupid if she called on me. Miriam also required us to write and present a paper to the class, garnering material from many sources, some of which were completely unfamiliar to me.

In distinct contrast to Miriam's quiet assertiveness was Rabbi Dr. Emanuel Gold, Manny as he chose to be called, another one of my esteemed teachers, with whom I first studied The Book of Kings and Jonah from the Bible. Ordained at The Jewish Theological Seminary, he was an academic who had studied with many of the impressive scholars of his era as a student, the men who wrote influential books, like Louis Finkelstein, Mordecai Kaplan, and Abraham Joshua Heschel, the men who continue to inform us to this day.

Manny was a bit of a rabbinic renegade. His knowledge base was astounding, and he was quick to tell us that the ideology he had assumed as gospel when he was younger had changed through the years. He shared that he had become more skeptical, less accepting, more questioning of the dogma of Jewish law and practice, wondering if all of the ancient rituals were relevant for our time.

Sitting in Manny's presence was, for me, much like an actor today would dream of being a student mentored by Ben Kingsley or Meryl Streep, and it was as instructive listening to his digressing stories about his days as a student at The Seminary as it was listening to his original ideas about the texts.

"The Red Sea parted when the Israelites left Egypt because of a tsunami, not because Moses raised his arm with his staff," Manny conjectured, long before the idea of tsunamis had reached Western consciousness. Maybe so and maybe not, but his scientific spin shook our long-held core spiritual beliefs. Many of us were not ready to give up our grounding in familiar stories, our mythology based on faith.

Leaving Egypt is one of the central metaphors of Judaism: *"We were once slaves; now we are free"* (*The Haggadah* from the Passover Seder). Messing with folklore was like saying that the Temple in Jerusalem never existed, though there is incontrovertible evidence that it did. Students argued with Manny mercilessly, challenging his opinions. Sometimes we rolled our eyes at his ideas, but no matter what we thought about his controversial or sensational reflections, he defied us to think creatively. And he was resolute.

"Listen up," Manny used to say. "You are the disciples of great scholars and thinkers, and you have an enormous responsibility to disseminate truthful information to the next generation." Whose truth was the truer or truest was a matter of opinion.

"Transmission, which has an extremely high value in Judaism, is in your hands. Be honest and know your material—all sides of it. There's a teaching I'm sure you all know about the Torah from the *Mishnah* (Rabbinic law codified in 200 CE by Judah the Prince). *'Turn it and turn it and everything is in it.'* Everything is surely in it! Now it's up to you to know the difference between facts and fiction. Look at the Torah right side up and sideways. Make it your own! Then teach it with conviction to your students. *B'Hatzlacha*. Good luck!"

Liebe Hoffman, another early teacher, was also a product of The Jewish Theological Seminary, one of the earliest women rabbinical students. The class she facilitated that semester was entitled "Sacred Texts," which concentrated on the teaching of the Piaseczno Rebbe, a young rabbi from Poland who perished in the Warsaw Ghetto. I had never heard about him before or examined his brilliant writings.

We learned that Rabbi Kolonymous Kalman Shapira, from the town of Piaseczno, was a rabbinic child prodigy, groomed like the Dalai Lama by his family and the community to be a great spiritual leader in his homeland of Poland. Sadly, he was thrown into the Warsaw Ghetto during the war and died there. Before his death, in his twenties, he delivered homilies in the ghetto on every Shabbat and Jewish holiday, which were recovered from their hiding places after the ghetto was liberated following the War. His teachings, especially for one so young, were genius, and inspiring.

I loved knowing about and having access to these beautiful texts with analyses supplemented by the lovely and insightful Liebe. I remember sitting in class, shaking my head slightly in gratitude for the gift I had received to be able to study at the Academy. It had become quickly apparent that these were the moments I had been seeking when I began itching, thirsting, and questing, all the way back in Chicago. Liebe's class was the reservoir that started to quench my thirst for learning and spiritual sustenance, which was now being fostered in a safe, respected academic environment.

◆◆◆

During the formative years of the Academy, when it was virtually a Mom and Pop operation, permanent classroom space hadn't existed and classes were often held ad hoc. A restaurant, a café, a volunteer's apartment, or even the ground beneath a tree in Central Park became part of the learning spaces of the school and afforded opportunity for the exploration and exchange of Jewish ideas and the wisdom of the rabbinic sages.

By the late 1990s, when I entered the Academy, it had moved into its rented space in the SAJ building with the proviso that the AJR students would vacate the building to make room for the Hebrew school children who filed into the classrooms after 4:00 p.m. Like the Israelites who moved their portable *Mishkan* (tabernacle) from place to place in the desert, students wandered about looking for venues to hold late classes.

On Tuesday afternoons, a senior rabbinical student invited us to study in her rented apartment at the Belnord, a famous New York architectural landmark. A Renaissance-style prewar building fronted by a superbly landscaped courtyard visible behind arched iron gates, it stood in stark contrast to the corner Starbucks in which most of us were used to meeting. Each week a small group of aspiring rabbis and cantors gathered around a large dining room table with light streaming in from an open window.

Our teacher, a delightfully cheerful man whose ruddy cheeks looked as though they had been scrubbed red with a rough sand brush, sat at the head of the table. He was a rabbi, but he wasn't wearing a kippah on his bald head, which felt odd to me. His name was Rabbi Bernard Zlotowitz, a Greek and Hebrew scholar who everyone called "Rabbi Zlotowitz" or "Rabbi Z." We never used his first name (Bernard or Bernie) as we did with the other teachers at the school—not that he would have minded. His style was in keeping with the Classical Reform training he'd received at Hebrew Union College where he was ordained in 1945, and he was a source of fascination for me. Part of his personal history was that his brother Meir, who was fifteen years younger, was an Orthodox rabbi and the founder of Artscroll publishers, headquartered in Brooklyn, which continues notably as one of the largest publishing houses of Orthodox books and holy texts. Despite their stylistic and denominational differences, the Zlotowitz brothers got along famously, a model for contemporary families facing a clash of internal religious orientations.

During my first semester, Rabbi Z was teaching a course titled, Translating the Book of Psalms, and he was simultaneously completing a book on the subject, one of many in his prolific career. Except for *Psalm 23*, which was read or chanted fairly often at funerals, the psalms were generally mysterious to me, their language esoteric, poetic, and difficult to access. Rabbi Z was an expert, familiar with every nuance of tone, intent, and meaning. I was eager to contextualize the psalms, to explore their layers, to translate them into spiritual texts for our time.

"Ms. Targan," Rabbi Z boomed on our first day of class, initiating the process of role-taking and the requisite introductions. I loved the newness phase of the classes, and I enjoyed hearing about the back-stories and journeys of my distinguished fellow classmates. I was listening intently to hear someone's name other than my own. "Ms. Targan," Rabbi Z repeated. "Are you a rabbi or a cantor?"

A rabbi or cantor? What? Are you talking to me? I looked over my shoulder. He had said "Targan," but was he addressing *ME*?

"Ms. Targan, are you studying to be a rabbi or a cantor?" he asked again, gently.

"I-I-I'm just studying," I stammered. "This is my first semester at the Academy as a nonmatriculated student."

"Very good! Are you planning to become a rabbi or a cantor?" he asked patiently, restating the question for a fourth time. The query threw me. Though I had been on the rabbinic road for a long time, it had been fraught with so many twists and turns and delays, that I was sure of nothing.

"A rabbi. I'm hoping that someday I can be a rabbi," I answered timidly.

"Well then, welcome, Rabbi Targan. Nice to have you in my class. Welcome indeed!"

It was the first time anyone had called me Rabbi Targan. The appellation sounded strange, but it made my blood surge. All of the valves and arteries of my heart began dancing in response. Apparently, he had no problem "imaging" me as a rabbi.

Rabbi Z became one of my early and beloved mentors at the Academy, and he continued to address me as a rabbi. "Rabbi Targan!" It had a certain lilt. I let the sound of it roll over in my mind, like a first taste of a fine wine swirling around the tongue. His naming gave me confidence, infused me with an assuredness that I was heading in the right direction, and made me feel comfortable enough in my own skin to feel somewhat authentic. As I listened to the lecture, I wondered if Rabbi Z was a messenger foretelling of success to come.

◆◆◆

Four months passed while I studied at Gratz, worked at my AJC internship, and took four intense courses at the Academy. At the same time, I continued my private Hebrew sessions with Tamar. I had to stay very focused and organized at all times, which was challenging. I listened to Hebrew tapes in the car, tested myself with flash cards while standing in line at the bank, read as I commuted to New York, and studied all day Sunday when Larry went to the Eagles' football games.

I had little occasion to chat on the phone with friends or family—just the facts ma'am. It was impossible to set up an appointment with a service company to fix an appliance, much less wait for the serviceman to show up late with the wrong parts. My house was suffering the effects of neglect, and so was I.

I didn't have time to take my skirts and pants to the dressmaker for hemming, get my hair cut, have my car washed, or purchase new sneakers when my running shoes wore out. Nothing but studies received my full attention.

I had no time to ruminate or to meditate, except during scheduled prayer time or Shabbat, if I wasn't working. My roster was packed like raisins in a box, but I was motivated and driven, and kept going like *The Little Engine that Could*. I didn't know where I was ultimately travelling, but I loved the ride as it was. Larry was happy for me, never complaining about skimpy dinners or the extra errands he had to run to pick up the slack.

After months of a frenetic pace, I was hoping to apply for admission to the Academy and elevate my status from a nonmatriculated student to a full-time rabbinical student. I loved the vibe at school more and more. The teachers, my classmates, the academics, and the spiritual infusion were like a continuous B12 drip into my venal system. It reminded me of being back at college, but with another level of spiritual depth. And now I brought the wisdom of age and maturity to my studies. From every indication, I was respected and well liked at the school, but would the teachers and administration accept me? I was convinced that this was my place, but after the earlier RRC disappointment, who could be certain of anything?

Every time a piece of mail arrived from the Academy I was afraid to take the letter opener and slice the top of the envelope, terrified that it would say, "We regret to inform you . . . You can't study here anymore." And that would be the end of it. A dream pulverized. But if ever I was to move ahead I would have to be fearless and take a big risk. "Feel the fear and do it anyway." Classic Letty again and again.

◆◆◆

During the last week in April, I finished my thesis for Gratz. A week later, the dean of Gratz told me that I had the highest grade point average of anyone in my class, and the teachers and administration had voted me class valedictorian! I was slated to deliver the valedictory address at graduation for my second master's degree in front of hundreds of people in the community, and share the stage with prestigious academic and community leaders from both Israel and America who were accepting awards the same evening.

Tears flooded my eyes as I considered the significance of my achievement. Redemption! Total Redemption! For all of the people who had doubted my abilities, who were patronizing, judgmental, insulting, lacerating, or rejecting, I could now say with the chops to prove it, "You were wrong about me. I am Number One in academic achievement in a class full of scholars earning master's degrees."

Success is surely the best antidote against detractors, the people who aren't supportive and push you down, don't take you seriously, place stumbling blocks in your way, and corrode your spirit. I had had a full complement of those characters in my world, and now I had achieved something that could never be taken away from me, ever, by anyone!

And it was not only redemption for me; it was redemption for my late mother, who had not been formally educated and had wanted her children to have the American academic pedigrees that she was never able to earn for herself. It was redemption for my father, who, abandoned by his parents, was forced to quit school in the eighth grade. It was redemption for Larry who had sacrificed and nourished me every step of the way. And it was a proud moment for me to be recognized by my children as a gritty, hard worker. A nonquitter.

◆◆◆

On the night of Gratz's graduation, May 18, 1998 (*22 Iyar 5758* on the Hebrew calendar), I was cloaked in my black cap and gown, sitting on the dais, looking out at the packed auditorium, my friends, family, teachers, *chaverim,* and colleagues before me. Dr. Alice Shalvi, an ardent early feminist Zionist, resident of Jerusalem and a leading figure in progressive Jewish education for girls, sat beside me.

When it was my turn to speak, I began, "The *Levitical* biblical mandate, *'Proclaim liberty throughout the land,'* has a familiar ring to those of us in Philadelphia. Perhaps because we know these words as the inscription emblazoned on the Liberty Bell not too far away from here in Independence Hall. You may also know that the words on the Liberty Bell were a quote from this week's Torah portion, *B'har,* on the mountain top, Mt. Sinai to be precise . . ."

It was my first *D'var Torah,* or word of Torah, in front of a large audience. The hall was quiet. I was in command of the room. The participants were invested in listening to what I was saying as I made the connection between freedom and responsibility, social action, and good deeds—*ma'asim tovim,* as they are known in Hebrew.

"Freedom is not freedom from responsibility. On the contrary, freedom embraces a deepened understanding of our moral and personal obligations. Knowledge without heightened social consciousness, and education without a commitment to service, is an incomplete package. Marian Wright Edelman says, *'Service is the rent we pay for living.'*"

There I was, feet firmly planted in front of the podium on the eve of my fiftieth birthday, born in 1948 like the State of Israel, speaking into the microphone, addressing a room overflowing with onlookers. I was sounding rabbinic. I felt rabbinic. When

I finished, people rose to their feet and clapped, and I heard a person on the dais say, "She can write it, and she can deliver it with a punch. My money's on her." It was a poignant moment.

Dr. Shalvi asked me if she could have a copy of my text. "Yours was a very interesting take on the *parsha* (Torah portion)," she said, shaking my hand. "Your first sermon—and it was really good, my dear. *Kol Hakavod lach*! All honor to you."

In addition to the diploma I received that evening, I picked up two awards for leadership and service as well as The Nettie R. Ginsburg and Nathaniel I.S. Goldman Prize, "presented to the member of the graduating class receiving a master's degree with the greatest academic distinction." That night I earned a lot of adulation from friends and strangers alike. My children were definitely proud of me, and my father, who was then in his seventies and increasingly sentimental as he aged, beamed like a lightbulb. My husband and mother-in-law were joyously tearful. But the most important aspect of that stellar Monday night was that I reclaimed my dignity, confidence, and self-respect.

◆◆◆

The next morning, I was back on the 6:50 a.m. express train to New York to attend my regular Tuesday classes at AJR, exhausted from the previous night's celebration, but as high as a helium balloon let loose in the sky.

The following week, I began the application process for official acceptance into the rabbinical program at the Academy, and at the end of June, I appeared in front of the admissions committee for my interview. Shohama sat at the head of the table next to one of my teachers, who sat next to the chairman of the board, also a rabbi, and a couple of other people whom I didn't know.

Having been through one of these sessions before, I was prepared for a rugged ordeal. But this meeting was nothing like I had anticipated—no gotcha questions, no confrontations, no antagonisms—just a very lovely and loving process. It felt natural; I was myself.

Before I left, Shohama made a statement to the rest of the participants on the admissions committee, "Lynnda has been studying with us for several months now. She is an outstanding student, very serious about her work, and an excellent writer. She has good insights and doesn't take up too much space with her opinions. She gets along with everyone. We would be well-advised to welcome her to our school."

Well, if this wasn't a rousing endorsement from the president of the seminary, what was? But still, there was no guarantee that I would get in. I'd been burned before, so I couldn't allow myself to be over-confident or too cocky about my potential admission. It became a daunting waiting game.

◆◆◆

I thought I would get a call the next day, but the next day passed, and the day after that. Uh-oh. After three days of silence from the school, I was beginning to wonder if something had gone wrong. Had I missed a nuance of disapproval in what had felt like a mutual admiration session? Was there a naysayer on the admissions committee who couldn't image me as a rabbi, or didn't think I had "it?" The suspense was wreaking havoc on my psyche.

I decided to call Shohama as we were driving to Westerly, Rhode Island, to spend the Fourth of July weekend with Leslie and Steve, who were friends from back in our Chicago days. I was taking a huge risk in making the call, but the anxiety of not knowing overruled my patience.

Shohama picked up the phone right away. "Hiiii Lynnda," she chimed, with her usual welcoming intonation.

"Hi Shohama," I responded, trying to sound upbeat, though my heart was pounding as if it would burst out of my chest. "I wanted to check in with you. I hadn't heard anything and I was wondering when I might? What's the process? When will I know if I was accepted or not? . . ."

"Oh Lynnda," she broke in. "Of course you were accepted! You were accepted with flying colors. Your acceptance was unanimous."

Was I hearing right? Was I in?

"The admissions committee was very impressed by you," Shohama continued in her relaxed manner, summoning calm and tranquility like a yogi.

"There was never a doubt amongst us that you are most welcome at the Academy! Your official written acceptance is in the mail. *Mazel Tov,* my dear!"

Poof! Just like that, I was in! I was in! I could study and become a rabbi. Self-actualize! Serve humanity! Serve God! If I hadn't been in the car I would have been arial somersaulting like an athlete on a trampoline.

Larry, sitting next to me in the driver's seat was elated, even giddy, bebopping behind the steering wheel. He knew that my acceptance would mean sweeping changes in our lives, and he was ready and willing to be a partner in my rabbinic journey. Upon hearing the news he gave me the high fives and the thumbs-up as he drove across the Tappan Zee Bridge.

While we cruised along the highway making our way to Rhode Island, I made several phone calls to my children, my friends, family, and teachers to share the good news. Beginning in the fall, I would be in New York three days a week for, what I jokingly called, "Text and the City," my personal spiritual adaptation of the HBO series hit, *Sex and the City.* It was going to be a long road to the rabbinate, four or five hard years of full-time engagement with ancient and modern Jewish texts, writings, and scholarship. Nevertheless, I was teeming with glee.

When we arrived at our old, dear friends,' we popped the cork on the bubbly. It was a great celebratory weekend, and as I watched the fireworks commemorating the birth of our nation the next night, I, too, felt reborn. The boom, boom, boom sounds and showers of colorful sparks seemed to illuminate my inner sparkle. Like our country that had been liberated during the War of Independence, my own internal war appeared to finally be over. I felt liberated from my motherlode of self-doubt, from my old unrealized dreams. I had found my place to study and learn. I was finally on the wholly holy path to the rabbinate . . . *Glory, Glory Hallelujah!*

The official letter, which was waiting for me when we got home, sealed the deal. I was ecstatic.

But the merriment would be short-lived. There were more challenges on the horizon, an unwelcome intrusion, more soap opera drama. *Like sands through the hourglass so are the days of our lives . . .*

Another test.

— CHAPTER 23 —

God Laughs Again

"God is with me. I shall not fear."

(Liturgy: Adon Olam*)*

*A*T THE END OF THE SUMMER, Larry and I took a magnificent cruise to Greece and Turkey that we had planned as a joint celebration for my fiftieth birthday and my acceptance to rabbinical school. On the boat we kept clinking our glasses with whatever we were drinking at every meal—wine, water, or ice-tea—making toasts as Larry kept repeating his daily refrain, "It doesn't get better than this." We both agreed. Life was good. Spectacularly good!

When the trip ended, we flew home, and I made final preparations for the AJR retreat in the Catskill Mountains that would precede my first official year of rabbinical school. There's a saying: "If you make a door for yourself, the teachings accompany you." And for the first time since the kernel of the idea of rabbinical school had begun to germinate in the flora and fauna of my soul, I absorbed the reality of being a full-fledged, full-time, matriculated rabbinical student. The door to learning was wide open. Walking with a grateful verve, I pinched myself that after so much uncertainty, everything had fallen into place; I was excited and moving forward. Or so I thought.

Late one night I was reading in bed, perched against the pillows in front of my headboard, and I noticed a high-pitched ringing in my left ear. It happened again and again, particularly when the room was silent. There's an old joke about ringing in the ears:

> Patient: I have a ringing in my ears.
> Doctor: Don't answer.

I tried not to "answer" by ignoring the ringing, but it was so annoying that I called my friend, Dr. Charles Rojer, a board certified otolaryngologist and plastic surgeon, and asked him to have a look. I couldn't imagine that it was anything serious, but it was irritating and needed to be addressed.

Charlie and I had been friends for years. I loved and respected him for his quiet, gentlemanly elegance, his European charm, and his perfect, professional bedside manner. He had been a hidden child in Belgium during the War years, and I had interviewed him for the Shoah Foundation's archives. As a result, we had a powerful bond and we trusted each other.

Charlie examined my ears with the otoscope as I sat on the high table in his pristine examining room. After a cursory routine examination, he said, "I don't see anything here that troubles me. Everything checks out fine clinically. Many people have tinnitus, a ringing in the ear, and there are a lot of theories about it, but no substantive cures."

I could live with that news, I thought, although the maddening ringing in my ears was going to be a continuing nuisance during what I anticipated would be hours of reading, writing, and studying into the wee hours. But so be it.

Then matter-of-factly he added, "Since the ringing is only in one ear, however, I would be remiss if I didn't check it out further . . . It's rare, but sometimes there's a brain tumor that grows inside the ear. It's called an acoustic neuroma."

"I know about that," I said, startled. "Remember, you diagnosed my brother-in-law Steve with that tumor."

The intensive surgery that Steve had undergone to remove the same tumor many years earlier, had damaged the nerve fibers and had left him deaf in one ear and paralyzed on the right side of his face, from his forehead to the bottom of his chin. His mouth on the paralyzed side didn't move well when he spoke, which, for a trial lawyer must have been painfully irritating, though he never complained, or let this disability impede his law practice or personal life. His right eye, which already had been fraught with a degenerative eye disease, didn't blink or tear appropriately. It seemed a big, irksome hassle for him, and he was always putting lubricating drops into that eye and adjusting his glasses with the custom-made cup that surrounded the lenses. His ongoing comfort was challenging for both him and his empathetic doctors to handle.

What were the chances that two family members, unrelated by blood, would grow the same benign but destructive tumor, generally diagnosed in much older people? I couldn't believe I was hearing the words "acoustic neuroma" in connection with some ringing in my ear.

"Ah, yes," Charlie said. "That's right. I forgot for a minute. It's really highly unlikely that you have one, but I do have to check. I'll schedule an MRI for you in a day or two."

This was not going according to the script I had written in my head. I was expecting a possible prescription for eardrops that would clear up the ringing—one, two, three—and then be on my way to a clean bill of health, approaching my studies, unfettered. It didn't work out that way.

◆◆◆

I had the MRI the following day, and afterwards we headed to the Jersey shore with friends for the Labor Day weekend. No sooner had we set foot on the wooden planks of the boardwalk when my cell phone rang. It was Charlie.

"Hi Lynnda," he said cheerily.

My heart began racing. "Hi, Charlie what's happening?" I asked, trying to stay calm.

"Well, I got your test results. There is no evidence of an acoustic neuroma. Your ear canal is clear. . . ."

Whew! I was relieved. I dodged a big bullet, I thought.

"However, there was, an 'incidental finding' on the scan," Charlie continued evenly, with not a hint of a French accent, his first language, which might have made the forthcoming news sound less foreboding. "We found a small parotid tumor—about the size of a dime. It appeared distinctly as gray matter against a vague background."

"What's that?" I asked, immediately starting to panic. "Is that like the carotid artery? Do I have heart disease?"

"The parotid gland is one of the salivary glands. Tumors in these glands are relatively rare, and most of the time they are benign. It's going to require surgery—no big hurry, whenever you can. But it's a very delicate operation. You'll need time to recover."

"What makes it delicate?" I asked, not really comprehending the myriad details he was dispensing. Larry was looking at me in bewilderment. The deep furrowed brow on his worried-looking face read, "What's going on?"

"There is one facial nerve on each side of the head which traverses the parotid gland. This nerve exits at the base of the skull and enters the face at the level of the jaw. There are five divisions of this facial nerve, which, depending on the location of the tumor in the gland, may impact facial function," Charlie explained. "We hope that the tumor is benign, but if there is a malignancy and the whole gland has to be removed, there is further potential for facial paralysis. We won't have absolutes until we get inside."

I was stupefied. I tried to absorb the details quickly. I have a tumor. It's probably not malignant, but it could be. The parotid gland is connected to five branches of a facial nerve that may affect form and function. My speech might be seriously compromised as a result of this surgery, or by allowing the tumor to grow. Woe is me! Moses, the great rabbi and hero of the Bible, had a legendary speech impediment, and it hadn't detracted from his oratory skills. It didn't stop my brother-in-law Steve from arguing and winning difficult cases in front of demanding judges. But I was about to enter rabbinical school and hopefully become a rabbi—a rabbi who might not be able to speak well! How was that going to evolve with facial disfigurement and speech impediments hanging around my neck like an albatross?

Larry's color faded as he heard my side of the conversation with Charlie. He didn't know what was happening, but he rightfully suspected that it wasn't good news.

"Lynnda, listen to me," Charlie ordered gently. "You're in generally good health, strong and hardy. You are going to do fine."

By the time Charlie's pep talk began, I had already mostly zoned out and was not fully present as I pondered the scary diagnosis and its frightening exigent treatment. I hung up the phone and started to explain Charlie's "incidental finding" to Larry.

"I'm fine," I said hastily, trying to hide my rising panic. "But incidentally, I have a rare tumor growing inside my head and neck. And incidentally, I need to have delicate surgery to excise the tumor before it gets too big and causes more damage.

And incidentally, the tumor is in a gland that's connected to five facial nerves, any of which can potentially cause facial paralysis or speech disorders. And incidentally, perhaps I'll now speak out of one side of my mouth. And incidentally, isn't facial paralysis just what every rabbi needs for vocational enhancement?"

Larry didn't know what to say. He just looked at me with vacant eyes. The news, like all bad news, was a vicious interloper in the ordinary rhythm of a day, a week, a month, the rest of your life. Bad news is like a demanding visitor that shows up uninvited on your doorstep with a large suitcase prepared to hunker down in your home and wreak havoc for an unknown period of time. And you have to deal with it graciously, because not doing so will make it worse for everyone involved. *Ohm . . .*

◆◆◆

I called my rabbi before Shabbat, and he told me that he would put me on the *mi sheberach* list, and read my name among the names of members of the congregation and their friends and family who needed healing prayers during Shabbat Torah services. He said that he would personally pray for me, and he offered the best piece of advice I would receive from anyone during the whole ordeal—a powerful statement in the form of instruction that I would return to again and again as I met future crises in my life. To this day I offer his guidance to others. He said matter-of-factly, "Lynnda, don't let this tumor take any more time than it has to!"

Hmmm. Brilliant! Such a simple prescription. I repeated it. "Don't let this tumor take any more time than it has to." Yes, there were surely going to be many unknowns coming down the pike. Unknowns were the worst—the most anxiety producing—not knowing the identity of the adversary is the scariest of the scary. It was undeniable—I was presently neck deep in the gray matter of life, the gray matter of my tumor. But I quickly resolved that this tumor was not going to take any more time than it had to.

It was important to me to be done with it. I didn't need a tumor messing with my head. I wanted to be a part of the new rabbinical school class coagulating for the current school year. I yearned to be situated in the community and hoped that the students and teachers would keep me in their circle of concern and be willing and able to pray for me. If I delayed the inevitable surgery, I feared that I might not start school for another year and that seemed like too big of a setback after all I had done to meet this milestone. I surely wasn't going to let that tumor take any more time than it had to.

◆◆◆

In September I attended AJR's three-day bonding rabbinical and cantorial retreat, during which time I reluctantly revealed to the community that I had recently been diagnosed with a tumor that required surgery. People were kind. Sami and Shohama were empathetic and reassuring. Everyone made me feel safe enough to be candid and vulnerable. My fellow rabbinical students were supportive. People made a point of giving me hugs and offering prayers.

One woman in particular, Joyce Reinitz gravitated to me and lingered more than the others. "I think I can help you deal with your crisis," she said with a welcoming smile. I discovered that Joyce was a well-respected Manhattan therapist, and an expert in healing imagery who had worked in the field for more than twenty-five years. Trained in New York and Jerusalem, she was now studying to become a rabbi to integrate her spiritual leanings into her academic and professional skills. Tall and solid, she had bright eyes, a face full of light, and an engaging presence and personality. We talked for a few more minutes, and she explained some of her techniques for healing and relaxation.

"Let me give you an image to help you calm down during this time of uncertainty," she said. "Would you like to try it now?"

"I'm all ears," I said, "no pun intended." I trusted Joyce instinctively, and I found that I was breathing noticeably easier after our conversation. She told me to concentrate on the last line of the prayer, *Adon Olam: Adonai li, v'lo era*—"*God is with me, I shall not fear.*"

With that, Joyce and I cleaved together. Employing her imagery, I acknowledged that my fate, as always, was in God's hands. My newly inspired mantra became, *"God is with me, I shall not fear."* And the tumor wasn't going to take any more time than it had to.

I left the retreat feeling close to my classmates. These would be the generous souls with whom I would study for the next five years, and who, if all went well, would be ordained with me. I prayed that the tumor would not impede my ability to stay synchronized and engaged with the community that had embraced me and allowed me to move forward with my studies. After all of my searching, I finally felt that I might fit comfortably into this lovely, welcoming, and joyful spiritual community. But first, the surgery.

◆◆◆

Fortunately, school was not scheduled to start until well after a month following the Jewish holidays. I sat in synagogue, on Rosh Hashanah, a Day of Judgement on the Hebrew calendar, praying for a good outcome. The next day I checked into the hospital before 6:00 a.m. for prep work before the scheduled 9:00 a.m. operation.

Larry accompanied me to the room, and my mother-in-law and sister joined us a few minutes later. As I undressed and changed into the sterile, flimsy, blue-printed cotton hospital gown, I tried to close my eyes intermittently and bring Joyce's imagery into focus. The exercise helped, but I remained scared and a blink away from a floodgate of tears.

I recovered my composure quickly, took several deep breaths and repeated my mantra from *Adon Olam*: *"Adonai li, v'lo era." God is with me, I shall not fear. . . . "Adonai li, v'lo era. . . . "*

◆ ◆ ◆

I was in surgery for more than five hours. I woke up in the recovery room to the sound of beeping body monitors and the soothing voice of my old friend Dr. Steve Barrer, an intense and well-respected neurosurgeon who had watched as Charlie and his colleagues performed the delicate procedure. Steve was one of the men who had accompanied me on the trip to Poland and Israel seven years earlier, which had become the catalyst for pursuing my rabbinical career. Over the years we had developed a caring relationship.

"You're fine, Lynnda," he said in a quiet, authoritative voice that droned over the din of machinery noises in the background. He leaned over the railing on my bed as I began to shake off the effects of anesthesia and told me, "The tumor was benign as we had hoped. The operation was successful. There's no nerve damage. You'll recover quickly, and we are not expecting any residual effects."

My head felt as though I had been clubbed by a band of marauders, but I fought to stay awake and process what Steve was saying. I heard him through a cloud of fogginess, but even in my semi-somnambulant state I was deeply grateful and relieved. "You're fine, Lynnda," he repeated again. "Your recuperation will likely be very uneventful. You're fit and strong. Remember, I saw you climb thirteen hundred feet to the top of Masada in Israel."

I tried to summon a smile as I closed my eyes and nodded back to sleep, hoping that I would wake up miraculously pain free and full of energy. But as the anesthesia wore off, the next day was a bear. Day three was worse. When I left the hospital on day four, the last drain filled with blood and gunk was still taped to my neck. My long curly hair was pulled up loosely into a ponytail on the top of my head like Bam Bam from the Flintstones, so it wouldn't stick to the adhesive tape on my neck or get matted with dried blood.

I wasn't climbing Masada any time soon, but I progressed steadily. A week later, I fixed my hair, put on makeup, and dressed up in a chartreuse green, two-piece skirt and blazer to attend Yom Kippur services at our synagogue. It felt marvelous to be back in my spiritual home for the holiest day on the Jewish calendar, uplifted by the music and the liturgy and the compassion of the congregants, who greeted me warmly.

Putting my best face forward was a positive healing strategy, but truth be told, following services, where I had been rising and standing—and in heels mostly rising—according to the liturgy, I was thoroughly fatigued. Following services, I collapsed in my bed, dog-tired.

I still had another two weeks to recover before starting school, and even though I was improving exponentially, I couldn't jiggle away the lethargy. My concentration was hazy, like deep smog hovering around my head. How was I going to commute to New York every week, *schlepp* my books and clothes, attend hours of daily classes, remain alert and aware, and sit doing homework for even more hours six nights a week? In the midst of my fatigue, the doubting voices burrowed in. It seemed dubious that I would be able to bounce back sufficiently to become a rabbinical student in the fall, if ever.

— CHAPTER 24 —

School, Finally

"I'm in a New York State of Mind."

(Billy Joel)

IN THE FALL OF 1998, with President Bill Clinton in the White House and a feeling of prosperity in the country, New York was a boomtown, teeming with people who were flocking to the Big Apple from all over the world to pursue their dreams and enjoy the city. During that period, it was extremely tough to find a vacant hotel room for a reasonable price, and even the expensive ones were difficult to book. Since I now had to be at school three days a week, and it was necessary for Larry to be in New York for work, we commuted Mondays through Wednesdays and stayed overnight on sofabeds with friends. Occasionally, out of necessity, we paid an outrageous price for a hotel room with amenities we didn't have time to enjoy. We became the proverbial wandering Jews, and I elevated the term "bag lady" to new heights, wheeling my rolling suitcase with one arm and carrying two other bags filled with books and course materials over my shoulders—although lugging heavy items was forbidden three weeks post-surgery. It was likely too early for me to be putting such a burden on myself, but I was determined to give it a go.

We started to think that perhaps finding an apartment for the next five years would be both prudent financially and physically self-preserving. Besides the uncertainty of not knowing where we would be sleeping each week, or where I might be able to study and crash after classes, dragging my toiletries, clean clothes, and books around with me all the time was proving to be a big strain. Even on a good day, most rabbinical school students in tip-top shape walk around in a state of mental and physical exhaustion. Recently flat on the surgical table and fifty-years old, I was fried.

After several weeks of moving from place to place, we learned from our brother-in-law Fred—a lawyer representing a real estate management company—of a rental apartment that had just become vacant in one of the properties that the organization owned. It was a small one-bedroom in the theatre district that someone had lived in for thirty years before his death. Embedded in the glorious Adlon building built in 1912 on West 54th Street between Broadway and 7th Avenue, the apartment was rundown, but the management company promised a sterling renovation, a face-lift for a craggy aging diva.

It was immediately evident that to convert the apartment into a habitable home and a serene place to study after the renovations would require a Rosie-the-Riveter style of rolling up sleeves, a lot of elbow grease, and a can-do attitude on my part. But the bones of the place had a lot going for it despite its frailties, so I vowed to make it a pleasant space for the three days a week it was necessary for us to use it. In addition, I could easily walk to the train or bus to get to school. There was a Starbucks across the street, bookstores in the neighborhood, and all-night kiosks offering Advil and fruit salad for late-night study sessions. And most important, there were plenty of synagogues around, accessible by foot and other modes of transportation. It seemed as though God was handing us this apartment at the appointed time with the proviso: "You wanted to be in New York, now by choosing to serve Me, you have it! Live wisely!" We signed on the bottom line and the apartment became ours.

The renovations were completed in a matter of weeks, and when the few pieces of furniture that I'd ordered arrived, it truly felt like home—a very small and cramped home, albeit cute enough and functional. Upkeep would not bite into my study time. I brought only what I needed, which was just enough to eat, sleep, read, and write. Minimalism offered freedom to the max. It became an excellent place to create the third act of my life

I realized very quickly, however, that for all of my excitement to be in New York, sitting in my apartment hour after hour, I could have been in Hong Kong and not known the difference. Most of my waking hours—and those were longer than my scant sleeping ones—were spent with my head buried in books, unable to partake in much of the city's other enticements. I scurried from one task to the next, one book to the next, one paper to the next. I was in my own little shtetl of morning *minyanims*, prayer, text study, homework, sermon writing, and working as a student-rabbi in a pulpit. It was indeed "text and the city" around the clock. There was no time for rumination and reflection. No time to read the paper or stay in bed an extra hour with a cup of coffee and a muffin, even if Carnegie Deli delivered the items to my door. Most days I never got to do anything cultural. Being in New York was a tease except for Tuesday night, which became a bit of a delicious date night for us. And despite the competing influences and everyday challenges, I was recovering well from surgery, profoundly involved with my AJR community, and supremely happy with my nonroutine routine. Deliriously, deliciously, divinely happy!

◆◆◆

As Sami had explained when I first met him, each semester course was worth one point, and a half-semester course was worth a half-point toward a total of seventy needed to fulfill smicha requirements. Based on a timeframe of a full-time, five-year study formula, rabbinical students were required to take at least seven courses a semester in a variety of disciplines, and with the half-point structure, perhaps more. It was a hefty load, but for all the insane pressure at school, I galloped off to school daily like a racehorse.

It was a year of diaphanous firsts. I learned about *Kabbalah* (the mystical interpretation of the Bible) and mysticism, and I bolstered my budding practice of meditation, silence, and stillness. I delivered my first school D'var Torah in the context of a prayer seminar at school, serving up inspiration straight from the narrative of the Hebrew Bible. The double Torah portion for that week was *Vayekel/ Pikudei,* which recounts the story of the Israelites building the Mishkan that followed them though the desert. The account motivated me to construct a mini-homily about women's contributions to building the Jewish community going forward. The value of womens' stories, the ones that were known as well as the less familiar ones, which continued to resonate as I began thinking about structuring my own rabbinate.

Joyce, the woman I had met at the retreat, and I continued to be secured as bffs. To have a sympatica to moon around with was one of the best finds of my early school days. Another woman of a certain age like Joyce and me, Tsurah, a former dancer, joined us as a triumvirate in our study sessions. Our little group regularly exchanged ideas and acted as sounding boards for one another when difficulties arose.

Together, a colleague and I created and led our first *Shacharit* (morning) service in front of our fellow students, teachers, and administrators using the Passover theme of redemption as a leitmotif. Despite my pre-performance jitters, our presentation turned out to be quite respectable, which prompted me to think that maybe, just maybe, I could develop into a competent prayer leader, a necessary skill beyond sermon writing.

Every day was a journey, each moment brought something new to assimilate. With so much to do and such a steep learning curve, there was always a certain amount of stress and strain. But I remained joyous. I hung out with the student cantors as much as possible. I found the music uplifting and a good mnemonic device for remembering material. "If I died today, God forbid . . . if I died today," I chirped to my family and friends, whenever they asked how I was managing the intensity and struggle of rabbinical school, "I would die a happy woman doing what I loved."

◆◆◆

By year two, my course offerings were an eclectic mix of subjects ranging from Biblical Narrative to Life Cycles (weddings, funerals, baby namings, and unveilings), Ritual Skills (putting on tefillin, leading prayer or funeral services, wedding ceremonies, knowing the various tropes or melodies for Torah readings), Conversion, Counseling II, Intermediate Talmud, *Parashat HaShavuah* (an analysis of the Torah portion of the week), Personal Theology, Bar/Bat Mitzvah, Liturgy, and Storytelling thrown in for good measure. We were required to take singing lessons to learn how to breathe and project properly, and we were offered many courses in crisis management. Trained to be generalists, we were taught to use every possible skill or source, sacred and secular, to engage and uplift an audience or congregation. As we students gained in knowledge and vocabulary, our courses were presented in even greater depth, building on skills we were perfecting a little at a time. AJR was adamant that they did not want us spewing back what was taught verbatim, and they guided us to find our own voices and gleanings. It was both a demanding and stimulating process to absorb all the material and to personalize the teachings.

We were the newly evolving tadpoles striving to swim well in unfamiliar waters while we mastered many specific rabbinic proficiencies like *homiletics* (delivering sermons) or Music for Rabbis, and then demonstrating our adeptness at the ritual skills. Writing was the easiest piece for me; demonstrating was horrifying. These terrifying mini-performances were graded with discerning comments, gentle but exacting, intended "for growth."

It happened one step at a time as more and more famous teachers, specialists in their fields, were hired for a semester or two, and they came with lofty expectations. Rabbi Meir Fund, an Orthodox rabbi, and Rabbi Neil Gilman, a Conservative rabbi, both noted authors of many scholarly books, would sit at the round tables dispensing wisdom like the enlightened ones, and we basked in their brightness. These classes were comported mostly as lectures, and we the students asked questions or commented sparingly only at the end so as not to waste one minute of hearing the great ones speak.

For most of the text courses, particularly Talmud, we studied in *Chevruta*. Chevruta learning is a rabbinic methodology where a pair of students engages in a close examination of a particular piece of text, which is dissected, parsed, and debated. Derived from the Aramaic word for "friendship," or "companionship," chevruta was the unique process utilized by the ancient rabbis of Jerusalem or Babylon in the famous Academies of Sura and Pembedita, in keeping with the *Sayings of Our Fathers,* "*Get yourself a teacher and find yourself a friend*" (*Avot 1:16*).

Chevruta partners, like Joyce and me, sat face-to-face in a roomful of pairs modeled by those early Jewish sages, and the conversation would transverse into hundreds of directions as every word, letter, and marking within a letter was dissected to find meaning in the passage. Like other religions, the overarching questions sought in those discussions were always: What does God want of us? How can we live the best, the holiest, most ethical life possible?

One of our teachers, considered a master, generally supervised the discourse. He or she walked around the room to add insights or share famous rabbinic commentaries, which generally enhanced our academic and spiritual explications. Sometimes no conclusion at all was established, the process itself being the endgame. In the holy space of a seminary, questions raised begot other questions. The totality of the experience inspired critical thinking and creativity so that when we were ordained and out on our own, we would have confidence to think both inside and out of the box.

Our seminary was also a place of personal conciousness-raising and self-centering, which refined our daily way of interacting in the world. Every session was intended to be personally transformative for us as leaders who aspired to cultivate sacred communities of empathy through love and forgiveness in the chain of transmission.

Someone once asked me if rabbinical students sit around a seminary and criticize other religions. Quite the contrary. We were taught to develop tolerance and respect for diversity. Our sessions were framed within a Jewish context, but the "seeking" questions were universal. How does God work through our lives for good? For me, *tzedakah* (righteous charity), honoring rituals, using respectful speech, limiting gossip, praying with intention, developing an internal culture of gratitude, and choosing the path of blessing and forgiveness became the internal imperative to my personal development and ultimate transformation.

Many of my friends outside of the institution were baffled by my all-consuming focus. "How can you spend so many hours a day grappling with such minutia?" one asked, mystified that someone with my energy level would sit so long while pondering the ineffable. I simply loved it. The rabbinic quest helped to clarify my path and purpose in the world. My colleagues and I who sat around the seminary table "got" each other. The power and potential for revelation was wildly difficult to explain to people who were not in the room, and still is. But it called to me then, and it continues to call to me now.

According to the rabbis in the Talmud, "*One who visits the sick takes away 1/60th of his or her pain*" (*Bava Metzia 30b*). The *mitzvah* of *bikkur holim*, visiting the sick, is considered an act of *lovingkindness* highly valued among the commandments of Judaism, and preparedness for pastoral care is one of the most vital areas of discipline that rabbis, cantors, and counselors must develop.

In our second year of school, after only a couple of assigned books to read and a few scantily supervised introductory sessions, our ten-hour-a-week's worth of service as student-pastors at Memorial Sloan-Kettering Cancer Center (MSK) began. It was inculcated to me that pastoral service was a critical piece of the rabbinate, but initiating the work as a novice in a cancer center made me nervous. The last time I had visited someone with cancer in a hospital it was my mother, and she had died. Stepping one foot over the threshold of MSK brought back a slew of stinging memories: the sounds of beeping machinery, the smell of medicine, the prevailing sadness, and the palpable encroachment of suffering and death. Seeing desperately sick children and young people made it even worse.

The first person on my visiting list was a man in his early forties who had been diagnosed with inoperable brain cancer. When I walked into his room, he smiled the smile of a soul at peace. "I'm ready to take the next part of my journey," he announced with quiet acceptance before I'd said anything beyond, "How are you feeling today?"

"What do you mean, Brian?" I asked timidly, wondering how best to engage him. Was he talking about his own imminent death? Should I flat out ask him if he was prepared to die? We were taught to take our cues from the patients. He seemed fairly clear-minded. When my mother was dying, I remember that we had all lied to each other and missed the opportunity to be real and in the moment, to acknowledge fate together, and help each other as the illness unfolded. I took the plunge into the deepest tunnel of darkness to attempt to find the light according to Brian's needs.

"What do you see as the next part of your journey?" I asked.

"It's obvious, I'm dying, isn't it?" he answered by posing a question.

"You're dying?" I inquired with trepidation. This wasn't an earth-shattering question since hospice was solidly involved in Brian's case, and he had already invited me into the finale of life conversation. Brian's aunt was sitting nearby in a chair at the foot of his bed, and when the dialogue began between Brian and me, she bolted from the room precipitously, her mouth covered with a silk scarf pulled up from around her neck. I stayed focused on Brian.

"Yes, I'm ready," he responded, his face awash in serenity. "I'm not afraid."

We talked for a little while, and I asked the question student pastors had been taught to pose before we left a patient's room: "What would you like to pray for today?" We also had been instructed to inquire about a patient's immediate desire: a good day, less pain, to be surrounded by love and healing. Other times they might cry and couldn't answer. We were warned that once in a while a patient might even wave us away unengaged. Brian wanted me to pray for a "good journey."

"Dear God," I prayed, holding Brian's hand. *"Brian has been sick for a long time and is suffering. Today he would like me to ask you for a 'good journey.' May it be your Will, God, that you grant Brian's wish. Thank you, God, for listening and for the power and peace of this moment. Amen."*

Brian smiled and thanked me for my tenderness. "I hope to see you again soon," I said as I turned to leave.

"Maybe, maybe not," he responded.

"Ken Y'hi ratzon. May it be God's Will," I said as I closed the door behind me, rattled, and praying again that I had offered Brian a moment of peace.

◆◆◆

As soon as I walked out into the corridor, Brian's aunt greeted me with hate-filled eyes. "We are trying hard to keep his spirits up, and you come in here and talk about dying. How dare you!" she screamed. "Who gave you the authority to do that?" She had already reported me to the front desk at the nurses' station. My supervisor was on her way up.

"It was his wish to talk about dying," I said calmly. "Believe me, it was not a conversation I wanted to initiate. Brian knows he's dying and needs support in the process. As clergy, I had to meet him on his path. I'm so very sorry for everyone's pain."

The aunt shrugged me away as I tried to put my hand on her shoulder.

Oh, God, I thought. Maybe I had done the wrong thing? Did I have a right to be so blunt with this poor, lovely terminal patient? Would it have been better or worse for me to ask Brian's aunt to leave the room while we talked? With virtually no experience, how was I to be sure that I had behaved appropriately?

My supervisor talked to Brian's aunt, and then took me aside to confirm that I had acted properly in the situation. She looked me squarely in the eye and said, "People need to express themselves in the finite moments." Nevertheless, I angsted about this episode endlessly and often wondered about my comportment. For years and years, I worried that I might have hurt Brian instead of helping him.

I saw Brian a few more times and met other members of his family. They were all pretty resigned to the inevitable. No one ever mentioned what had happened on that first day. Then soon after, when I arrived to do my rounds, I was told that he had passed away peacefully, surrounded by loved ones.

Years later, a famous Israeli singer came to our synagogue to perform a concert. Following the show, I went to a table managed by the singer's wife, who was selling her husband's CDs. She seemed vaguely familiar and looked up at me with recognition on her face.

"Are you a rabbi?" she asked.

"I am," I said, still trying to place her. I'm not spectacular with names, but faces I rarely forget. "How did you know?"

She looked at me again more intently and the tears welled up in her eyes. "I remember you clearly now," she said, this time with certainty. "You were the chaplain that was extremely kind to my brother Brian as he lay dying at Sloan Kettering. He talked about you and said how much you had diminished his suffering when he was about to die."

"You're Brian's sister, of course! So good to see you. I think about Brian a lot. He was a beautiful soul—so brave." We embraced each other.

Later, I reflected that, after what felt like an eternity of doubting my pastoral skills, I had received validation from Brian's family that I had been suitably present for a dear, sweet man, too young to die, who had lost a fierce battle with a malignant brain tumor. I hadn't added to his anguish as I had often imagined with sorrow. I had, in fact, eased his misery because we had been honest and forthright with each other in the murky territory.

It made me recognize how much I had evolved since the time of my mother's illness, and how much truthfulness, apt in its time, can serve the greatest good. I was growing as a spiritual being. Even past age fifty, my rabbinic training—less than half complete—was infusing me with invaluable life lessons, which would help me in serving others. But, boy, was there a long way to go.

— CHAPTER 25 —

The Making of a Rabbi

*"Every soul needs to express itself. Every heart
needs to crack itself open."*

(Rabbi Alan Lew)

THOUGH IT HAD NEVER BEEN MY GOAL to be a pulpit
rabbi, rabbinical school includes training to be one. In
the summer of 2000, after I'd finished my second year at AJR,
I was jogging on the footpath of a park down the hill from my
home in suburban Philadelphia, when I encountered a woman
I'd seen walking previously on many mornings. Our strides
met each other, and we started schmoozing. Soon into the
conversation, after I introduced myself as a rabbinical student,
her antennae shot up. "Wow, we could use someone like you at
our synagogue for the High Holidays."

What could she mean? Her name was Rina, and she was
the wife of the former president of a vibrant Reform suburban
synagogue, one of the most renowned in the area, led by a beloved
South African, Rabbi Robert Leib. I knew him peripherally from
his well-respected work in the community. And from what I had

remembered, his endearing rabbinic persona was only enhanced by his gorgeous South African cadence.

"Our associate rabbi, a woman, is ill, and just retired," she told me. "People will miss her at the holidays."

Now my antennae shot up. Working as a pulpit rabbi on the High Holidays was a school requirement, but not until year four or five. It was a little early for me to be tackling the job with my nascent rabbinic skill set. But opportunity was opportunity. It was a conversation worth pursuing.

"How do you know they're looking for someone?" I asked, my pulse jumping. And why might they want me? I wondered to myself. I'm a second-year rabbinical student with no pulpit experience, and I belong to a Conservative synagogue.

"I'm going to tell them about you," she answered. "We could use a fresh face this season."

At age fifty-two, I hardly felt fresh-faced, but nabbing a High Holiday student-pulpit opportunity at Old York Road Temple Beth Am would be an amazing coup.

I became proactive and called some friends of ours, congregants at the synagogue, who maintained an intimate relationship with the powerful executive director who was always in the loop and a part of important decision making. "Is it true that the associate rabbi is gone and they're looking for someone to replace her at the High Holidays?" I asked my friend Maddy, half hopeful, half terrified.

"Could be," she said. "I'll do some investigating."

A couple of weeks later, without advance warning or any background information about their conversation, Maddy summoned me to her New Jersey shore house, which was close to ours, to meet the executive director who was leaving to return to the city shortly. I was right in the middle of a run on the Atlantic City Boardwalk, but I hightailed it to her house in a few minutes. There in rumpled, sweaty running clothes, my hair pulled into a ponytail with renegade wisps streaming down my flushed cheeks and behind my ears, the executive director of Old York Road Temple Beth Am confirmed me as a "fresh face."

The next day, I was asked to meet with the current president and the president-elect of the synagogue. A day later, Rabbi Leib proclaimed, "My dear Lynnda, we at Old York Road Temple Beth Am would be honored to have you on our bima for the High Holidays." One day after that, I signed a contract.

Poof! In less than a snap I became the rabbi *sheni*, the second rabbi, who would share the High Holiday pulpit with the esteemed Rabbi Leib, Rabbi Harold Waintrup, the Rabbi Emeritus, and the beautiful and talented Russian/American Cantor Elena Zarkh, whose enchanting voice soared to angelic heights. It was astounding good fortune to have landed a job in a prestigious synagogue that boasted some 1,800 congregants with wonderful clergy. I had no time to rest on my laurels.

Midsummer is very late to be hired as a rabbi for the High Holidays that would surge in just weeks. Many rabbis spend months thinking about and drafting the sermons they'll deliver at the holiest and most well-attended services of the Jewish calendar year. For me, the dawdling rhythm of summer quickly morphed into rabbinic madness.

My days were filled with preparations of all kinds: sermon writing, learning the liturgy, securing a white rabbinic robe, buying comfortable shoes for the long hours of standing on my feet, and attending meetings with Rabbi Leib and the other clergy members to rehearse and set our intention as team members. I learned how important it is that congregational clergy work together on the pulpit and maintain an interconnected chemistry to transfer to the congregants at arguably the most sacred time of the Jewish year.

◆◆◆

On September 29, the secular date of my mother's death and the night before Rosh Hashanah—also known as *erev Rosh Hashanah* when the holiday comes in at sundown—I was slated to deliver the High Holiday opening sermon. What a way to be plunged into congregational service, I thought, comtemplating the meaning of wisdom and renewal while personally reframing a heartbreaking anniversary.

I looked to the insights of an early mentor, my congregational rabbi, Sidney Greenberg, for writing my first High Holiday sermon as a student-rabbi. "When you develop your talk, put one eye on the traditional Jewish sources and another on pop culture," he advised me. "Make your sermons current and relevant to the times, but always look at our treasure trove of Jewish wisdom for thematic inspiration."

I wasn't rich on rabbinic experience, but I was chronologically mature and experienced in life. I had suffered abandonments, lived in both poverty and financial plenty, survived exploitation, sustained losses of loved ones, suffered miscarriages and delivered premature babies who spent weeks in NICUs, borne rejections, moved from city to city to city, endured several minor operations, battled a rare tumor, negotiated friendships and relationships, raised two children, returned to school in midlife, and maintained a long marriage. I had been to the far corners of the earth, developing my humanity and by this time was reasonably well read in the Jewish texts, having studied with a coterie of brilliant teachers, both religious and secular. I still had a lot to learn, but I had intuition about many of the ways of the world, or so I hoped. Delivering an inspiring High Holiday sermon to a packed congregation at Old York Road Temple Beth Am would be my maiden voyage. I prayed that I wouldn't sink like the Titanic.

I'd always objected to hell, fire, and brimstone homilies, which are as toxic as secondhand smoke. My goal was to be a facilitator who guided people toward reflection and spiritual elevation as they left the sanctuary at the beginning of the New Year. I had no desire to send them on a guilt trip. We all know what we've done wrong; we want to be forgiven our trespasses and start anew with God's blessings. The human experience in many of its guises embodies most of life's universal themes. Amen.

As a unit, the ten days between Rosh Hashanah and Yom Kippur are viewed optimistically as a spiritual journey punctuated by threshold moments. It is a temporal time when Jews starting a New Year cycle are at their most vulnerable, and the liturgy informs us that a person's fate for the following year is determined during this period of liminality. *"On Rosh Hashanah it is written and on Yom Kippur it is sealed. Who shall live and who shall die?..."*

My grandmother used to tell me that each person carries with them a little *peckle,* a symbolic bag, like the bags they brought over from the Old Country. No matter how charmed a life appears, the peckle contains disappointments, woes, challenges, and burdens. Even as a rabbinical student I was astute enough to understand that each and every congregant enters the sanctuary with his or her peckle of stuff.

Some people limp in lifelessly, having just lost loved ones, others are facing debilitating illness; some people's children have not lived up to their parental expectations; some have aging parents requiring exhausting, time-consuming care, and may be struggling with financial instability. Particularly at the New Year, which is a solemn time of reflection and questing for spiritual resucitation, the contents of the peckle come into focus for worshippers. A significant segment of the population doesn't feel they have a great reason to ring in the New Year. In synagogue they mix with the lucky ones, steeped in gratitude for having danced through a season of good fortune.

As clergy we are challenged to address the diverse needs of the community, striking a balance between what is read in the fixed liturgical pages, the *kevah*, and what is offered as *kavanah*, a set intention. Serving as a prayer leader demands textured choreography between prayers of expression and prayers of empathy, while encompassing the universal themes of the holiday. Much is expected of the clergy in shepherding the group through the various passages on this journey, especially during the High Holidays when synagogue attendance peaks. I always felt that our job was to uplift, restore faith, and offer hope for the coming times ahead. Proffering a dystopian reflection or disappointing the flock wouldn't be fruitful. And, the expectation that clergy would inspire listeners to take action invited a lot of tangential pressure.

My sermon was about reality shows, which at that time didn't dominate the airwaves as inescapably as they do now. They were beginning to creep into the mainstream, and in my opinion, were creepy. By posing a series of pertinent questions, my talk was intended to engender thoughtful timely introspection. "What do we want the reality of our lives to be? How do we recreate ourselves after tragedy, trauma, and loss? What will we leave behind in the old year, and what will we bring with us into the realm of the new? What in our peckles can we dump out into the dumpster and what can we salvage or recycle? How do we secure meaning, purpose, and joy in the ho-hum?"

I looked out at the crowd of about eight hundred, and no one was sleeping. Everyone was quiet and seemingly attentive. I could feel the mood of the congregants with me, taking it all in, thinking. It was heady and powerful. I made my closing statement and ended with a simple poem I'd written for the occasion. "Judaism, particularly at this time, enjoins us to understand the ordinary as extraordinary, the unremarkable as memorable, the mundane as miraculous. All of it is bound up together for good and bad. We have choices to make.

> *"Look into your hearts and observe what you see.*
> *A precious creature of God, that's you, that's me.*
> *We've all made mistakes, that's human frailty.*
> *But this is the time to change destiny.*
> *Count your blessings; say you're sorry where you must.*
> *Forgiveness is the basis of relationship and trust.*
> *Know that you're being watched by a Presence above.*
> *And may you live the next year in the sweetness of honey*
>   *and love."*

When it was over, I was proud of myself, confident that I had hit a revelatory nerve. I didn't feel like an imposter playing a role. What I gave from my heart was authentically me. The hearty applause was intoxicating. It was a great beginning to the spiritual quest of the High Holiday season, and I garnered high-fives, thumbs-up, and kisses blown through the air to my "fresh face" from people even at the rear of the chapel who were watching on wide-screen monitors.

My father made a surprise cameo appearance, and from my vantage point it was easy to discern that his heart muscles were undulating with pride, a far-flung image from the one his wife had once perpetrated—i.e., that he had a bad heart, and I would put him in a pine box prematurely with my cries for attention. Beth and Larry were also there and applauded as wildly as if I had just delivered an acceptance speech for the Nobel Peace Prize in Oslo.

It had been a yeoman's job to get to this moment, but it turned out to also be a sacred and holy experience, more personally gratifying and meaningful than anything else I'd ever done professionally. Our tradition teaches, *"To save one soul is to save the universe"* (*Talmud Sanhedrin 37a*). To lift someone up, to shine a light in darkness, to inspire, to make a difference in the life of an individual or a community, and to be a moral agent enacting social change are chief among the highest Judaic values as a spiritual leader, a *kli kodesh*, a holy vessel. There are no words, no medals, no awards, and no amount of applause that could ever be concomitant with the satisfaction I felt.

When traditional Jews enter the synagogue on a typical day for services, and the threshold between the private and the public is traversed, a verse is recited from the Bible: *"How goodly are your tents"* (*Numbers 24:5*). It's a vision of being blessed by God in an atmosphere of Divine space. I was standing in the midst of it.

After my student pulpit High Holiday internship ended, Rabbi Leib, with his cheery disposition called to check in regularly. "My dear Lynnda . . . We here at Old York Road Temple Beth Am miss your presence. There isn't a day that goes by that someone doesn't stop me in the halls and says, 'Is that pretty rabbi who gave that wonderful sermon coming back?'"

Hmmm.

I suppose I had been successful in presenting a "smart, serious, fresh face," the "image" of a rabbi, after all, pretty or not. And the High Holiday synagogue experience, which had also been such an uplifting personal spiritual endeavor, made me wonder long and hard about rethinking the pulpit rabbi option.

— CHAPTER 26 —

Busy and Blessed

"Listen and be attentive, do not be haughty."

(Jeremiah 12:15)

After the high of the High Holidays, Rosh Hashanah and Yom Kippur dissolved into a simmering whoosh and I reentered my school community for the third year in time for the holiday of *Sukkot*, which follows four days after Yom Kippur. Originally framed as a harvest holiday, Sukkot is designated as *The Feast of Tabernacles* or *Ha Chag*, THE holiday, which stands in joy as a stark contrast to the fasting and breast-beating of the *Days of Awe* that had just passed. During the existence of the Temple in Jerusalem until the year 70 CE, it was one of three festivals besides Passover and Shavuot on which the Israelites were commanded to perform a pilgrimage.

An intersection between Divine time and space, according to the Bible, Sukkot commands Jews to live in "booths" for eight days, enjoying the camaraderie of friends and invited guests, both real and spiritual. *"All Jews are responsible for one another,"* is a major theme pertaining to Sukkot. It is my favorite of all of the holidays in the Jewish calendar year.

At school, students and faculty alike could always count on Reb Shohama to start the school year off with a spiritual lilt, nourishing us after the marathon of the New Year experience. On the first day of classes, teaming up with Cantor Ken Cohen, the head of the Cantorial school at that time, she created our first early morning service for the community. Vintage Shohama, it was orchestrated to establish a meaningful kavanah for the new academic year: *Klal Yisrael*, inclusivity, Jewish pluralism, the gestalt of our school.

Cantor Ken was traditional but open to liturgical experimentation, which was one of Reb Shohama's strengths. Together they coordinated the flow of davenning, modeling the mantle of prayer leaders, teaching us how to watch the clock and take the pulse of the congregants simultaneously, and weave together various aspects of a stimulating service—uplifting music, choices in the prayer book, a snippet of wisdom, and measured silence for thoughtful contemplation.

At the end of our session, Shohama sent us off to our studies with an objective: "This year, be aware of the God moments in your lives. Meditate. Sit in silence. Stay centered. Be mindful. Record your Divine encounters and stay present. Breathe peacefully."

Of course, once classes resumed there was barely time to breathe, much less peacefully. In addition to the work associated with the frenzy of taking seven courses, I was also chosen, along with Joyce, for a prestigious fellowship as an intern for The Center for Leadership and Learning (CLAL), a pluralistic organization originally founded by Rabbi Yitz Greenberg, and Holocaust survivor and author Elie Weisel to invite interdenominational conversation. It was a really impressive honor for me, but while it offered a generous stipend, it also came with time-consuming assignments and lots of responsibility. Further, as a third-year rabbinical student, I was also primed to work ten hours a week in a field service placement for the duration of the year. As I considered my unfolding schedule, I wondered where I would find the quiet "God moments" Shohama suggested.

◆◆◆

At the behest of my old friend Cyd Weissman, who at that time was the director of education at Beth Am Israel, a wonderful Conservative-affiliated synagogue set in the woods of suburban Main Line Philadelphia, I jumped into a student-internship with my trustworthy friend and early rabbinic mentor, Reconstructionist Rabbi Marc Margolius, whom I was to shadow for Torah study and life cycle events. A relaxed, informal Shabbat-centered synagogue with a quiet, casual rabbi—who was also a thoughtful former civil rights attorney—was ideal, and I was thrilled with the placement. For each Shabbat, under Rabbi Marc's supervision, I prepared a short lesson and led a section of the morning service.

I'd always imagined that when people decide to become rabbis, God hands them a special present—the gift of remembering names. However, I must not have been in line that day, because I am simply horrible at names, a shared trait in our family gene pool. It's a terrible disadvantage for a rabbi, and it causes me endless worry that people don't feel valued or important if I bungle their names. I never forget a face—but names. Oy! It's an embarrassment, and it has gotten worse with age.

The first morning I led a service at Beth Am Israel, I forgot the Bat Mitzvah girl's last name, and stumbled all over myself trying to retrieve it. For some unknown reason it hadn't been in my notes, and writing in a Conservative synagogue on Shabbat is forbidden. Finally, the Blumenthal family corrected me from their seats as I blathered on, growing redder and redder in the face.

Later I cried to Mark, "What is wrong with me? What a nightmare! I diminished the family in front of everyone at their *simcha*. I feel like I failed them AND myself."

"Lynnda, don't be so hard on yourself," he reassured me. "You're a rabbinical student doing ten thousand things at a time. . . . You'll get it."

"But the family . . ." I pressed on. "It's such a noble responsibility to hold them spiritually in our hands. I didn't want to disappoint them in any way. I wanted everything to be perfect."

"Forget perfection. Just try to be a little more self-forgiving, more *zen*. Relax a bit," he counseled. "Beth Am Israel is a very nurturing place. Everyone here wants you to succeed. We all know that rabbis are human, too."

The congregants, many of whom were liturgically more knowledgeable than me, were indeed kind, tolerant, and eager for me to have a safe place to learn and grow. They gave me permission to work through my performance anxiety, find my voice, and forgive myself when in future services I stumbled on the Hebrew, lost my place in the prayer book, or forgot to turn to the *Psalm of the Day*. And because they were so generous and forgiving and I didn't want to disappoint anyone, I practiced over and over again to get it right. And I did—mostly. Whatever Shabbat liturgical skills I now possess, I owe to my year at Beth Am Israel, and the kindness of the congregation.

◆◆◆

Meanwhile at school, the day-to-day cycle of classes and homework was predictably tedious, and there was a normalcy to business as usual. Shohama and Sami and the supporting staff did a brilliant job of nourishing us to become competent rabbis and cantors in the Jewish community and the community at large. Then midyear, in February 2001, trouble began brewing at school. AJR had been becoming increasingly popular, and more and more students were being accepted. As a result, the administrative load was overwhelming.

The economic reality is that it costs money to run an institution, lots of it, and there were bills to be paid. A well-known Jewish teaching says: *"Without wheat there is no Torah"* (*Avot 3:17*). The stockpile of wheat seemed to be diminishing quickly. As a school unsupported by denominational funding and not academically accredited, it was almost exclusively dependent on private donations. Whereas many schools counted heavily on affiliated synagogue denomination dues, well-endowed endowments, and alumni giving back to the coffers, AJR's alums, in general, were generous, but not people harboring deep pockets.

With a few noted exceptions, rabbis—many of whom staffed the school at that time—do not universally count business acumen among their greatest strengths, nor are they extremely savvy about building boards of directors, facilitating stewardship for fundraising, handling public relations, and marketing and promoting outreach to new students. The budget at AJR was so tight it didn't allow funding to hire additional professionals who could do these jobs either. The entire staff was constantly in multi-tasking mode, pushed to their limits. Shohama was teaching, running the school with Sami, and also doing the taxing job of fundraising.

With too much on the administrators' plates, important tasks began falling through the cracks, and still little money emerged to hire helpers. The usually upbeat climate at the school began to plummet. The economic pressure was penetrating. Lots of complaining brought tension to the previously tranquil corridors, and students were divided about what was to be done. Petitions to change the administration started swirling, and a few letters were sent to the board.

With lightning-like velocity, our beloved President Shohama and Dean Sami were gone, overrun by their own success. It was a mystery to us exactly what had transpired behind the scenes. Afterwards, two presidents were put into place, one after the other, without long-term prospects, and finally one of our beloved teachers, JTS scholar Dr. Ora Horn Prouser, stepped up to organize and handle the administrative details and keep the school functioning and solvent.

These ongoing changes continued to polarize the otherwise cohesive community. Sadness filled the air. The touchy-feely atmosphere of our seminary seemed to dissipate precipitously without Shohama's warm presence, and the *raison d'être* of the school became increasingly more text-based, and for many pupils it felt denominationally Conservative-leaning. On balance the academic and administrative changes were positive, Dr. Prouser was stellar, but the new climate in the school seemed challenging for a constituency of the students who thought they'd signed a different spiritual contract.

Initially we walked around shell-shocked, unable to adapt quickly to the school's transformation. The upheavals left hurt feelings and scars like a pox. Shohama's calls for God-moments seemed to vanish and were hidden like forgotten treasures in an attic. For a time, the students even wondered if the school might close and if our *smicha* was in jeopardy. Eventually, Dr. Prouser stabilized the school, and in hindsight the reorganization made our authentically pluralistic students textually and academically better-qualified rabbis in the marketplace. Dr. Prouser remained the adored, solid guiding light and spirit of the school and later became the CEO and Academic Dean. Shohama made cameo appearances, continuing her role as *Maschgiach Ruchani*, the school's coveted spiritual advisor, which she had assumed while she was president. After a short separation, she was invited to teach meditation and her specialty classes again. When she returned she brought her unique light back to the campus. But those days of internal institutional uncertainty took their toll. And there was a lot to learn about the process of transition and transformation.

— CHAPTER 27 —

Year Four

"Just to be is a blessing, just to live is holy."

(Rabbi Abraham Joshua Heschel)

O<small>N THE FIRST DAY</small> of my fourth year of school I was in
an uncharacteristically miserable mood, which no matter
what I did to try to shake, stuck to me like tar on the sole of a
shoe. In prior years I had leapt like a gazelle at the potential of a
new semester—filled with excitement to return to my un-routine
routine at school, to my soul-seeking fellow students, and to the
brilliant, colorful cast of scholars and teachers who had guided us
through the beloved ancient texts of our Jewish people.

However, the beginning of this year seemed different from
the outset. For starters, I was more exhausted than ever. Sleep
deprivation, the universal adversary of rabbinical students
everywhere, perpetually loomed large. Stimulation, academic
growth, and spiritual fulfillment aside, the mounting pressures
of the last three years of school combined with the increasingly
difficult demands of balancing school, work, and family life
were beginning to wear thin. This semester also presented an
additional commuting hurdle.

The SAJ building reclaimed its afternoon rented classroom space back, and AJR, growing in demand and popularity, was forced to move its headquarters. Over the summer, the campus had shifted from the Upper West Side of Manhattan opposite Central Park, which had been a comfortable walking distance from our midtown apartment, to rented space with its own wing on the campus of the College of Mount Saint Vincent, a private Catholic liberal arts college in Riverdale, New York, some forty-five minutes away from Manhattan by car, depending on the traffic angels.

Public transportation to AJR would now involve a one-and-a-half-hour commute on the subway from midtown Manhattan, followed by a hefty five-block walk. The thought of lugging armfuls of heavily bound Bibles and Talmudic volumes to Riverdale was already weighing me down both physically and psychologically, and promised to be even more challenging in inclement weather. I wasted lots of energy fretting over why the administration had not found space in Manhattan to fulfill its needs, which I felt would be a better option for everyone in the long run. But financially, space in Manhattan was not feasible.

On top of these issues, Joyce, my fantastic chevruta partner, had left for a year of learning in Israel with her newly retired husband. At the time, terrorist bombs were detonating frequently, turning public spaces in Israel into war zones, killing innocent civilians in their bloody path. Besides missing the prospect of my confidante and confidence-inspiring buddy for two pivotal semesters, I was also worried about my friend's safety, and I questioned her and her husband's judgment for choosing to be in Israel during this new spate of gratuitous violence—even though a big part of me secretly yearned to be studying there with her.

Over the summer, I had considered making this year at AJR my last. With credits I had earned from my two master's degrees, it was conceivable that I could acquire my rabbinic degree within the year, but it would require Herculean efforts. If I took nine courses instead of the usual seven, worked the yearly required ten hours per week as a student rabbi at a synagogue—which, like my duties the year before at Beth Am Israel, would involve sermon preparation as well as teaching classes—took a series of seven challenging comprehensive exams, and wrote a book-length senior thesis, it was theoretically doable. But working even harder than usual seemed beyond the realm of possibility. Ultimately, I decided that given the new rigorous commute, I needed the additional year to stay healthy.

◆◆◆

Day one of the new semester was carefully orchestrated to cope with the new commuting challenges. I boarded the express train from Trenton to New York and sat down in a seat with room enough for my wheelie, stuffed with weighty textbooks too heavy for me to put in the overhead compartment. Taking this particular train would leave me plenty of time to disembark in Manhattan and make my way to the Lincoln Center area to meet up with my friend Sara, a cantorial student who had promised to drive me to the new campus so I could avoid the subway. Ten minutes into the ride the train jerked, lurched forward, and came to a screeching halt. The lights went out and the air-conditioning stopped. My fellow commuter neighbors groaned and looked at their watches, as did I. What was happening?

For several minutes there was great confusion in the cars as people tried to get information. Finally, the conductor's voice came over the loudspeaker with the requisite announcement: "Due to unanticipated issues beyond our control, the train's equipment has to be evaluated and serviced. We hope this won't take very long, and we apologize for any inconvenience."

I prayed, *"God grant me the serenity to accept the things I can not change,"* as I wiped the sweat off my brow that was fast dripping down my flushed cheeks. We were in the midst of an end-of-summer summer-like day and the car became stifling. Twenty minutes passed. No news. The commuters were getting restless. The window of opportunity that I had to meet up with my friend and secure a ride to the new campus was rapidly closing.

Finally, after an hour the lights went back on and the air-conditioning began humming. The conductor's voice came over the loudspeaker again: "Well, folks, as you can see, we're making progress here, and we should be on our way momentarily." No sooner had he finished his little *spiel* when the lights went out again. Now what? People were pacing up and down the aisles, hot and really bothered. It was not a serene scene.

In the end, the train was one and a half hours late when it pulled into Penn Station. Sara called on my cell and told me apologetically that she had waited as long as she could and would have to leave without me or be late for her first class. Not an auspicious beginning.

And the situation went from bad to worse. As I started walking toward my apartment, the wheel broke on my suitcase that was filled with books. I tried to drag it along for a block or two, but the metal screeched like nails on a chalkboard. I picked up the suitcase and tried to balance it on my two outstretched arms. The taxis I hailed whizzed by without noticing me, and I continued to walk, struggling to carry the many pounds of books.

All of a sudden it started to rain. Not just a little drizzle, but a veritable monsoon, steady and relentless. I was drenched to the bone, my clothes clinging to me as though I was participating in a wet t-shirt contest. I became a comedic caricature in my own out-of-control day, arriving at my apartment exhausted and limp as a noodle.

My first impulse was to lie on the sofa and watch mindless TV all day, but that really wasn't a viable choice. As I was drying my hair a thought came to me. Josh!

Josh was a fellow student, a free spirit and confirmed night owl. He always scheduled late classes, regularly bouncing into AJR's halls at his own appointed time. Perhaps he would be driving to the new campus soon? Sure enough, Josh was still home and willing to pick me up near the West Side Highway on his way to Riverdale. Success!

I always enjoyed Josh's company. He was spontaneous, upbeat, and fun, an heir to a long line of rabbis going back many generations on both sides, and he was an accomplished musician. Like his maternal grandfather who had written the well-known Shabbat song, *"Shalom Alecheim,"* which welcomes the Sabbath angels to the weekly holiday of peace and rest, Josh wrote many of his own tunes, both secular and liturgical. In Josh's company there was always a lot of singing, and it was hard not to be happy.

I stepped into his car on 10th Avenue near the West Side Highway, thanking him profusely, then immediately recounted my miserable morning.

"Thank you, Josh, thank you," I began. "What would I have done without you? The train was stuck on the tracks for more than an hour with no light or air-conditioning in this heat," I *kvetched*. "I missed a ride to Riverdale with Sara and then got caught in the pouring rain and had to carry a heavy suitcase filled with books all the way to my apartment. I was drenched."

My complaining droned on, faster and faster, like a queen bee among a swarm of annoying buzzing bees. Josh looked at me out of the corner of his eye, bemused.

"I can't do this Josh. I can't do this for another two years. I won't make it."

Without missing a beat, he responded: "You know Lynnda, you don't have to do this for two more years. You only have to do it for today. Just today. You don't know what tomorrow will bring." A lesson in mindfulness to stay focused on the here and now.

Josh had a way of cutting right to the heart of the matter. My litany of complaints sounded ridiculous. I could feel the agitation melt like hot butter in the sun as I contemplated his advice: What was the use of angsting about tomorrow? Or the day after? There were too many variables, and it was futile to obsess in a sea of negativity. I reminded myself to remember what I had learned after my mother died so young—step forward consciously and positively, one day at a time. We do not live in this world with total control. Only God knows what's coming around the bend. Enjoy the good in this day and celebrate it.

"You're right, Josh," I agreed, leaning back into the seat, grateful to be softened into a constructive place. "Today we only have to worry about today. Ahhh-men." The next day was September 11, 2001.

— CHAPTER 28 —

September 11, 2001

"In my distress, I called to the Lord."

(Psalm 118:5)

MUCH HAS BEEN MADE about the sky that Tuesday morning. It was clear and crystalline blue, like the wings of a blue jay in flight. The few clouds above looked like powder puffs, and early in the morning the Indian summer heat seemed to diminish. The air was September-mild with a wispy breeze rustling through the verdant green leaves still grasping onto the branches of the trees. Daybreak was filled with the first *nitzaot*—sparks of sun—and was so breathlessly inviting that I seized the opportunity to take a short power walk through Central Park, where late blooming flowers maintained their palette of vibrant colors.

Tuesday was day three in the order of God's Creation and biblically it had a special place in the week. After creating vegetation and seed-bearing plants and trees of every kind bearing fruit, *"God saw that this was good"* (*Genesis 1:12*). And it seemed good in this promising sunshine as well.

Aside from the commute, the new campus where I had attended classes the day before, with its spectacular views of the Hudson River, was vastly superior to the prior facility the school had been renting. Never before had a Catholic college housed a rabbinical seminary, and the potential for interfaith dialogue and academic partnerships facilitated by this unique arrangement seemed limitless. In addition, AJR now had the space to develop its own library as well as access to the college's vast holdings, which meant a move in the right direction for accreditation.

As I prepared for the day's classes, I was in a much better frame of mind than I had been the day before. Josh and I had arranged to meet at the same spot on 10th Avenue at 9:30 a.m. At 8:30 a.m. I was dressed and standing in front of the television watching the news on the *Today Show*. At approximately 8:50 a.m. a report came in without much fanfare that a plane had hit the North Tower of one of the Twin Towers in downtown Manhattan. The *Today Show* host read an Associated Press account, which speculated at first that a small plane had veered off course slamming into the building between the 93rd and 99th floors.

Knowing that Josh would be coming from downtown, I called him to warn of possible traffic snarls. He hadn't heard the news but said he was leaving soon. His voice was characteristically upbeat and reassuring.

An avowed news junkie from my PR days, I stood by the television with my latte waiting to see where the story was going. At 9:03 a.m., with the camera focused on the fire in the North Tower, I saw a plane hit what I thought was the same tower again with the force of a volcano erupting, leaving a mushroom cloud of red and black flames behind it. Was it an instant replay of the impact of the earlier plane? Or could this be a second plane hitting the tower? The newscasters were confused, too.

"It appears as if a second plane has hit the second tower, the South Tower," the TV host reported almost as soon as the image was transmitted. "This is now being called a terrorist attack."

I watched for several more minutes then went outside to wait for Josh. Midtown traffic was immediately bottlenecked. Josh was late. I kept trying to call him, but he didn't pick up the phone. Finally, I heard his voice. "Looks like the world has changed," he said. "I'm going to wait downtown to see what happens."

I went back into my apartment. The unfolding news was getting worse and worse. The U.S. was now obviously under attack. A plane hit the Pentagon at 9:37 a.m., and a fourth plane, presumably targeting the White House or the Capitol in Washington, D.C., crashed in an open rural field in Schanksville, Pennsylvania, at 10:03 a.m. Meanwhile, Larry was in the air on his way to Miami for a fabric show, and at 9:40 a.m., the army ordered all airborne planes to be grounded. I went outside again and stood close to the police station near the corner of 54th and 8th.

I didn't know what to do, where to go, or who to call. We were almost at the end of the month of *Elul* on the Hebrew calendar, traditionally preparation time for the upcoming High Holiday season. Every morning, along with the sounding of the shofar, *Psalm 27* is read as a daily reminder. I started praying from the familiar psalm silently: *"Oh, God, I seek your face. Do not hide your face from me . . . do not forsake me; do not abandon me. . . ."*

My cell phone rang. It was my daughter, panicked. "Mom, are you okay?"

"Yes, I'm fine. What's going on there?" I responded trying to sound steady.

"We were evacuated from school. They said there's a terrorist threat against schools, historical sites, and high-rise buildings in Philadelphia."

Beth was now a first-year law student at Temple University. She lived in a high-rise building in the center of town, and Philadelphia—at the seat of national history—was brimming with historical sites. I was petrified.

"I think you should go to Mom Mom's," I advised. "Mom Mom" was the term our family used for Larry's mother, the matriarch of the family.

My mother-in law and her husband lived in the burbs. I thought Beth would be safer with them—responsible adults in case the rest of us perished.

"Check," she said, spooked enough not to offer any resistance.

"Did you hear from Daddy?" she asked.

"No, not yet, but I'm sure he's fine," I said with bogus motherly reassurance. "You know Daddy—he's cornered the market on street smarts."

Then the phone went dead. Damn. Just as I had experienced in Israel during the bombing attack in the market that Beth, her friend and I had narrowly missed, the circuits were overloaded and the phones were spotty. Nothing like a communication blackout when the country is under siege and you want to reach out and touch someone.

I walked outside again near the police station on 54th street. A man in front of the police station listening to a radio started shouting, "Oh my God, the tower went down! The South Tower went down!"

What? The South Tower went down? What did that mean? How many people were in the building? I didn't know what to do. I was immobilized by panic and anxiety. I wanted to flee, to get directly out of town, but the tunnels and bridges were already closed down tighter than a hermetically sealed casket.

I went back to the apartment. Colleagues from school started to check in. AJR was scheduled to be closed for a month after classes the following day, in honor of the upcoming cycle of Jewish holidays. Many of my colleagues had rabbinical gigs scheduled for this time. Already it was possible to hear the collective rumble of rabbis worldwide ripping up their prepared sermons to write new ones, registering the catastrophic events unfolding before us. I heard from a friend in the know that school was now suspended indefinitely.

I felt as though I might want to go home to Philadelphia and never come back. New York, New York—a bright light in the narrative of my own life—was now dark in death and destruction. How could I abandon the city in her time of need? But how could I stay locked up in a tiny apartment, alone indefinitely, worried, and trembling with fear?

The phone rang, jarring me out of my reverie. It was Larry. I started to cry when I heard his voice just as he had when he heard mine after the bombing in Israel's shuk. Air traffic controllers had brought his plane down in an emergency landing in Jacksonville, Florida.

"Call a car service," he told me. "Get the hell out of there if you can."

"A car service? Do you think I would be here if I could get out? The tunnels and bridges are shut down. Manhattan's in virtual lockdown, and we're all just sitting here waiting for the Apocalypse!"

I was watching the television out of the corner of my eye. The news with its images of the people at the scene was searing. Work colleagues were holding hands, jumping to their certain deaths out of high-story windows rather than being burned alive. It was horrifying and close. So incredibly close.

"Take it easy, honey. You'll be okay." His usual calming demeanor did nothing to ease my anxiety.

After hanging up the receiver, I opened the yellow pages, which is what we did in the days before Google became the go-to locater. I called several car services at Larry's suggestion, but as I suspected they were immobile, unable to get in or out of New York. A few of them took my phone number and said they would call me if the bridges or tunnels opened up. Yeah, right.

I made some attempts to go to the hospitals to volunteer my rabbinic services, but friends told me it was to no avail. The EMTs were just bringing in bodies. As an aspiring rabbi I wanted to help, to offer support, to do something for someone else in this horrific situation, but I sat alone in my apartment for hours, fielding frantic phone calls and pacing. All I could do was pray. And pray.

Later in the day, my neighbor and friend Nancy left work and made her way back to her apartment in our building. Her husband was in the Middle East, and her ten-year-old son had been dismissed from school and was waiting for her at home. She insisted that I join them in her apartment, with a proviso: "Lynnda, we must be as calm as possible. I don't want Adam to be more alarmed than he has to be. We're not watching the news anymore," she told me as I followed her up the stairs to her fifth-floor apartment from ours on the second.

No news?

Disconnecting from the news freaked me out, but I needed the comfort of Nancy's tranquil presence more than anything else at that point in the day. Her equally serene cousin came to join us soon after. I continued to field call after call from people who told me that trains had started randomly running out of New York. I thought about boarding one of them. How would I even get to Penn Station more than two miles away? Was Penn Station another vulnerable target for attacks? Could I bring my broken wheelie? I was going to be officiating at my first wedding in Philadelphia in a couple of weeks, and all of the material was with me. It would be impossible to leave papers behind. My thoughts tumbled around in non sequiturs.

I went outside to check out the midtown vibe. The city was completely abandoned like an eerie ghost town. Starbucks was dark; the all-night restaurants were empty and mostly shackled tight. Hardly a soul was on the streets that were normally buzzing with tourists and working professionals. A few passersby moved silently, like zombies.

I stayed with Nancy, her son, and their cousin until after dinner, periodically running down to my apartment to check the news, respond to the landline phone calls, and pray. Joyce called from Israel. It was the ultimate irony that she had left the familiarity of New York's peaceful chaos to study in Jerusalem during a spate of escalated Israeli violence—and now New York was also a war zone. Joyce's family was in downtown New York, and what quickly became known as "Ground Zero" was engulfed in smoke and flames. It was too soon to imagine the numbers of dead and maimed—but there were many, probably thousands, and countless missing. The magnitude of the morning's events was still too horrible to absorb.

At 7:00 p.m. there were reports that the George Washington Bridge on the Upper West Side would reopen, signaling a vehicular avenue out of the city. With that news my cell phone rang. It was one of the car services I had contacted earlier that morning. For $400 a driver would take me to Philly as soon as the bridge opened. Four hundred dollars! In the morning when I'd called, he'd quoted me $200. Highway robbery! But I wanted out so badly that I might have given up my engagement ring to escape the city and reunite with my family.

The driver picked me up at 9:00 p.m., and as we crossed over the George Washington Bridge into New Jersey, I took a deep breath as I looked behind me. An enormous billow of ash and smoke rose up from the site where the majestic twin towers of the World Trade Center had stood until that morning. I let out a moan like a dying animal, moving one open hand to my forehead and the other fist to my mouth, trying to steady myself. Tears streamed down my face for most of the ride home.

Save for the TV, which was set to CNN at the back of the limo, there was silence in the car until we pulled up in the driveway of my unscathed suburban Philadelphia house around 11:30 p.m. I paid the driver and walked through the garage, carrying my broken wheelie like a baby, which I then set down inside the door. I went straight to my bedroom, exhausted and numb, grateful to God to be home.

As I flung myself on the top of the bed, still wearing the clothes I'd worn all day, I thought of Jackie Kennedy wearing her bloodstained pink Chanel bouclé suit and pillbox hat long into the night after her husband, our young president, had been assassinated. Like that day, November 22, 1963, September 11, 2001, immediately became a symbol of collective innocence lost.

How would our nation and the world ever recover from this tragic event? As a rabbi-in-training, I knew that people were going to look to me for solace, for spirituality, for answers, wisdom, and prayers amidst this ongoing horror. I was in uncharted territory. Would I be able to dig deep beyond my personal shock and grief to find my soul and be of value to others?

— CHAPTER 29 —

September 12, 2001

"Over these do I weep."

(Lamentations 1:16)

I WOKE UP ALONE and saw that the TV had been on all night. Larry had called and left a message saying he was en route home from Florida by car with three men he had met on the plane earlier the morning before. Beth went back to her apartment in Center City. TV cameras on the streets of New York recorded images of a city in shambles. People were looking for missing family members; others were making funeral arrangements for the confirmed dead.

At the final count, almost three thousand innocent people lost their lives that morning to suicide terrorists, violent murderers claiming to be working in the name of God. But not according to my theology. The heinous acts were not commandeered by the benevolent, merciful God whom I understood. The day's events on 9/11 had been self-serving and blasphemous to God, taking the name of God in vain.

As a religious leader, it was my job to make that known. It saddened me that people were blaming the 9/11 attack on organized religion. "Wars are fought all over the world because of organized religion," they said. "It just never happened here before."

But if anything, three years of rabbinical school and forty years as a synagogue congregant had convinced me of the merits of organized religion. Organized religion is "organized" to form a community of caring people. Organized religion is organized for people to thank God for blessings. Organized religion is organized to find a sacred space in which to ask God to be with us in our time of need. Organized religion is organized to be a presence for people in the community during their joy or sorrow. Organized religion is organized to take care of widows and orphans and the downtrodden. Was a war ever fought to support widows, orphans, and refugees? No, wars are fought solely over land and power. Land and power!

Truly religious people do not create hundreds of widows and orphans by piloting planes into buildings and killing thousands of innocent people. Or detonate bombs loaded with nail heads in shuks in Israel or other places in the world—the shared trauma between all suffering nations made them unduly connected in blood.

Many of my Israeli friends began calling me the way I had called them so many times before when they had been besieged by terrorist incidents. "We're all Israelis now," they said over and over again. "Now you know what it's like to have terror on the soil of your homeland. It's a God-awful way to live."

God, whom we may or may not experience through organized religion, I thought, can lead us *"through the valley of the shadow of death,"* as *Psalm 23* says. But when we're in a religious community, we traverse the valley of the shadow of death together. Religious institutions of all kinds were already being asked to bring solace and community to a bewildered world. Navigating the valley of the shadow of post-9/11 death,

I needed my faith community as much as an infant needed to suckle its mother. And people needed me.

During the days that followed, the bride and groom whose wedding I was to officiate at called me frantically, imploring, "How can we have our wedding in the aftermath of such horror? How can we be happy when so many people are suffering?"

I had the same flickers of uneasiness, too, but according to enduring Jewish beliefs, cancelling a wedding for a tragedy is considered a bad omen. Life must go on. I assured them that they had every right to celebrate, maybe even more so in light of current events. Judaism tells us to "choose life," and as far as I was concerned, a wedding, a family-building enterprise, was the perfect antidote to the poison of hatred and destruction that had been thrust upon us in recent days.

◆◆◆

The wedding took place as planned at the gorgeous Four Seasons hotel in Philadelphia. The lighting in the room was dim and romantic. The chuppah was covered with flowers. The mood of the ceremony, elevated by the honey-like voice of my friend Cantor Elena Zarkh, whom I'd asked to co-officiate with me, had the requisite air of reverence and the perfect balance of respectful gaiety in the shadow of the 9/11 tragedies.

While we were all under the wedding canopy, I spoke these words to the bride and groom: "We know from the period in which we are living that you have to cherish your time and space together, to live in the moment, as we are now, to find joy, friendship, wonder, and delight in each other—to be nourishing and supportive during sunny days and stormy nights . . ."

I was talking to myself and to the two hundred wedding guests as well.

To be an agent of legal and spiritual change, and to be at the center of love, contributing to happiness in such a life-affirming ritual was uplifting and validating in the current climate. I adored the experience. Larry, who came to watch me officiate at the wedding, told me that I "was born to do this work."

"When the bride and groom returned home from their honeymoon they wrote me a letter:

> *Dear Lynnda,*
> *What can we say . . . You were absolutely amazing at our wedding ceremony. We have to admit, we were a little nervous since it was your first wedding, but no one would ever have never known the difference. You were a natural up there! We definitely think this is your calling. Everyone was raving about how great a rabbi you are . . . And believe it or not, many of my friends said they actually learned something while listening to you at our service . . .*
> *We can't thank you enough.*"

The letter was confirmation that my instincts were correct, that I could trust myself to create an uplifting Jewish spiritual life cycle experience using my developing skills, even beneath a horrific cloud of national tragedy. When I reflected on the words in that letter, it boosted my confidence, and it was significant in helping me to clarify a vision of my future rabbinate.

◆◆◆

Following the wedding, I kept myself distracted from the 9/11 miasma by preparing for Sukkot, which besides its many other names is also described as the "Holiday of the Ingathering." Hospitality, particularly to strangers in the *sukkah* (the booth—or tabernacle—where one stays, shares, and prays with others during Sukkot), and some guests known according to the Kabbalists as *ushpuzim,* embodies one of Judaism's highest values. For a full week, Sukkot offers unprecedented opportunities to invite and to be invited as guests.

For years, living in our suburban home, my husband and I had taken on the *mitzvah* (commandment) of sukkah-building. Each Sukkot, at the appointed time, we erected a beautiful prefabbed sukkah with the help of our friend and neighbor Neil. The loose structure, reminiscent of the temporary dwellings used by the Jews in the wandering days, was big enough to seat twenty or so people in a crowded box-like containment on top of our deck. One side of the sukkah buttressed up against the house adjacent to the kitchen, the other three sides were made of loose canvas panels, which were handpainted with flowers and pomegranates on the inside by my friend and Hebrew tutor, Tamar. The top was covered with the required *skhakh,* bamboo, a once-living substance that allows for light in the day and the ability to see the moon and stars at night.

On each of the seven nights of the holiday, I'd always entertained more than twenty people, cooking and serving comfort food to different groups of friends, along with a dollop of learning. This year, more than ever, people wanted to huddle close together in our cozy sukkah and share thoughts and prayers about recent events, about vulnerability and fragility, healing and hope. We all seemed to need the sustenance of one another, as well as the routine and rituals of the holiday to be able to plough through the sorrow we were all experiencing personally and collectively.

After Sukkot, it was back to school. I hadn't been in New York for a month after 9/11 and I missed it desperately. I longed to be studying with my teachers, friends, and colleagues. At the same time, I was filled with anxiety about returning to Manhattan. I worried about taking the train with its haphazard security, fearful that it might become a "soft target" for more mass casualties, as had happened with public transportation in other countries. I felt exposed and susceptible there.

I hated entertaining negative thoughts, but they were present, and I was working hard to banish them with Joyce's mantra that I'd used when I had my tumor surgery: *"God is with me, I shall not fear."* Each day was a struggle. Life had taken on new meaning, with new urgencies and a redefining of priorities. It was hard to stay focused. A lot of people asked me "why" following the 9/11 attacks. "Why would God allow this tragedy to happen?"

What I knew was that it didn't make sense to ask "WHY?" Why did Joe Smith miss the subway to cheat death that 9/11 morning? Why did Cantor Fitzgerald, a global bond trading organization, lose 658 of its innocent employees, two thirds of its workforce, to cataclysmic terror?

Only God knows. I didn't know where God was during this crisis, I told people, but I did believe that God would be with us in the reconstruction if we were able to be there for each other and open to the possibility of God's presence even in the most trying of times.

When the school semester reconvened, our teachers were very sensitive to the students' feelings. They planned community events and bereavement sessions to help us, and to help us help others. Counselors were brought in from the outside, and we tried to process what had, heretofore, been unfamiliar territory for us as spiritual leaders. One of our teachers was Arline Duker, a social worker whose daughter Sarah Duker had been killed with her boyfriend, Matt Eisenfeld, on bus #18 in a Jerusalem terrorist attack. She modeled resilience and recovery, and we trusted her.

We developed crisis management strategies and found Jewish texts to offer comfort both to us and to those who might seek our counsel. In particular, many of the psalms took on added meaning during this time, giving us words where we had none. One special one was *Psalm 4*: "*When I call, answer me. You have relieved me in my distress. Let the light of Your face shine upon us.*" Just saying the words had a soothing effect. But getting through the "normal" day-to-day of the school year, post 9/11 trauma, was exhausting.

Many of us wrote our own poems, prayers, and additions to the traditional liturgy to reflect the spirit of the times. I adapted a meditation before the Kaddish to fit the new reality of our world. The text was later adopted by the New York Board of Rabbis, printed in its memorial booklet and recited for years at a board of rabbis sponsored memorial service held at Ground Zero.

9/11 Kaddish

by Rabbi Lynnda Targan

This one thing I ask of you . . .
Say *Kaddish* for them.

Fathers and Mothers, Sisters and Brothers,
Sons and Daughters, Family and Friends,
Spouses and Lovers . . .
Say *Kaddish* for them.

Seized in the calamity of inhumanity . . .
Say *Kaddish* for them.

Demolished with their dreams in the
debris of death and devastation . . .
Say *Kaddish* for them.

For they are the holy ones, whose souls will rise
As we stand and say *Kaddish* for them . . .
Please stand and say *Kaddish* for them.

Wherever you go, and whenever you can,
for as long as you live . . .
So that we don't forget . . .
Say *Kaddish* for them.

Please, stand and say *Kaddish* for them.

Amen.

— CHAPTER 30 —

The Final Year

"Remember whence you came, where you are headed,
and before whom you must give an account of your life."

(Avot 3:1)

*M*Y FINAL YEAR OF RABBINICAL SCHOOL sauntered in at a different pace than the previous ones. Over the summer, I had completed the rigid comprehensive exams required for ordination. There were seven in all: two in Hebrew, two in Codes (Jewish law), two in Bible, and one in Talmud. The entire season had been dedicated to studying and passing these exams, with the exception of my coveted early morning bike rides on the Atlantic City Boardwalk about ten miles from our beach house on the other end of the island.

Larry and I had recently taken up biking, and we loved it. It was great exercise, a chance to breathe in the healthy, salty ocean air, and a terrific bonding experience. As the summer progressed, we ventured out to various bike paths and more exotic scenery until we geared up to biking about twenty-five to thirty miles per day. I found it relaxing and meditative, a form of prayer, which put me in the right frame of mind to study and write exams indoors for the rest of the day while the sun shone outside.

As a reward for completing my dreaded exams, Larry booked an organized biking trip for us to Puglia, Italy, a stunning, then lesser-known area located along the boot of the Adriatric coast. One by one as I passed my exams and checked them off, we moved closer to our Italian biking venture and my ordination.

Italy was a dream amidst beautiful scenery. Every day we rode our bikes along the Adriatic coastline, and we capped every night with locally caught fish and farm-fresh vegetables sautéed in freshly made olive oil, all of which was accompanied by tasty, vintage wine. We had plenty of time to talk about my upcoming final academic school year. When we returned from Italy, school was in full swing, and I was feeling relaxed. Larry had joined the board in the aftermath of the school's transition period, and I was over the moon to have been elected as a trusted president of the student body.

Our little polity shared in the responsibility of the school's fundrasing, and my friend and colleague Dorit and I founded the first student newspaper, *Gesher l'Kesher* (Bridge to Connection), and wrote and summoned articles to fill up its pages. We also began the establishment of a library, another advancement toward AJR's hopeful accreditation.

Since I had completed all of my basic course obligations the year before, I registered for a roster of interesting electives, *l'shma* (not for any grades), which meant that I could continue learning without pressure, while I worked on my book-length thesis supervised by my beloved advisor, Dr. Livia Straus. Time filled up very quickly.

It became a year dedicated to holiday celebrations and senior cantorial and rabbinical student presentations that were essential to satisfy the school's mandatory requirements. With drug and alcohol addiction so prevalent and growing in society, I presented my thesis, "Addiction in the Jewish Sources," to great acclaim in March of that year. Two months later I learned that I had won the prestigious *Chana Timoner Creative Liturgy Award* for it.

◆◆◆

The week before my ordination I visited my mother's grave on Long Island, alone. I stood in front of her headstone, which was nestled close to the rest of our extended immigrant family in Mount Golda Cemetery, knowing that I had been the fulfillment of their immigrant dreams for American Jewish life. I was the first of my generation to have graduated from college. I'd also earned two master's degrees, and now I was on the precipice of becoming a rabbi, a voice in American Jewish continuity. My family couldn't even have imagined such a possibility in their day.

I left the cemetery feeling blessed by their legacy, and their spiritual presence went with me to the ordination activities.

◆◆◆

The next day, twelve of us participated in the annual "blessing circle" for rabbinical and cantorial students. As difficult and stressful as the process of studying to become a rabbi is, being birthed out into the world as an ordained rabbi after being protected by the rarefied air of a seminary is a bit scary. While our community surrounded us under a canopy of fabric—much like a chuppah—teachers, alumni, and fellow students offered bessings:

> *"May you go from strength to strength."*
> *"May you have clarity of vision."*
> *"May you be supported by God in all of your endeavors."*
> *"May you enjoy the blessings of good health."*
> *"Be strong and courageous."*

It was a very compelling and deeply emotional experience for the entire school community. We hugged and kissed. Most of us cried. We had been through so much as a group, well beyond the difficulty of huge course loads, homework, tests, papers, and working and commuting. Most of us had been challenged to negotiate our way through concurrent outside problems: a parotid tumor, cancer, losing a parent, divorce, the death of a child, surgery, financial issues, and struggles with children. The blessing circle was validation that we were survivors. We had trudged through the tough stuff with resilience and could now look back at the arduous journey with gratitude and pride.

After the blessing circle closed, I left school and went to the *mikveh* in Bucks County, Pennsylvania. The ritual bath, traditionally used for purposes of "family purity"—i.e., cleansing after menstruation in preparation to assume marital sexual activity (which is prohibited during bleeding), and for conversion, had lately also been reappropriated for other purposes. These days modern women were using the mikveh to mark a separation or change in status—a divorce, the conclusion of chemotherapy, and even the ordination of a rabbi.

I had immersed in the mikveh on the Upper West Side of Manhattan prior to beginning my rabbinic studies. It had made me feel spiritually clean, like a blank slate. I wanted to conclude and bracket my journey to the rabbinate with the same holy ritual. For this sacred transition, I wrote a special meditation:

Prayer Before Immersing in the *Mikveh*
As a Prelude to Becoming a Rabbi

Dear God:

I am about to enter a new phase in my spiritual journey.

More than ever I am seeking a life of kedusha, holiness,

Which I hope to be able to transmit to others.

The possibilities are exciting and I am feeling

the sense of awe while I prepare

to make this important change in status and transition in my life.

As I immerse in the flowing waters of the mikveh,

I pray for energy, renewal, and readiness,

To take on my new role as Your vessel.

May the past that I wish to shed be washed away,

And may I emerge from the waters transformed,

Open to the presence of You,

In all aspects of my forthcoming responsibilities.

May your guidance help me be the best I can be in all that I offer.

Thank you, God,

For the power of this precious and calming moment. Amen.

— CHAPTER 31 —

Ordination

"This is the day that God has made,
let us exult and rejoice on it."

(Psalm 118:24)

ON THE MORNING of the day of my ordination, I awoke in our New York apartment in the wee hours, filled with excitement and trepidation. The day I had anticipated, worked toward for almost ten years, prayed about, and struggled to attain, had finally arrived. My emotions were so highly charged that my skin felt prickly.

I looked at Larry sleeping next to me and was flooded with gratitude. He had given up so much to help me succeed in my mission to become a rabbi, to reach this pivotal moment. Our lifestyle had changed when I began the journey to the rabbinate, and the social, cultural, physical, and financial adjustments had become a normal part of our relationship as the process continued. We were newly bound by certain regulations that governed kashrut and Shabbat and holiday observances, which Larry had never voluntarily sought on his own—but as time passed, we'd discovered that we had evolved together into a refined version of our earlier selves, polished like sterling silver for a holiday meal. It was good.

My daughter was sleeping close by in the living room on the pullout couch, curled in a fetal position, her head covered by a soft, malleable pillow, the way I remembered her lying in her bed or ours since childhood. We'd never fought as mothers and daughters often do. Beth was an easy, sweet, caring child, and except for the partying days at college, when she was dressing to go out as I was brushing and flossing for bedtime, we were as in sync as "Heart and Soul," the duet we used to play on the piano.

She was a grown-up young woman now, a survivor of her own struggles and challenges, and a second-year law student living solo, on track to become a lawyer the following year. With a full heart, wry humor, and a finely nuanced level of maturity, she had come to New York from Philadelphia the night before ordination to support and celebrate with me in my time of achievement. As I walked into the room, she sensed my presence and lifted her head with tousled hair to see me smiling down at her.

"Hey rabbi," she whispered with a morning gravelly voice.

"Not rabbi yet," I cautioned. "But it looks like it's going to happen." After a brief pause, I added, "UNLESS they call me and tell me it was all a mistake. That they've reconsidered, that I don't look like a rabbi and they're not ordaining me. 'So sorry.' In any event, I'm not answering the phone."

"Oh Mom, you're crazy," she said, rolling her eyes with bemused impatience. "You're the school president; you're winning three awards today. Get a grip!"

"What if they call and say, 'We've decided against your admission to the rabbinate?' Five years ago, as you know, I received a version of that letter from another school."

Indeed, despite my success on all fronts, and the culmination of my dream just hours away, that earlier rejection letter could still sting as painfully as if I had stuck my head in a hornet's nest.

I knew that feeling well; I had done it as a child. As I stood on the precipice of success, I hoped that experience had now been reconciled as the moment when I knew that hard work would allow me to prevail.

It was, however, going to be a bustling day, and I was ready to get to it. "Rise and shine everyone. Let's make the beds and put everything in order." Larry and Beth, not exactly ready to be roused, set themselves in motion like good footsoldiers so as not to rattle me. Eric would arrive later on the train from Philadelphia.

I showered in the tiny bathroom and applied my makeup carefully, even though I imagined I might cry it off later. I put on a grey, polished-cotton pencil skirt and matching jacket, which, weeks earlier, I had picked out with my sister for the occasion. The saleswoman told me she had never dressed a rabbi before. My black medium-heeled pumps with the diagonal t-strap fit well and were comfortable enough to stand in during a long day. When I was finished dressing, I was happy with how I appeared in the mirror, a good blend of stylish chic and the requisite modesty of a woman about to be ordained as a rabbi.

I gathered my tallit, the long, flowing, white prayer shawl that I'd bought on the Lower East Side with my friend and chevruta partner, Joyce, before she'd left for Israel. I had affixed to it a special *atarah*, a maroon and gold colored collar band, AJR's school colors, with the school's motto: *"All shall unite to do God's will with an open heart,"* a reminder of our rabbinic undertaking.

My friend Judy had sent a blue thread, known as *techelet* from Israel, made with a specific blue dye produced from a snail-like marine creature known as a *chilazon*, to tie to the *tzittzit*, the specially knotted fringes of the prayer shawl, to remind the Jewish people of the 613 *mitzvot*, the commandments we are expected to uphold. Of the 49 times that *techelet* is mentioned in the Hebrew Bible, forty-four of them have to do with the priesthood. It was fitting. My friends would help me weave together the appropriate blue knots once I arrived at school.

Larry stayed behind to wait for Eric's train in order to drive him to the school's campus. In the meantime, Beth and I made our way to Riverdale. I had appointed her my *shomeret*, a guardian to keep me sane, which on this day was an indispensible service.

It was a stunning morning. Up at the school's grounds, the floribunda trees were in full bloom around the verdant greenery with the Hudson River glistening in the background. The fifth floor of the College of Mt. St. Vincent, AJR's rented space, was already abuzz with frenetic, but well-scheduled and coordinated activity. The smell of honeysuckle wafted in through the open windows as the sunlight streamed in like a canopy.

As soon as we stepped out of the elevator, my colleague, Terry, who would succeed me as president of the student body, presented me with a beautiful kippah that she had crocheted for me out of gold and silver metallic threads. It was such an unexpected, generous gesture. The first of many tears of gratitude began to flow.

Our class, consisting of eight rabbis-to-be and four cantors-to-be, was the largest class to be ordained to date. Among my august compatriots were a former dancer, a concert musician, a famous Talmud teacher from The Jewish Theological Seminary, a native Israeli born of secular Zionist parents, and a philosophy and English professor. Many of my colleagues already served pulpits in the capacity of "student-rabbi," and their status and paychecks were about to be inflated exponentially with their upcoming formally elevated professional status.

A jabbering gathering of associated alumni, teachers, administrators, and ordinees' family members generated an animated excitement in the halls, like a scene before a big wedding. Indeed, in the Talmud and Midrash the process of ordination is compared to marriage. The ordinees, like brides and grooms, are viewed Kabbalistically as fragile spiritual beings needing protection until the ceremony commences. All are seen as partners in Creation with God in shaping a marvelous world. The expectation for brides and grooms is to create and build beautiful new families. The hope for rabbis is to help those brides and grooms build and generate families to comprise burgeoning holy Jewish communities and a compassionate, ethical humanity.

For years, Beth had jokingly referred to me as a geek, "my mother the rabbi-geek," but on this day something shifted. Her eyes held the magic of recognition. The AHA moment that was a nod to the old adage, "It's not what you say, it's what you do," that applied to both of us. She was unabashedly proud of me and truly delighted to be a part of the spirit of the scene, performing her job as shomeret with authority, guarding me to make sure that everything was in its proper place and that I was calm and appropriately hydrated with water, but not so much that I would have to go to the bathroom in the middle of the ceremony.

The first official ritual of the day was the signing of the ordination certificates by members of the *Beit Din* that certify and witness the ordination process. I chose a Conservative rabbi, William Horn—the father of our adored dean, Dr. Ora Horn Prouser—to head up my Beit Din as *Av* (the senior member). Besides being a *mensch* (someone of utmost integrity and honor), he seemed a logical choice, mainly because I had spent much of my religious life in Conservative synagogues. His presence was symbolic.

The Beit Din was completed by a Reform Rabbi, Rabbi Bernard Zlotowitz, the beloved teacher who had first called me "Rabbi Targan" five years earlier during my introductory class with him on Interpreting Psalms, and Jewish Renewal Rabbi Shohama Weiner. She was now AJR's venerated President Emerita, who had recognized the spark and passion within me to become a rabbi early on and had mentored me to fulfillment. My Beit Din was a true pluralistic representation, one that modeled the pluralistic mission of the school—to assemble many denominations together—and reflected my personal inclusive Jewish philosophy of post-denominational *Klal Yisrael,* the concept that everyone is expected to be equally respectful to everyone else no matter their rituals, practices, and customs.

◆◆◆

After a light lunch, our community was called into the *Beit Midrash,* the study hall, for a final afternoon prayer session, known in Hebrew as *mincha,* which means "gift." This would be the last time I prayed as a member of the laity. I was about to become clergy, and with it came enormous responsibility, not just in appearances, but in righteous action. Our tradition projects many expectations onto rabbis: *"To stand in the presence of Adonai, and to serve and give blessing in God's name."* Mincha was a reality check that in a short time, the cocoon of rabbinical school would burst open like a ripe pomegranate on a tree in its season, and our group of twelve ordinees would now be expected to plant rabbinic mitzvah seeds all over the world.

As students, we could be forgiven our flaws, our little mistakes, our intermittent *faux pas,* but as full-fledged rabbis we were expected to be "on" all the time—to say the right words at the right moment, to remember people's names and know how they were doing, to deliver Pulitzer Prize-winning sermons and, most of all, to model exemplary moral and ethical behavior. If excellence was possible, we were to embody it. It was simultaneously thrilling and daunting.

I welled up with tears as I looked around. Like Moses at the top of Mount Nebo surveying the Promised Land, I reflected on the five years I had spent studying at AJR. I thought about my teachers, my colleagues and friends; the texts I had chewed on, struggled with, and tried to digest; the papers I had written; the happenings I had experienced. But unlike Moses, I was gaining entrance into my Promised Land, and yet was far, far less worthy than Moses had been. "God," I prayed, "let me be deserving."

My compatriots and I had shared a lot together. We were united through the desire to serve through our many years of study, joy, success, expectations, tragedies, loss, and triumph. We had all become cherished friends, supporters, and champions of each other in a way that wasn't possible with others outside of the community. On this day of ordination, filled with pride, accomplishment, and gratification, I felt blessed by what I had received. I was plumped up with love and admiration like a life preserver in water. Akin to being chosen the valedictorian of my master's degree class, today was a reckoning, a redemption in the face of doubters, naysayers, and dream busters who didn't think I could go the distance, or couldn't image me as a rabbi because they believed that I wasn't smart or serious enough.

◆◆◆

A little before 4:00 p.m. the twelve ordinees got dressed in our caps and gowns and boarded a small charter bus that would take us to Cardinal Hayes Auditorium, a building adjacent to the Main Administrative Building, where the ordination was scheduled to commence in a matter of minutes. As the bus started moving we all broke out in spontaneous song like the Jews crossing the Red Sea. Judaism is a singing religion. Music elevates the soul and brings the spirit close. *"Let us sing to the Lord," Psalm 95* says. It was so emotional that I gulped for air, lest I pass out.

Three minutes later, we dismounted the bus in front of the building—still singing—and began climbing the stairs, ready to march into the auditorium to take our places in our reserved seats. Standing at the door, catching me off guard, was my friend Genie, an old soul mate from Chicago. I was so touched and delighted by her surprise visit that my colleagues had to pry our hug apart to pull me back in line and push me over the threshold into the auditorium. The ordination ceremony was about to commence.

This was the quintessential liminal moment, and I was conscious of its significance. I was about to acquire a new title, a new status and lots of responsibility. As Dr. Prouser had always reminded us, "Remember, when you become a rabbi you are always a rabbi, whether you are on the bima or not, inside and outside, you are a rabbi." These words played in my head. My ordination was moments away, and I was still wondering how I had arrived at this juncture, if I was really about to become a rabbi. Might this all be a dream?

We marched into the auditorium singing and crying, taking our seats down in front as the audience rose and broke into thunderous applause. I caught the faces of my friends and family—nearly a hundred, scattered throughout the crowd. Seventy-five people had traveled by chartered bus from Philadelphia to the Riverdale campus, thrilled to be witnesses to a unique ceremony, one which would change my life forever. I was humbled by the number of people who had taken time off from work, traveled for hours, and gathered all around me with their hands together in admiration. Eric stood tall next to Larry and Beth. I caught the eye of my father behind my right shoulder, and by the look of pride on his face, I thought that THIS might really be the time that his "weak" heart would burst open.

Like graduations from high schools, colleges, and advanced graduate degrees, ordination is filled with the requisite pomp and circumstance. But the process of rabbinic ordination, similar in feeling to the classes I'd taken in rabbinical school for the past five years, went beyond the academic to the mystical.

◆◆◆

Recitation of both the American and Israel National Anthems preceded the Invocation offered by Rabbi Zlotowitz. After the obligatory administrative greetings, awards were presented along with the requisite speeches, punctuated by selections of beautiful liturgical music sung by our inspired Cantorial choir.

And now THE FINALE was about to begin, the actual ordination. The process is inspired by a passage in the Book of Numbers (*27:18–23*) in the Bible: *"God said to Moses, 'Take to yourself Joshua Son of Nun, a man in whom there is spirit, and lean your hand upon him . . .' Moses did as God had commanded. He took Joshua before Elazar the Kohen and before the entire assembly. He leaned his hands upon him and commanded him, as God had spoken through Moses."*

Thus, the precedent of laying on of hands, or *smicha*, to ordain a rabbi was set. Just as a worthy successor of Moses had been appointed as a leader in the Jewish community to enter the land of Israel as the full expression of the Covenant, a layperson is elevated to the status of rabbi with the same ritual.

Since we were such a large class, we were called to the pulpit (the raised area where the Torah resides in the arc, or in this case the stage), in two groups of six for the actual "laying on of hands" by a *Somekh/Somechet*—in my case Rabbi Horn—along with the other two members of my beit din who were infused with the authority to change my status from lay leader to rabbi by this specific act of confirmation. When I took my place, Rabbi Horn was in front of me, his hands holding me tightly, one on either side of my cheeks as though he were holding up the weight of my head. Rabbis Zlotowitz and Weiner stood behind me, touching my shoulders. Tears flowed from my eyes like tributaries from a river, meeting in the indented philtrum above my lip, the area where the Midrash says God's finger infused every human with wisdom that needed to be acquired throughout a lifetime.

Our ordination certificates were read as a collective, declaring us, "Rabbis and Teachers in Israel," and the *Priestly Blessing* taken from *Numbers 6*, was recited softly as a Benediction by each individual Somech/Somechet. Rabbi Horn, still holding my cheeks snugly between two warm palms whispered:

> *May God bless you and safeguard you.*
> *May God shine an illuminated countenance before you*
>   *and be gracious unto you.*
> *May God's countenance be lifted before you and grant you*
>   *peace. Amen.*

Thunderous applause erupted while the audience rose again, clapping wildly for more than five minutes. My smile was so broad that I thought my face would crack as tears continued to roll down my cheeks and into my mouth. It was one of the proudest, most awesome and overwhelming moments of my life.

One by one, the newly ordained rabbis took seats and waited to receive ordination documents and to be called by our "presenter" to deliver our first, albeit very short *drash* (sermon) as an official rabbi. With twelve ordinees it was a long process, and I was the last to be called alphabetically. I chose Larry to be my presenter, since he had been my most vigorous supporter, and the most directly impacted. He deserved the honor, and he was the person I wanted most in the world to be next to me in our time of shared *simcha*.

When it was my turn, I quickly left my seat and ascended the bima to meet him in the center facing the audience. He took my right hand and held it high as he joyously stated, "*Ladies and Gentleman, it is my honor to introduce to you for the first time ever . . . Rabbi Lynnda Targan.*"

The audience leapt to its feet and remained standing for what seemed like an hour. I could discern each of the faces of my family, friends, and colleagues looking up at us on the stage, genuinely proud of me and my accomplishments, happy to be part of the communal experience.

I turned to walk away from Larry as he made his way back to his seat on the stage next to songwriter Debbie Friedman, and I headed to the podium to speak to the crowd. The audience's whooping became so loud that it seemed like the rock star Jon Bon Jovi had jumped on stage amidst pyrotechnics and thunderous drum rolls. But remarkably, astonishingly, the audience was going wild for just l'il ole "Rabbi" me.

Larry was nearby. We looked at each other, tearfully, and walked to the center of the stage again, taking each other's hand for an astounding encore moment. I bowed humbly before everyone who had supported me on my rabbinic journey—the ones who had seen the "Divine spark" within me and encouraged me to "go for it," pushing me along the way when I was tired and doubtful; the ones who had comforted me as I dealt with failure and rejection; the ones who hadn't objected when I bought flash cards to the movies; the ones who'd understood my disconnection during long periods of study. Now, they were with me at the crossing of the finish line, and we all knew that I wouldn't have been vertical on this holy ground without them.

As I stood behind the podium, my voice was loud and full of joy. People told me later that I was lit up like a menorah on the last night of Chanukah. During the course of my brief talk, I thanked some of the people who were present in the auditorium by name: my cherished rabbinic role model, Rabbi Robert Leib; Cantor Elena Zarkh; and Marcie Goldman, now deceased, who was the executive director of Old York Road Temple Beth Am, where I first worked as the "fresh-faced" student-rabbi. I recognized the internationally renowned cantor,

Nathan Chaitovsky, who used to walk home from our Dresher synagogue, Temple Sinai, with me on Shabbat, still singing after services in the early days of my wondering. There were my kids, Eric and Beth, and Larry and my mother-in-law, my dad and my Hebrew tutor, Tamar, as well as a couple of key professors from AJR—my thesis advisor Dr. Livia Straus, and Dr. Prouser who had birthed me into this new phase of my life and taught by example the true meaning of commitment and holiness.

I dedicated my ordination to my mother, Bernice, and paid homage to my beloved grandparents, Bella and Hymie Yaskolka, who had infused me with a passion for *Yiddishkeit,* brought to America from Poland, which kept my sister and me stable after my parents' marriage collapsed when we were little girls.

In my first official sermon as a rabbi, I spoke about holy time and sacred space, and how the process of becoming a rabbi was a holy accounting of how I had spent my last many years pursuing my passion for Judaism and Yiddishkeit, hoping to inject it into others.

Psalm 90:12 says, *"Teach us to number our days so that we may acquire a heart of wisdom."* According to the lunar Jewish calendar, at the time of ordination we were at the midpoint period between the holidays of Passover and Shavuot known as "the counting of the *omer,"* a ritual that enjoins us to mark time as we move up spiritually as a community from redemption in Egypt to revelation on Mt. Sinai. Daily, for fifty days, we have the opportunity for self-reflection, asking ourselves, "What counts in my life?" I told the audience that realizing my goal to become a rabbi at this juncture was how I became accountable to God, and by extension to the people who counted on me.

I said that this particular day in the counting, the 33rd, was a separate minor holiday, *Lag B'Omer,* a harvest holiday which had been reframed by the sixteenth-century Kabbalists as a day of joy, spiritual yearning, and a time of praise for students, teachers, and Torah scholars. It was fortuitous and intentional that our ordination was planned for this day. On the secular Gregorian calendar it was Tuesday, May 20, 2003—Tuesday, a "good" day according to the Creation story in the Bible. The number "20" was also significant, having the Hebrew numerical value of *Adonai*, God. Coincidentally, it was also the 18th day of the Hebrew month of *Iyar*, "18" being a lucky number, *chai,* equivalent to "life."

And so it happened amidst much glorious fanfare, that on May 20, 2003, twenty years to the day after I became an adult Bat Mitzvah, I was officially accorded an ordination certificate that named me *"Rabbi and Teacher in Israel."* I was also granted three awards. My life had been transformed. I felt strong and appropriately vested to step into my leadership power, to serve in the name of God.

◆◆◆

The ceremony was followed by a light buffet meal in the large banquet hall where there was more kissing and hugging. Later in the evening, several beloved friends, including my oldest one, Sheila, from Madame Duvall's ballet class in Reading, Pennsylvania, when I was seven years old, joined a group of family members and came back to our little Manhattan apartment where I opened cherished gifts—books, a silver *yad* (pointer) for *leyning* (reading) Torah, candlesticks for traveling, a pin from my sister, trees planted in Israel, and many contributions to various charities in my honor.

Beth presented me with a humbling scrapbook of laudatory testimonial messages that had been written by friends to mark my ordination. She had arranged it as a surprise. It blew me away.

Even now, decades later, I access those tribute letters whenever I need a boost. They wrote:

> *You have been a cherished friend, teacher and student all rolled into one.*
>
> *To have reached this day required many of the qualities I have always known you to possess—among them, your intelligence, your love of learning, your curiosity, faith, spirit, persistence, commitment, good humor, your ability to comfort, and your capacity to love . . .*
>
> *You are the stellar example of how motivation and hard work lead to the pursuit and the ultimate realization of one's dreams . . .*
>
> *You have inspired me with your willingness to say, 'This is really hard,' then you do it anyway . . .*
>
> *I learned from you that things worth getting are worth fighting for...*
>
> *People play many roles in the course of a lifetime, but few have the courage to pursue a new role of incredible complexity at the midpoint in their lives . . .*
>
> *Your energy, dedication, talent, and zest for life have enabled you to arrive at this pinnacle.*
>
> *You are a wonderful role model and you proved that it's never too late to follow your dream . . .*
>
> *Mazel Tov!*

— EPILOGUE —

*"Everything has its season, and there is a time
for everything under the sky."*

(Ecclesiastes 3:1)

FOR DAYS after the official ordination festivities ended, I pranced around in a sustained state of wonderment at our beach house, pushing sand beneath my feet, reveling in joy. Mindlessly, as though my brain had taken a holiday, I walked for hours up and down the water's edge, collecting beautifully colored sea glass and unusual shells of different sizes and shapes, silently thanking God for allowing me to reach my season of bliss.

It occurred to me that I had made numerous sacrifices and many changes in pursuit of the rabbinate. Forfeiting my business and the income it provided had nipped at my financial independence. When I had stopped writing a newspaper column, I lost the connection to thousands of engaged readers, although I would later learn that many could be recaptured on social networking sites like Facebook, Linked-In, Twitter, and blogging. During my years of study, I had stopped sitting on most charitable boards and lost my influence in directing philanthropic funds, which had always been a satisfying endeavor.

For almost a decade I'd had barely a thimble-full of free time and rarely saw my friends, and when we did connect, I was usually distracted and stressed-out. Reading popular novels and devouring the *New York Times* from cover to cover was a far-flung notion. A neat, well-managed house became a fantasy. The job of paying the bills, which dictated where our family money was allocated, had gone to my husband, who had his own system that I could no longer access. The worst part for someone like me was negligible downtime and self care, especially post surgery for my parotid tumor. But I learned that, when in pursuit of a life-changing makeover, we sometimes need to forfeit many previously comfortable situations and routines in order to achieve our deepest aspirations.

On the plus side of the ledger, achieving a lofty goal had sent my self-esteem index soaring. I'd modeled commendable behavior to my children: to be a hard worker and a lifelong learner, to be strong and resilient, and when transformation is required, to "Go for it!" Most significant was that I had strengthened and developed my ongoing personal relationship with God.

In the short aftermath of my momentous journey, I craved the luxury of a summer of just *being*, of not *doing* anything monumental. What I needed was a vacation from frenzy to spend time with family, sip iced soy lattes with friends while I caught up on the latest news, tend to what had been neglected in my home, go to the dentist, have a mammogram, and read some of the popular bestsellers I had missed while my nose was buried in Jewish sacred sources. And in due time, enveloped by the serenity at the beach, I began preparing for my next professional steps.

I leapt into rabbinic life immediately following the high season at the Jersey Shore, and began teaching and offering rabbinic services as the summer evanesced into the fall. I was a pastor and teacher at the Golden Slipper Senior Center in Philadelphia where I also led High Holiday services. On an alternative day, I led High Holiday services at The Actor's Temple in New York with my friend Rabbi Josh Simon, my 9/11 compatriot, who, sadly, was diagnosed with brain cancer soon afterwards and succumbed to his illness a short time later.

For several years I worked at the famous 92nd St. Y on Manhattan's Upper East Side, teaching in one of its most successful programs, *Derekh Torah*, 30 learning sessions offering outreach to interfaith couples and singles. The prestigious class was created by Rabbi Rachel Cowan, a *Jew by Choice* who is now deceased, and was designed for people who wanted to convert to Judaism, but hadn't yet amassed the vocabulary to ask the appropriate questions. It was also meant to address the needs of Jewish individuals or couples who wanted to deepen and enhance their Jewish learning. I was privileged to meet many amazing souls in my classes who were recreating their lives and transitioning onto a new Jewish path, just as I had done.

One of my favorite quotations from the Bible states, *"Those who teach righteousness to the multitudes will be like the stars forever and ever"* (*Daniel 12:3*). During the thirty-week Derekh Torah sessions, I guided dozens of couples on their spiritual journeys and arranged for many of their conversions. I am proud to say that I brought several people into the fold of Judaism and into the body of the Jewish community, and they are happy with Judaism's blueprint for living. One couple who Larry and I now see socially from time to time still tell me whenever we meet, "You changed our lives, and we can never thank you enough."

On days that I brought someone to the mikveh, a final step in the process of conversion to Judaism, I was so moved by their raw emotion that I was brought to tears. For each of them, I wrote individual prayers that reflected my internal pride and joy. Years later, my students continue to call me to officiate at their life cycle events, which I have performed at a myriad of gorgeous venues all over the country and in Europe. I also worked as a rabbi on a Passover Caribbean cruise, and was the rabbinic presence and served on two missions to Israel.

◆◆◆

And now?

And now, life is good. And I say that having recently traversed another life-threatening health calamity, the aftermath of a brewing tooth infection beneath a crown that had been treated with a root canal. In the emergency room with a high fever, after more than six weeks of unexplained debilitating symptoms, I was diagnosed with life-threatening endocarditis. The infection from my tooth had hit my heart and eaten through two valves, which had to be replaced. In critical condition, I almost died before the surgeons performed lifesaving open-heart surgery, and spent the rest of the summer recovering and thinking about where I was headed after the operation that had left me weak and compromised. Would I have to retire? Would I be able to be of service again in the same way I had been for the last fifteen years after my ordination? Could pure will again help me recreate my professional and personal life after surgery?

Fortunately, I had been in good shape, fit and strong before the symptoms of illness began appearing, and by the fall, buoyed by my faith, I was able to dive back into the world I had created for myself after ordination. Life was on track again (although I say quietly *bli ayin ha rah,* against the "evil eye," thought to be the jealous evil satanic rival of goodness). One of our ancient teachings comes to mind: *"Rabbi Ben Zoma asks, 'Who is rich? One who is satisfied with her portion'" (Avot 4:1).*

I love being a rabbi because I love knowing that I am living a life of service. According to Dr. Martin Luther King, "Life's most persistent and urgent question is, what are you doing for others?" In ministering to and serving the Jewish community and the spiritual population at large, I think that I am realizing the plan God had for me in this life. In serving humanity, I continually serve God. I have the opportunity to be a voice for good and an agent for change during times like these when society demands reflection, ethical leadership, and faith in an optimistic future.

Arriving at this point, having negotiated my way through many "tests," I have learned how to survive trying transitions and transformations. As a result, I have morphed into a self-motivated, powerful advocate for a happy and fulfilling life infused with depth and substance, for myself as well as for others. I've noted that in the process I have become more generous, more satisfied, more peaceful, more aware of ethical ambiguities, and wiser in ways of the world. I feel blessed that my studies have taught me how to deal strategically with rejections and failures, illnesses and compromise, and to be contrite and apologetic when I err.

As a woman still seen by many to be working in a man's profession, especially in the era of the "Me Too" movement, I'm pleased to have a modicum of authority in these difficult cosmic conversations, and to bring newly cultivated power to social issues that matter.

Of course, not everything goes my way. Alas, the rabbinate also bears some ownership in the problems of sexual harassment, pay inequality, access to institutional Jewish life, gender discrimination and expectations. Though we are proportionately small in number compared to men in the rabbinate, women rabbis have been organizing and working together to achieve parity on all fronts. Little by little, we are making progress.

My profession keeps me busy and balanced, grounded in faith and rooted firmly in my family, friends, and Jewish tradition. The passage of time since my ordination, along with my life-and-death heart surgery, have only deepened my hunger for Judaism: the calendar, the Jewish life cycle, Israel, and the enduring wisdom of the sages. Having turned inward and upward for so long after I began my journey to the rabbinate, it is a privilege to be able to give back to the world as I had hoped, to tend to it through the spirit of *tikkun olam*, repairing the world. At this juncture of my life, I have less to prove and much more to give.

Albert Einstein once said, "To keep your balance you must keep moving." Since I was ordained eighteen years ago, I have created a unique and diverse rabbinic portfolio that keeps me motivated and pushing forward. Blessed to officiate at many life cycle events (including my own children's weddings and grandchildren's baby namings), I feel that my mission of becoming a rabbi is realized on these sacred occasions as I stand with people in their transitional moments. Whether accompanying them and their deceased loved ones to their final resting place in the cemetery, greeting a bride and groom under the chuppah, or conferring Hebrew names on Jewish babies, I am an abiding rabbinic presence—often a joyous facilitator, and at sad times, an empathetic and consoling minister. As my husband watches me perform in my rabbinic roles, he continues to express his validation towards my work. He tells me again and again, "You were born to do this."

Though I am not the rabbi of a pulpit in a synagogue, I have maintained a close personal and working relationship with Old York Road Temple Beth Am, and with my friend and mentor Rabbi Robert Lieb in suburban Philadelphia where I co-officiated as a student-rabbi during High Holiday services in 2000. For the past six years, I have been blessed to deliver a High Holiday sermon there on the second day of Rosh Hashanah.

Simultaneously, a large portion of my rabbinic work concentrates on *keruv*, bringing an unaffiliated Jewish population—which at this juncture in history is the largest segment of contemporary Jewry—to the community through *Mussar* (ethical self-improvement practice) and various study opportunities.

A few years ago, I cofounded *The Women's Midrash Institute* with my friend and colleague Rabbi Margot Stein. Though she has gone on to other rabbinic work, I am pleased to present a diverse menu of classes to highly motivated, mostly women adult learners, and to engage other rabbis in the process. Some of the classes we've taught are entitled: "Biblical Women as Moral Agents," "Pursuing Happiness," "The *Parasha* from a Feminist Perspective," "Pluralism in the Bible," "What I did for Love: Love, Lust, and Longing in the Jewish Tradition," "Jewish Ethics," and "Maintaining Balance."

It is particularly gratifying that I have been able to realize my goal of focusing on women whose Jewish educations, like mine, had been uneven or even summarily dismissed. I am guided by a teaching principle from the late, great Maya Angelou who said, *"You learned it, teach it. You have it, give it. When you get, give. Each of us comes from God with wisps of glory."*

My days are never the same. I love the diversity of the Jewish experience, and the many disciplines such as prayer, Mussar, meditation, and Torah study, which support the Jewish ethical tradition and the Jewish people as a "light unto nations." I am honored to facilitate an ongoing Mussar practice with a very special group of amazing women. I learn from them every time we meet.

Writing remains an integral part of my rabbinate, and in creative moments, or when circumstances arise, I compose poems, meditations, prayers, and original services which I disseminate in an evolving body of liturgy for events at which I officiate, or in specialized publications. Indeed, writing this book has become another emergence, an ongoing reimagining of my life.

Reflecting back at my disappointments, rejections, failures, and denials, on the road to becoming a rabbi, I accept responsibility for what I didn't handle well, took for granted, or didn't understand. I've come a long way from my spiritually and financially impoverished childhood, and I'm satisfied with who I've become. My personal growth and wisdom, informed by my rabbinic training, has enabled me to forgive people who were unkind, dismissive, and even hostile to me. I carry no bitterness towards my father's wife and others who knowingly or unknowingly were obstructionists. People evolve as products from where they emerged. And those are their stories. I am grateful to be close to my brother and his family despite the difficult early family dynamics.

It was not my intention either to paint RRC in a bad light. I no longer view my rejection as a catastrophe, or believe that the people there were mean spirited and "against" me. I recounted that story in this book to convey how difficult my struggle was, and how hopeless it occasionally seemed that I would ever realize my dream of becoming a rabbi. In hindsight, my rejection from RRC was *hasgacha pratit*, Divine intervention. It was not the end of an ideal, but the beginning of a new path, which ultimately fit my feet like comfortable shoes that I could walk in forever. In fact, my rejection experience, like my parents' divorce, prepared me for the travails of leadership. It fortified me and made me resilient, as well as more empathetic. Those same people who I thought hurt me are now my colleagues and friends, and today we collaborate on many shared endeavors. They are good people with good intentions, and we have mutual respect for one another.

As one of my friends told me in the midst of my rejection despondency, "This will turn into good," and it did. That's life! You don't always get what you deserve, and you don't always deserve what you get. We all have to learn how to lick our wounds and move on, otherwise happiness eludes us.

This book was intended to inspire people to cultivate their own life image, to grow and change and to develop fortitude and tenacity. To reach beyond their comfort zone in order to achieve fulfillment. I wanted to challenge you, the readers, no matter where on the age spectrum you fall, to confront yourself, ask tough questions, make hard choices and perhaps give up what feels superficial and superfluous in order to stay focused on important personal and professional goals. In the process, there will be bumps in the road and fears to face. But you can step into your own power and possesss your own authentic life. Someone once said to me, "Don't ever *should've* all over yourself." I've learned that success can always be achieved if you don't let others define you, and you don't settle for less than who you want to be.

One of Judaism's most famous statements posits, *"It is not incumbent upon you to finish the job, but neither are you free to desist from it"* (*Avot 2:16*). Even as I write this final chapter in the narrative of the book, I recognize that every transition and transformation is an ongoing process. Though I have achieved the title of rabbi, I am perennially incomplete, living in the gray, and traveling on an expedition of learning, always trying to improve myself and self-actualize as God's vessel in the world. The German expressionist artist Max Beckmann once wrote, *"It is the quest of ourselves that drives us along the eternal and never-ending journey we all must make."* And it is an especially vital expectation that rabbis continue to learn beyond school, and to perennially expand as human beings and professionals.

Of this I am certain: In *Olam Haba,* the world to come, God will not ask me why I was not Moses or Rabbi Zusya, which is a variation of a famous story; God will expect that I was the best Rabbi Lynnda Targan I could be. I'm trying. Day by day. Moment by moment.

I still have work to do.

— ABOUT THE AUTHOR —

 Rabbi Lynnda Targan was ordained by the Academy for Jewish Religion in Riverdale, New York, in 2003 after earning master's degrees in Jewish Communal Studies and Jewish Liberal Studies from Gratz College. Before assuming the path to the rabbinate, she was a journalist, oral historian, and the president of LT Communications, which facilitated public relations and marketing campaigns for professionals, nonprofits, and small businesses. Several years ago she co-founded the Women's Midrash Institute to provide a setting for women and men to study Jewish texts in a context that encourages feminist inquiry and spiritual reflection. She sits on the executive board of Women of Vision, a division of Women's Philanthropy of the Jewish Federation of Greater Philadelphia, is a member of the National Council of Jewish Women, and a Life-Member of Hadassah. A sought-after teacher and speaker, she officiates regularly at public and private lifecycle events. Rabbi Targan is a member of the Board of Rabbis in New York and in Philadelphia, and she lives between both cities with her husband, Larry Targan. The couple have two married children and two grandchildren.